WOR
Stories from all round Australia

Angela Goode

ABC
BOOK

ACKNOWLEDGMENTS

For all their invaluable help in a variety of ways, I thank alphabetically: Ross Bain, Stephen Bilson, Geoffrey Blight, Peter Bull, Charlie, Lance Clifford, Rusty Connelly, Lyndon Cooper, Chris Davison, Byn Dinning, Ian Doyle, Barry Giffen, Jean Green, Nancy Halsall, Rex Hocking, Malcolm and Chrissy Holt, Mavis, Ron and Garry Kerr, Neil and Helen McDonald, Rob Macklin, Stuart Neal, Eric Plane, Don Robertson, Tim Rowe, Helen Semmler, Chris Stapleton, the ABC, the *Weekly Times*, Judy Welbourn and Nancy Withers.

Published by ABC Books for the
AUSTRALIAN BROADCASTING CORPORATION
GPO Box 9994 Sydney NSW 2001

National Library of Australia
Cataloguing-in-Publication entry
Working dogs.

ISBN 0 7333 0327 7.

1. Working dogs—Australia—Anecdotes. I. Goode, Angela, II.
Australian Broadcasting Corporation.

636.730994.

Edited by Jo Jarrah
Designed by Helen Semmler
Set in 9½/12 Schneidler Old Style Light by Midland Typesetters,
Maryborough, Victoria
Printed and bound in Australia by Australian Print Group, Maryborough, Victoria

1695

9 8 7 6 5 4 3 2 1

CONTENTS

INTRODUCTION

This book takes you on a vast farm tour of the nation. Bumping along in utes, sitting in trucks, driving a header or riding the stock routes, you'll meet an energetic bunch of characters that many reckon are our greatest rural heroes—working dogs.

Along the roads from Girilambone to Geraldton, from Cummins to Bruny Island, in deserts, wheat fields, shearing sheds and on mountains, you'll see them at work—droving, minding a flock of sheep, chasing pigs, pulling down wild bulls and sometimes even at the wheel of the ute itself.

The wonderful thing about this third collection of stories about our once-unheralded stars of the bush is that their owners and friends have through their stories, not only paid tribute to working dogs, but also given us a taste of life in remote regions of Australia that few can visit. The contrasting types of farm work across this huge land, dictated by soil, terrain and rainfall and sun, very often determine what type of dog is found on those farms—from hairy and agile in the mountains, to sleek and tough in the tropics.

I am not able to say whether the humans of these stories follow the same patterns, but there certainly are many rich and interesting characters amont them. They range from eleven year old Kathy Boyden of Moonlight Creek Station to Emmie Cripps of Northampton who died at 82, just months before publication.

You'll meet aboriginal writer, Jannial Thunguttie Kamilaroi, former drover Lionel Hewitt, station wives, aerial musterers, shearers and truckies, stock inspectors and jackaroos—and city slickers like Gundars Simsons and Paul Holst who needed dogs to show them the lie of the land.

The appeal that working dogs seem to have goes far beyond the farm gate. The reason, I believe, is that Australian farm dogs are the only animals which continue to work large scale in a close commercial partnership with humans. Once, our streets rang with the sound of delivery horses, bullocks strained at their chains to drag wool to market, donkeys and camels pulled carts and carried loads, and in the paddocks, men sat behind the huge rumps of Clydesdales to plough, sow and reap. And in the mines, a canary would warn of failing air. All those have gone, except as novelties. Dogs, however, are perhaps even more valuable in the working partnership than in generations before. When most farms have cut their human workforces to absolute minimums to cope with the 60 per cent drop in wool prices, terrible droughts, mouse plagues, weather destruction of crops and the legacy of crippling interest rates, a dog that will reliably carry out stock work—and provide a shoulder to lean on when the spirits are low—is essential.

The respect rural people have for their working dogs is very evident from these stories. Apart from the fact that these workers never hit the grog, rarely go on strike, don't care about holidays, seldom answer back, never ask for a pay rise and scarcely take a sickie, they are always ready with delirious joy to start the day.

Enterprise bargaining to a dog means to look longingly at the offcuts when a ration sheep is slaughtered. A productivity increase will be willingly achieved—if the gate to the bitch's cage is left open. Workers' comp is an extra blanket in the 44. A superannuation payout is an old chair on the back verandah in the sun.

No machine could ever take the job of a working dog—and who ever heard of a machine that could tell you it loved you? So it would seem working dogs' positions are safe on their farms for some time yet. Mind you, a machine wouldn't bark all night or get pregnant at shearing time.

During the course of compiling this book I visited two writers who featured prominently in *More Great Working Dog Stories*, Ron Kerr of Borroloola in the Northern Territory and Geoffrey Blight of Narrogin in Western Australia. Living in vastly different climates and doing very different work, they epitomise the diverse nature of living off the land in Australia. Like every other writer in the book, though, they are equally dependent on their dogs to earn their living.

To underline that diversity, I have written profiles of these two fascinating individuals which accompany more of their very fine contributions. I also spoke to mountain cattleman, Rusty Connelly, Queensland musterer, Shirley Joliffe, acclaimed border collie breeder and trialler from the red gum region of South Australia, Byn Dinning and from the twisted mallee country, dog philosopher Neil McDonald.

After five years of reading, editing and compiling working dog stories I can confidently say it has been a marvellous journey. I have had the pleasure of speaking to a great many of the 750 people who sent in almost 2000 stories to the 1992 competition sponsored by the ABC's South Australian Country Hour. Over the phone, laughing and talking to the warmest, friendliest humans imaginable, story editing was never so much fun.

I hope you enjoy this volume as much as I have.

Angela Goode, 1993

HISTORY OF THE BORDER COLLIE

Stephen Bilson, Orange, New South Wales

On the border of England and Scotland in September 1893, almost exactly 100 years ago, a pup was born that has changed the way sheepdogs work right around the world. It was a 'Working Colley' pup called Old Hemp—an exceptional dog, recognised as the father of all modern Border Collies.

Old Hemp himself resulted from an amalgamation of bloodlines from many different sources, for the history of the Border Collie goes right back to the Roman invasion of Britain in 55 BC. The Romans brought with them their own breed of sheepdog, described as large and heavy-boned, and carrying either a long or a short coat. They were usually black with tan and white markings. These dogs spent most of their time fending off wolves and foxes and guarding the shepherd's possessions and sheep from other humans. It is thought that these dogs resembled the large Bernese Mountain Dog that is still popular today.

In AD 794, Britain was invaded by the Vikings, who brought with them a small Spitz-type breed of dog. Over the centuries the Romans' sheepdog and the Spitz-type dog were crossed and various strains of Working Colley were bred to suit the conditions in each locality. Many of these strains specialised in particular jobs. For instance, Welsh Greys were good for feral goats. The Welsh Hillman was a breed that evolved and was then crossbred with dogs coming from North Africa. We also know that in 1514 Polish Lowland sheepdogs were introduced into some of the working strains in Britain. Another Working Colley strain was the Highland Collie, which was left unchanged until Queen Victoria took an interest in the breed in the late 1800s. The Queen was even reported to have attended sheepdog trials. With its new popularity, this breed, too, was crossed.

During the long period from the Roman invasion to the 1800s, people in Britain did not travel much and dogs in various districts generally remained mostly unchanged for centuries. When nationwide trade began to have an effect on British farmers, it also had an effect on their sheepdogs. Many of these dogs were cross-mated to produce better dogs. This also meant that over the years some of the Working Colley strains disappeared in favour of more efficient breeds. The Working Colley in Britain still had many different strains and these, with various cross-matings, produced the Bearded Collie, the Smithfield, Shetland sheepdog, Australian Kelpie, American McNab, Old English Sheepdog, Rough and Smooth collies, English shepherd— and very likely played a strong part in the development of other breeds such as the Australian shepherd, the Corgi and the German coolie (or German Colley, as it is sometimes called.)

The Australian Kelpie was bred up from crossbreedings of different strains and imports to this country. In 1869 John Rutherford of Yarrawonga, Victoria, used a pair of imported Scottish dogs as a foundation for the Kelpie breed, intermingling their blood with dogs imported by other breeders such as Messrs Elliot and Allen of Geraldra station and George Robertson of Warrock station. Another influential breeder was G S Kempe of South Australia.

Without doubt, though, Border Collies are the British Working Colley's most noted sheepdog ancestors in the world. As the name suggests, the Border Collie was found in the region of the Scottish and English border. All Border Collies trace back to that single dog, Old Hemp. He was bred by Adam Telfler and was described as being jet black with a very small amount of white on him. His coat was long and similar to a lot of Border Collies today.

Old Hemp began to compete in sheepdog trials at twelve months of age, and in his entire life remained unbeaten. It has been reported that he didn't excite the sheep but instead held them with complete control by his intense gaze. No-one had ever seen a dog work sheep so well. It was also reported that he was a good-tempered dog but with a tendency to be excitable—in fact it was noted that he sometimes trembled as he worked.

As a result of his talents, his services as a sire were widely sought after and soon everyone wanted a pup by Old Hemp. It is estimated that he sired more than 200 male pups in his lifetime before he died in May 1901. His importance is further enhanced by the fact that his offspring also showed many of his outstanding characteristics and the line continued holding many of these traits that we now take for granted in the modern Border Collie.

Hemp's sire was a black, tan and white dog called Roy. He was described as being a plain working but easily handled dog. Hemp's dam, Meg, however, was described as being very sensitive, intelligent and showing style and eye when working. She was an all-black bitch. Both were from old, solid lines of Northumberland Colleys.

In Britain the first sheepdog trial was held at Bala in Wales on 9 October 1873. It was reported that most of the dogs used a lot of barking while working on the course, but the dog called Sam, who scored third place, was said to have shown eye when working. This characteristic is what we now know to be a typical trait of the modern Border Collie. The term 'eye' refers to the way a dog can persuade the sheep to move by looking intensely at them instead of rushing about. This trial was won by Mr James Thompson with his black and tan Working Colley called Tweed. She was a small black and tan dog with a white forefoot, compactly built with an intelligent, foxy head and a fairly thick coat. There were ten competitors and up to 300 spectators. For many years this was thought to be the first sheepdog trial in the world, but we now know there were trials as early as 1866 in New Zealand and a few years later in Australia.

In 1906 the International Sheepdog Society was formed. Scotland, Wales and England each had their own National Trial, which was the highest award for each country. A little later Ireland also joined. The best sheepdogs in each country then competed for the highest award in the combined countries, which was called the Supreme Championship. Many of the Supreme Champions were exported to New Zealand, which indicates how high the standard was of early Border Collies in New Zealand. The imported dogs included Moss 22 (1907 champion, later known in New Zealand as Border Boss); Sweep 21 (1910, 1912 champion); Don 17 (1911, 1914 champion); Lad 19 (1913 champion); and Glen 698 (1926 champion).

The first Border Collie to come to Australia was Hindhope Jed in 1901. She was first imported into New Zealand by James Lilico and had already won three trials in Scotland. At the time, she was in pup to another of the 'new' border strain called Captain. She was also the first of the Border Collies in New Zealand. She was purchased soon after her arrival for 25 pounds by Alec McLeod of the famous King and McLeod Kelpie Stud in Australia. Hindhope Jed was placed fourth at the Sydney Sheepdog Trials in 1902. She then won the event in 1903 against a field of thirty-two. Jed was later mated to some pure-bred Kelpies by McLeod.

The next Border Collie imported into Australia also came through New Zealand. This was Maudie, a daughter of the famous Old Hemp. Later the King and McLeod partnership also imported Moss of Ancrum, Ness and Old Bob from Britain.

The name Border Collie was used as early as 1905 by King and McLeod in an advertisement for their dogs in Australia, but the name did not become official for the new breed until much later. The Border Collie today plays a large part in Australian sheepdog trials and on farms across the country. Even though Border Collies have been bred here very successfully, some breeders still import new dogs from Britain, and to some extent from New Zealand, to add to their bloodlines.

A BLACK AND WHITE CASE
FOR A QUIET WORKER:
A PROFILE OF BYN DINNING

Angela Goode

When champion sheepdog trialler Byn Dinning was a lad of ten he remembers riding through scrub with his father on their block at Bordertown, South Australia. With them were always a few dogs whose job it was to flush sheep out of the scrub. This was in the early 1930s, before much clearing or fencing of the land had been done in those parts. Their block consisted of one paddock of 16 000 acres. Mustering had to be done with great skill and care to ensure that all the sheep were brought out of the scrub for shearing.

Byn maintains that was when he first learnt the value of a good dog—a quiet, gentle, but forceful dog that wouldn't push the sheep too hard, was able to probe them out of the undergrowth and was tough enough to walk them the twenty miles they sometimes had to travel to get to the shearing shed. Those dogs were always border collies.

Sixty-two years on and Byn Dinning's respect for the black and whites is as strong as ever. Hardly surprising. He and his team over the past 45 years have won most major sheepdog trials in the nation, as well as run several farms without much outside labour.

To emphasise what it is about border collies that he loves, he tells a story about something that happened when he was a boy. Byn's father was out mustering in some rough country when his horse fell and rolled on him. His father broke his pelvis. His dog, Bot, one of a string of particularly good dogs on the place, went after the horse, grabbed the rein which was hanging down and brought the horse back to him. Byn's father was able somehow to climb aboard and get home. Byn maintains his father wouldn't have survived if the horse had left him. After that, no other breed of dog ever got much of a look-in, although Byn has had the odd kelpie on the place from time to time.

'It's a popular misconception that the border collie can't take hard work,' is his answer to the common belief among kelpie owners that the black and whites are soft. 'It's all in the strain. Some are soft, some are tough. I have only ever had tough dogs.'

In his 45 years of trialling, Byn has had success right from the start: 'At the first trial I went to, I got in the prize money. And I won the next one with a seven-month-old pup.' (That pup that gave him his first win carried the bloodlines of the Homeleigh stud in Victoria where Arthur Kemp, one of the very early serious border collie breeders, turned out many champions. That bloodline is still pulsing through Byn's dogs today.)

But it's not Byn's own prowess this solid rock of a man is boasting about—it's the dogs he's proud of. He squirms a bit in his chair when the spotlight is put on him and his undoubted ability to breed and train extraordinary animals. However, while Byn is not given to boasting, there's an amazing array of ticking clocks, silver platters, silver cups and championship ribbons arranged all around the room we are sitting in to do his boasting for him. To ensure that everyone realises they're a result of the dogs, not him, there are large, hand-coloured, ornately framed photographs of his greatest champions hanging around the walls.

So it is only with quite a bit of effort that the truth can be excavated from the rock. After a bit of jackhammering, the big man with the gentle face walks off and returns with a pile of exercise books. But the books don't record Byn's wins—just the dates and names of dogs, the trials they entered and where they were placed, all methodically tabled in a neat hand.

This man with the big kindly face needs more prompting to talk about his achievements, so I start reminding him: in 1992 there was 'A Dog's Life', the television series on the ABC in which he competed as South Australia's representative with Old Mill Laddie. He didn't win that trial—a minor lapse—but he helped put dog trialling on the television map. And what about the Canberra National?

From there Byn starts talking. Yes, he won the National in 1992— regarded as the supreme test for working sheepdogs. It was his first win out of only three attempts. But he regards his major triumphs that year as winning the Commonwealth Championship at Koroit, Victoria, rated as one of the biggest trials in Australia and the South Australian championship at Roseworthy Agricultural College.

In 1991 and 1992 he represented Australia against New Zealand with three other team members. Warming to the theme, he brought out the green blazer: embroidered in gold on the pocket are the words 'Australian Sheepdog Workers' Association—Test Team'. In 1991, the New Zealanders won, but only by a few points despite the Australians having had no time to acclimatise or loosen up before the tussles in Palmerston North and Christchurch got underway. You get the feeling, though, that he was sorrier for the dogs that tried their hardest in difficult conditions than for the handlers. In 1992, in Bendigo, the Australians evened the score.

He gets rid of further talk on the subject of his successes by waving his hand dismissively: 'I won open trials all over the place.' And that's the end of it. So we focus on the dogs, and the going is easier.

Old Mill Laddie, he volunteers, the dog bred by Damien Wilson of Littlehampton, has been in the prize money 28 times since July 1990, and has won more than $5500. Although he is a well-known dog because of the television trials and the Canberra National win, Byn doesn't reckon he is the greatest dog he's had. 'He'd be in the top ten,' Byn says, leafing through his exercise books.

At the top of his list is Glenromian Judy, a bitch he bred, who reached the finals twelve times in fifteen competitions between 1949 and 1960. Glenromian, Byn's stud prefix, is made up of the names of his three offspring: Glenice, Roma and Ian. Then there was Glenromian Jack, followed by Kenton Hope, with whom he won his first South Australian State Championship in 1963.

He lingers over the names of Navarre Wally and Penmore Bradman, a dog who won nineteen opens. Then Kynoona Deane (a Queensland-bred dog), Glenromian Tamie (named after Tamie Fraser), Kelton Tom and Glenromian Cindy. The last two dogs became famous as a breeding pair, with progeny sold in five Australian states. One pup of the same strain was exported to Montana in the United States to work sheep in the mountains.

When I caught up with him, Byn was reluctantly taking a bit of a forced break from farming and trialling because of some 'nonsense' with his heart which he didn't want to go into. The doctors were ordering him to town for tests and making him rest. However, his Naracoorte house backs onto a lake and some scrub, and he's got room in the back yard for a small mob of quiet wethers. Tied up in the yard was a young bitch he had bred who was just starting to work. All his other dogs had been farmed out amongst his friends while the heart was getting attention. But the bitch was giving him something to do—and she was coming on well.

He was a bit dark that he wasn't in Canberra that week to defend his national title, and that he wouldn't be taking on the New Zealanders in the Test Team: 'It's good to give some of the young ones a go coming on up,' he says. But it's blatantly obvious he'd rather his wretched heart hadn't got in the way.

Despite the trophies, ribbons and clocks, Byn maintains that trialling has never been anything more than a hobby, one he took up in 1948. 'It's the people I've met, that's been the thing for me,' Byn says. The weekends away at trials with other farming people pitting their dogs against each other for a bit of sport have made him friends all over Australia—people he feels comfortable enough to drop in on and sling a swag on their floor. 'They're a great bunch of people, the three-sheep triallers,' he says.

Not that he's got anything in particular against the yard dog triallers—though he does reckon many of their dogs are a bit too pushy, too noisy and waste an awful lot of energy rushing about to achieve their ends. 'And yard dog triallers are a lot more commercial than we are. They're in it to sell pups and make a living.

'There's a lot more finesse in what we do. Sure, the yard dog has a place. But I know what I like and, really, you don't see the same level of skill. The test that we get our dogs to do means that if they can do that, they can do the other—and usually without all the yapping.

'I've got to have quiet dogs. I hate these yap, yap type of dogs that hustle and push the sheep around, making them bash themselves on the side of the yards. You don't get the job done any faster stirring the stock up—it's probably slower.'

It runs deep, this love of the border collie. While he admits there are good kelpies around, Byn's love of careful dogs, ones that are biddable—he calls them 'press button' dogs—makes him, he admits, a bit one-eyed. 'I've never bred dogs commercially,' Byn points out. 'I breed dogs when I'm looking for a better one for myself and just sell off the surplus.'

On the properties he's run since 1945 near Bordertown, Lucindale, and others near Naracoorte and Edenhope, he says he's only employed labour spasmodically. His good dogs, he reckons, are worth up to three men: 'I was the lazy one. I could sit in the ute and let the dogs do all the work. And these have always been the same dogs I've won trials with.

'My best farm dogs have also been my best trials dogs. They are always the first dogs I let off when I've got hard work to do—and sheep or cattle, it doesn't matter to them.

'No, there's nothing soft about a border collie. They might be quiet workers, but they're tough.'*

* Byn Dinning was selected to represent South Australia in the Supreme Australian Working Sheepdog Championship held between 27 September and 4 October, 1993 on the lawns in front of Old Parliament House, Canberra. The photograph below shows Byn with Old Mill Laddie and Glenromian Flag.

PART 1

WHERE THE BIG GUMS GROW

In dappled shade mobs of sheep sit out the heat of the day. Cattle chew their cud contentedly. Big gums with peeling bark reveal smooth new skin beneath, and gum oozes from unhealed wounds where branches have snapped off in wind or still heat. Creeks and dams mirror tangled branches, red and white coloured bark and glossy leaves. Grasses wave. In the air hangs eucalypt scent. Blue seedlings erupt after flooding and big rains. Under thick brown bark, small lizards and ants live, while hollows shelter noisy corellas and galahs.

A huge gum—dense canopy against bright blue sky making grey purple shadows underneath—epitomises grandeur and stateliness. This is the country where the topsoils are deep, water is plentiful and the seasons relatively predictable. There are vineyards, pine forests and irrigated crops, and predators like foxes, rabbits, bushfires . . . and tourists. There are also neighbours close by and pubs.

The dogs of big gum country have a particular tale to tell.

MESSIAH OF THE LAMBS

Garth Dutfield, Wellington, New South Wales

We run about 4,000 sheep on 'Stockyard Creek', our property on the shores of Burrendong dam. The views of its waters from most of our paddocks are great but it's in winter, when the hills are cloaked in fog, tht I find myself overawed by the beauty around me. On cold crisp mornings, shrouded in mist, I ride through mobs of lambing ewes to ensure that all are safe and to retrieve any lambs rejected by their mothers. Many a cold wet orphan lamb has been revived with a warm bottle of milk by the open fire in the homestead. And so to my dog tale . . .

As a young man I saw many funny incidents involving dogs, but I reckon that Sam, the whippet-beagle cross, one of the members of the rabbit pack, gave me the biggest laugh. Sam's position in the pack was semi-fast rank outsider in any chase, with very little chance of ever coming up with the prize money. He was a likeable dog, pure white with black patches stretching up over each eye to cover his large floppy ears. This description is important.

Mustering and lamb marking time had come around again—a time of year most of us sheep men don't much like. This particular year we were a bit late and the lambs were wild and large. As the bellowing ewes hung back, all trying to find their lost lambs in the mob, the lambs started to ring the edge of the mob, with more and more joining in the 'frisky' run. I knew we were in trouble. I had turned the surging tide back into the centre three times. Sheepdogs and motorcyclists were becoming frantic when strolling across the hill fair bang in front of the mob came Sam.

You can't imagine what I called him. Sam knew he was in trouble and turned for home. At the same time, however, the lambs broke and, seeing a pure white comrade (albeit with black floppy ears) making a beeline away from the mob, they followed. Sam glanced back but was not impressed to find upward of 300 charging lambs bearing down on him and a further 400 screaming ewes coming after them. Sam changed into a higher gear and headed for home.

I was thinking murderous, unprintable, blasphemous thoughts about 'white rabbit dogs'. But being dimwitted as sometimes I am, I hadn't recognised heaven-sent assistance when I saw it.

Sam bolted for home. The lambs followed as though he was the annointed Messiah of all sheepdom. The faster Sam went, the faster the lambs went. He tried to lose them at the creek, but the leaders cleared it like Olympic long-jumpers. Sam stuck to the road like glue except for a smart circular move through a patch of scrub which he had learnt from chasing foxes. But, because the lambs were strung out through it, he ran into them wherever he turned. He soon dodged back to the road at even greater speed.

The gates had all been left open and Sam made full use of them—but still the lambs followed their leader, propping and bucking with glee. As we watched in astonishment from the rise where it all started, we could see Sam approaching the yards. The lambs were gaining on him. My mother looked up from the homestead garden and was aghast to see a line of 300 lambs heading for the yards with no ewes in sight. They were strung out far behind, all panting.

Finally, after being pursued for a mile, Sam hurdled the gate at the sheepyards and escaped to the safety of his kennel. All we had to do was pick up a few exhausted ewes along the way. When we finally reached the yards, my mother had already closed the gate.

This event happened about twenty years ago, but I can still see the tears of laughter rolling down my dad's cheeks. Sam probably had recurring nightmares.

EXPOSING DAD'S HABITS

Anthony Honner, Brentwood, South Australia

Dad's home property was at Brentwood and he had a scrub block, called Paling Hut, 22 miles away. Once a week Dad and Spike, his kelpie-collie cross dog, would check the water and stock at Paling Hut.

In 1949 Dad left for a trip to England. Mum kept an eye on the farm at Brentwood and a sharefarmer checked the scrub block. After about three weeks the dog went missing, and while Mum was on the phone to the sharefarmer she mentioned this. He said that when he had checked the sheep the previous day a friendly dog had been circling them. The dog then went over and lay down by the trough. As it had done no harm, he thought no more of it, except that in hindsight the dog did indeed look like Spike.

Mum then rang a few Warooka people and a local identity said he had seen Spike hanging around the Warooka Hotel all day two days earlier. He'd been there again that day—lying on the mat at the hotel front door.

Next morning the dog was home again.

Mum put two and two together, and realised the dog must have though that no-one was checking the sheep in Dad's absence. Spike had therefore set off on foot on the usual trip—which rather exposed Dad's habits. First he went to Warooka and had a long wait at the hotel. Then he went twelve miles south to Paling Hut to check the sheep and water, before returning to Warooka for another long session. He then returned home.

And we had thought Dad's long day was all to do with sheep.

THE DUCK HUNTER

Peter Chantler, Casterton, Victoria

Aron (pronounced A-Ron) was a sheepdog of great repute, known for feats of bravery while facing savage mobs of rampaging wethers, not to mention keeping packs of irate rams at bay. His most memorable feat, however, occurred one Saturday during the duck season.

A good mate of mine, 'Coop', came out to our place to go shooting on a large billabong which is usually chock-a-block with black duck. Coop had brought out his new duck dog, Heidi, to show off her skills. From what he'd been telling me, Heidi was going to do everything except shoot the ducks. I'd been taking in this drivel for several days by then and finally, thank God, the dog's day had come. I couldn't have handled too many more stories about the utterly amazing superdog Heidi.

So off we went to the billabong, Coop and me, with Heidi waddling along behind. As expected, there was a stack of ducks swimming around among the weeds, and we were able to bag a few. One duck, however, landed smack in the middle of the water.

'No problem,' said Coop. 'This is exactly what I brought Heidi along for.'

Well, I rolled my eyes and thought to myself: 'Lordy! Surely I don't have to listen to this all over again while Wonder Dog is freestyling out to bring the duck back to the bank, do I?'

My silent prayers were interrupted by the volume and tone of voice that Coop was using to command Wonder Dog to bring home the duck. After a couple of minutes, Heidi's parentage was being seriously questioned, and I don't think the dog was too impressed with the 25-kilometre walk home that Coop was generously promising her. Needless to say, Heidi was on the bank out of arm's reach from Coop, and the duck was still in the middle of the billabong.

As neither of us was too keen on giving Heidi a practical demonstration of how to do it, I said rather jokingly that perhaps Aron could show us how to do it. So I ran back to the house and brought the other wonder dog back to the scene. Coop had that 'don't be an idiot' look on his face, but I was becoming quite convinced that Aron was up to the job.

Luckily, he loved to fetch sticks and balls and return them to the thrower. So I grabbed a stone and threw it in the vicinity of the floating duck. Aron took a mighty leap into the water and made a beeline straight for the duck. As the only thing floating out there was the duck, he immediately assumed that I had thrown out a dead duck for him to fetch back. And he did just that, dropping it right at my feet.

I just looked up at Coop and smiled. I never did hear another Heidi story.

THE SHEEP AND HAT DOG

Graeme Bassett, Newstead, Victoria

I was bringing in some sheep one day for drenching. I was on a motorbike and had my dog helping out. As I approached the creek I noted another mob on the other side coming toward me. I did not want the two mobs to mix, so I left the mob I was following with my dog to bring them to the creek. I accelerated swiftly to cross the creek and head off the second mob. As I did so, my woollen beret fell from my head onto the ground.

I could not stop to pick up the beret. Instead I intended to leave it there until I returned to take the sheep to their paddock. I proceeded to escort the first mob to the shearing shed for drenching.

About half an hour later I came out of the shed to get on my motorbike. There, next to the bike, was my dog, looking quite proud of himself. At his feet was my beret. The dog had gone back over the creek, got my beret and brought it to the shed. It was wet from where he had swum the creek.

The breed of dog? A fox terrier.

RABBIT HABIT

Helen Sutherland, Scotsburn, Victoria

A rabbit pack consisting of ten or fifteen dogs of various descriptions—greyhounds, whippets, fox terriers etc—was always to be found on properties of any size in Victoria in the 1920s. Where my husband lived on his parents' sheep farm, such a pack was kept to keep the rabbit population in check.

As a small boy he remembers the great interest aroused by Bruce, one of the dogs. Bruce was a Russian collie and he had a most unusual habit. When he caught a rabbit he would trot off to the nearest waterhole, hold the rabbit under the water until it drowned, and then return in an unhurried manner to present it to the man in charge.

NO LAUGHING MATTER

Brian Kilford, Kersbrook, South Australia

This story was serious, dead serious, while it was happening, but when I tell it, everyone laughs!

I was about to leave to do some wool classing up round Broken Hill when I found the battery in the one-tonner truck had gone flat. I took the battery from the car, put it alongside the truck and jump-started it. As soon as the truck started, I hopped out to remove the jumper leads and close the bonnet.

Jack, our border collie, thought, 'Here we go. It's time for work.' He bounded into the cabin, knocking the handbrake off in his rush. I couldn't get back inside because the truck was already moving down the slight slope in front of the shed. Bracing my foot against a young pine tree behind me so I could stop the truck, I yelled to Marj, who was down at the house, to come and help.

'Jesus, I'm gunna lose it,' I thought as I struggled to hold the truck from rolling into the dam. Then the pine tree snapped, my legs buckled and I fell backwards just as the truck rolled on over me, its wheels going right over my thighs. I thought that would be the end of the truck. But next second, the engine was revving. Marj had seen the danger the *truck* was in, had jumped in, revved it up and reversed it back—*straight over my legs again!*

Luckily for me there was a ditch around where the pine tree had been standing and my legs went into it. Otherwise I would have had two broken legs for sure, and not just bad bruising. What's worse, while I'm rolling around in agony, Marj decided it was funny. And Jack, well he just loved all the shouting and swearing and revving—and jumped all over me with delight.

It was two months before we did any more work together. And I still can't understand why it is that everyone laughs.

HELLO, DINGO

Cavell Keevers, Sandgate, New South Wales

Having lived in a forest area on the north coast of New South Wales where dingoes were plentiful, I have developed great respect for the intelligence of our native dog. Its cunning is extraordinary.

Our family has had several half-bred dingoes, but one stands out in my memory. We called him Dingo. He was the result of a furtive mating of my father's blue heeler bitch by a big red dingo which had forced its way into a locked slab barn.

Dingo, who was red like his father, was a wonderful household pet and a very intelligent farm working dog who seldom left my father's side. Because of this he frequently used to hear my father shouting 'Hello-o-o' to the neighbours when a telephone call came in for them. This was in the early days of telephones, and the neighbours had not yet installed one. The dog would sit by my father's feet and echo this call.

One day a friend living on a heavily timbered property nearby came to me very distressed, saying, 'Something seems to be wrong across the road from me. I can hear someone calling out "Hello-o-o" repeatedly, as if he needs help. I have searched the scrub and called out, but got no answer.'

When I told him that it was probably Dingo, he was most indignant, but had a laugh about it later.

After my father's death I lived by myself in the forest area. This half-bred dingo became very protective of me and would snarl and bark savagely to prevent any stranger from entering the front gate. I well remember the look of disbelief on people's faces when I told then to say 'Hello-o-o, Dingo' to be allowed inside. As soon as they did, however, the snarl would be replaced by a smile and a wave of the red tail. I must admit, though, that they always kept a close eye on the dog as he followed them up the garden path.

The other member of that same litter was not like Dingo in any way. He had thrown back to his mother's looks but, although a blue heeler in appearance, he had all the ways of the wild dingo. He was a thieving devil and, if caught at any wrongdoing, would freeze and stare at you in such a manner as to be really frightening.

A LEANER CHRISTMAS WITHOUT LENA

Christine Stratton, Strathalbyn, South Australia

In September 1978 we bought two dozen day-old turkeys to fatten and sell to help bring in some cash for Christmas. It had been a lean year for us. We put our two working collies, Lena and Sonny, on guard over the turkeys to ensure their safety.

At 11.30 one late November night, about two weeks before the turkeys were ready to kill and dress, we heard a terrible squawking coming from the barn where they were kept. We had thought they would be safe in the well-protected cage we had made. The dogs had been asleep on the old settee outside the back door. They took off, barking. As they ran toward the turkey cage they were met by a large fox with one of the biggest turkeys in its mouth.

The fox raced through the fence and into the paddock, with the dogs in full pursuit. We could do nothing but listen to the dogs barking as they chased the fox toward the dam. In the moonlight we could see the dogs circling the top of the dam wall and the fox swimming for its life. The dogs refused to let it leave the water and we found next morning that it did eventually drown.

'Well, there goes our Christmas dinner,' I said to my husband. We had taken orders for all but one turkey which was to have been ours, so it looked like we would have to eat chicken.

Just then I felt something warm against my leg. There were the dogs looking very pleased with themselves, tails wagging like windmills, as Lena dropped the large white turkey at my feet.

That Christmas, no turkey ever tasted better. But I did swear the kids to secrecy until after the guests had eaten, even though I think the bird must have died of fright. There wasn't a mark on it when I dressed it.

'I'LL HIT HIM WITH THE SPADE'

Ian Ward, Keppoch, South Australia

My wife, Jenny, and my mother were going around the ewes and lambs when they came across a large foxhole. They had no spade, so decided to come back later and fill it in.

When they returned, Kiwi the sheepdog, unseen by them, jumped off the ute and disappeared down the hole. The women then started stuffing screwed-up newspaper down the hole with the spade handle.

As they were about to start filling the hole with dirt, they heard a rustling and scratching noise.

'Quick,' shouted Jenny, 'call Kiwi. I think the fox is coming out. I'll hold him down with the spade until the dog gets here.'

She jammed the spade handle against the paper and they called and called to the dog, who of course didn't come. The more they called, the louder the scratching became.

Finally, Jenny gritted her teeth, stood back and said, 'I'll hit him with the spade as he comes out.'

Poor Kiwi suddenly shot out of the hole, narrowly avoiding a spade on the head—and terribly thankful not to have been buried alive.

COINCIDENCE?

Murray Staude, Naracoorte, South Australia

Some years ago it was our good fortune to have a thirteen-week overseas trip. Our son, whose property was five miles away, took Talbot, our working dog, to his place to care for him.

Not once during those thirteen weeks did Talbot attempt to come home. But on the morning after we arrived home, I walked out the back door and there he was, lying on the mat, delighted to see us.

I still wonder if it was a coincidence—or did he somehow know we had come home?

He is still with us, fourteen years old and still working sheep—although he's badly in need of a hearing aid.

A TOUCH OF TELEPATHY

Barry Field, Tilba, New South Wales

Chad wasn't born a sheepdog. He was a German shorthaired pointer—a hunting dog. He lived with us on a small property overlooking a lake in southern New South Wales. He had been a gift to us.

He was ever keen to please and performed all the tasks a good working dog should. He was my constant companion and possessed an uncanny ability to understand everything I asked him to do. For instance, I was working on a fence line one day and I told him to fetch my jumper, which I had left on a fence post a couple of hundred yards away up the hill. Chad returned a few minutes later holding the jumper gently in his mouth.

Another time my son and I were again working on the fence line, repairing broken wires, when we lost a pair of pliers. We searched for about fifteen minutes, then gave up and continued down the line using an old pair from the tractor tool box. Chad had been watching keenly while we searched. About half an hour later, to our great surprise, he turned up with the pliers in his mouth.

SUNDAY STOWAWAY

Beth Henke, Mumbannar, Victoria

It is extraordinary what lengths your best friend will go to so she, too, can go visiting on a Sunday afternoon—despite having been told to stay home. Wocky, our blue heeler cross, was as broad as she was tall and reckoned she knew as much as her boss. On this occasion, she outsmarted even him.

We set off in our old XR Falcon ute to journey across country to the parents-in-law for the afternoon. Wocky was determined to be part of the visit. She came with us to the first gate, but was growled at and told to stay home. We shut the gate and when we couldn't see her, didn't think much more of it. We thought she had slunk off through the rushes and swamp for home.

We travelled on, opening and closing seven gates. We stopped to change a flat tyre but then continued on across country and into a pine forest. We were stopped there by tourists who asked questions about the lie of the land. Suddenly the old XR died. We opened the bonnet to investigate the problem—and there was determined old Wocky, sitting between the engine and the mudguard.

The tourists looked a little stunned, but the boss just casually remarked, 'Oh, that's where we carry our dogs in this part of the bush.'

In her keenness to meet the tourists' labradors after her cramped and bumpy journey of twenty miles, she had wriggled the petrol pipe off the engine block.

KEEPING AN EYE ON THE JOB

John Bodey, Edenhope, Victoria

My wife and I run a sheep husbandry contracting business. We have a black and white shorthaired border collie named Bob. He is a forceful dog who helps move sheep into sheep handlers for teeth-trimming, crutching or foot-paring. When one of our staff nicknamed him 'Wonder Dog' I was quite pleased until I overheard the explanation: 'Bob is called Wonder Dog because we wonder what he's going to do wrong next!'

Bob has a habit of staring at any one sheep that has been separated from the mob. This frustrating trait reveals itself all too often. A client may remove a stray lamb from a mob of ewes or a frightened sheep can jump out of the forcing yard. Until that sheep is returned to the mob, Bob's attention, to our extreme annoyance, is fixed only on it.

One day on a property near Coleraine in western Victoria, Bob's bad habit turned to great advantage. Our client's sheep had footrot, so our team was employed to eradicate this highly contagious disease. This requires *every* sheep on the farm to be mustered, then thoroughly foot-pared, inspected and treated.

Bob was pushing sheep through the force into our sheep-handling machine for foot-paring. He had been doing a great job but, quite unexpectedly, completely lost interest in working on the four-year-old wethers. Instead, he was staring out into the paddock, the boundary of which we could not see as the land was hilly and dotted with huge red gums.

I thought that for Bob to have gone on strike there must have been one sheep that had jumped out of the forcing pen, escaping out of view. I mentioned this to my client and suggested that he check the paddock. Sure enough, ten minutes later he returned in his truck with one sheep, Bob's eyes still firmly glued to it.

Bob didn't know it, but he probably saved the entire footrot eradication program from ruin.

PART 2

HEAD WOLVES AND UNDERDOGS

As in any effective organisation, someone has to be in charge—and it certainly can't be the dog, even though that's what most of them would like.

The secret to success, according to livewire dog trainer Neil McDonald, is to emulate the dynamics of a pack of wolves, close relatives of working dogs. In a pack, the head wolf takes authority and punishes insurrection amongst his underlings.

Getting to the stage, however, where the human is revered as head wolf by the working dogs is not always an easy path, particularly if the wolf is a mere woman. It's highly likely she'll be blatantly discriminated against by the working dogs if they're anything like Suzie, Sam or Ringer.

And while the aim might be to lift your dogs to a higher intellectual plane, there'll always be creatures like Boxer and Boots to drag you down to size. Indeed, the question of who is actually supposed to be doing the educating is worthy of deep consideration.

With a good mix of genes, character and training, theory has it that all you need to do is point your working dog in the direction of the quarry and issue commands. But as the bloke at Peter Murphy's trial discovered, boasting about a dog has its hazards.

If it weren't for dogs like Peter Mercer's, that demonstrate they can think as well as obey, many would wonder whether the agony of transforming a dog from freeloader to useful employee was worth it.

THE WORKING DOG'S JOHN CLEESE: A PROFILE OF NEIL McDONALD

Angela Goode

If you're ever way out in the backblocks and you see a bloke in a ute with about 50 kelpies on board, you've probably stumbled on Neil McDonald of the Sherwood stud on his way to another working dog training school. This South Australian dynamo with a John Cleese streak has for the past four years given schools all over Australia—about a hundred in total—plus numerous talks and working dog demonstrations. I caught up with him just before he loaded up and headed for central Queensland for schools at Julia Creek, Richmond, Hughenden and anywhere else on the way.

Out of his 33 years around dogs and the bush, Neil has stitched together a training philosophy that obviously makes sense to plenty of hardened dog handlers. In his three-day schools, the twenty or so participants get plenty of exposure to the colourful McDonald turn of phrase, coming out at the end of them, according to Neil, with a new approach that will make their dog's life happier, and save them money on their farms.

The fact that Sherwood dogs have earned glory no doubt gives the message some clout. Sherwood Ace, owned by Rob Macklin, has won South Australian Dog of the Year twice and Sherwood Macka has won three open yard dog titles. Sires Wabba Kelp and Capree Beau have produced numerous trial winners, among them the rising star Sherwood Adios.

McDonald sees his task as training the handlers, not necessarily the dogs. 'I observe in my travels that most people feel they're too big and tough to be affectionate to their dogs. The dog's the thing they laugh at. It's neglected the most.

'So when I go somewhere, I play their game and say, "Well, you've gotta get your dog, bash him round with a crowbar, smash him down with a shovel, put him around some sheep, then run over him with the ute a couple of times"—and you see them sit up and take notice and say, "Right, we'll start listening to this fella. He's on our wavelength."

'Then I suggest we crash-tackle a few beasts. So I call all the rough, yahoo dogs out and, unsurprisingly, they find they can't shift the stock because they apply too much force in the wrong area.

'So I come out with a couple of sneaking, pussyfooting dogs and, amazingly to them, my cattle or sheep flow. The good stockmen amongst the group quickly see that what I'm on about is a softer approach and that it produces more desirable results.'

At about that stage, Neil says he sees the tough guys slip to the back of the mob.

Basically the only thing wrong with most handlers, he says, is that they don't know how to play and be affectionate with their dogs and how to discipline them. 'The guts of the issue is—good

20

dogs are bred, and champions are made. To get there you have to put them under your wing and make a companion of them. But if I bowl up into Proserpine and say, "Look here, you fellows, grab yourselves a little puppy dog and we'll spend two to three hours patting it and talking to it", they'd laugh you out as a wimp.'

When he arrives at a school, Neil says the usual scene is of dogs fighting, piddling all over the place and straining on their chains.

'I usually tell them that if they think it's a dog training school, they've been tricked. It's a course on how to make more money through getting cooperative livestock, and you get them by having good dogs.'

According to an old stockman friend of Neil's, only about five per cent of the population is capable of working a dog. 'And I reckon that's generous,' says Neil.

The John Cleese streak finds expression in the McDonald impersonation of the 'normal farmer', the 95 or so per cent who don't get as much as they could out of their dogs. Standing at the back of the mob doing star jumps, model aeroplane-style manoeuvres and making insane whooping noises earns McDonald more than a few queer looks, but this bloke doesn't care what sort of galah he makes of himself so long as he gets his message across. For it's those Cleese-type antics that an awful lot of farmers perform unknowingly in their yards at home. However, if they stand in the right place in the yards, the dog will do the work for them, the stock will flow and everyone will feel more relaxed.

Although he is away from his farm at Keith in the south-east for months at a time, he finds teaching people how to work dogs suits him well. 'Even if I won a million dollars, I'd keep doing this just for the fun.'

So having tapped into the minds of the handlers, Neil takes the school off to remote central Africa in a story to help them plumb the minds of their dogs: 'If we were all wolves at the waterhole in central Africa 300 years ago and we spotted five antelope, we'd hardly jump in the air and say, "Oh! what a feeling, antelope!", because the noise would scare the antelope away.

'We would recognise the antelope are a bubble to be patted, just as livestock are a bubble to be patted—because they've got eyes in the side of their heads. If we make a heap of noise, the antelope run off. So the boss wolf is going to tell his team that if they make any more noise, he'll crush them. Naturally he gets a bit of order in court.

'In the pack there might be an enthusiastic young wolf called

Caroline who spots the antelope and wants to impress the boss wolf by getting them. She launches herself straight at them, and when the antelope look up at her and see her coming flat-out, they show her a clean set of heels. So when she comes back, the boss wolf says, "Do that again and I'll cripple you. Instead, go out wide, past the tree and the dam, so they don't detect you coming. If you have to, go on your belly and make sure your scent will not blow onto them."

'So now, as the boss wolf, I'm putting a plan into action. It's not a matter of just hoping we get some antelope today, because this time the antelope see a semicircle of Carolines, and they run away from her. Antelope take the spot where there's no pressure. All Caroline has got to do is stay back and run the antelope into where the others are waiting to pounce.'

That understanding of the basic hunting instinct that propels or motivates a sheepdog to work, the desire to go and shepherd stock and bring them back, is what Neil believes all working dog handlers should absorb. 'What self-respecting young wolf would ever get a mob of antelope and chase them away? He'd get killed by the others in the pack, and they would all starve.'

All too often, the first thing many stockmen do is get a pup, get a mob of sheep, stand at the back of the mob and send the dog around to tuck the wing in. Of course the pup goes too far, so they call him back and punish him. They try to teach him to 'come behind' before he gets a chance to follow his instincts.

'Every time you tell a young dog to come behind, you dampen his enthusiasm. Blokes will say to me, "Geez, it was a real keen young pup. All he wanted to do was work sheep, and he's sort of gone off. He must have got bitten by a snake or it was too hot." What's happened is, he's stripped the wolf out of him by continually telling him to come behind. In doing so, he stripped the work out of him.'

For a young pup, you need to break in four or five sheep or cattle so that when the pup is introduced to them, he becomes a winner right from the start and can use his instinct to herd them back to you, the head wolf.

The head wolf, Neil says, is like a football coach. If he doesn't have respect, he's got no team players. 'A spongy old wolf that's friends with all his pack will cause them to die because he hasn't got enough authority over them to stop them running straight at the antelope.

'If you look around at the majority of the prominent trial people, they're egotistical, they've got to win at all costs and they're a bit schizophrenic. Those factors have a lot to do with their success. A dog's got to see a good side and a bad side of you. Someone that just mopes around and is the same all the time doesn't give their dog any up and down, any contrasts.

'A dog's got to see what happens if he doesn't perform. I'm pretty tough on my dogs for sniffing, for marking out their territory, spinning their wheels and flicking up clouds of dust, trotting past another dog arrogantly, snarling at another dog, ignoring me. I give them an open hander for any antisocial manners.

'Too many people let their dog get up to all the most horrible habits under the sun, like licking another dog, sticking its nose into its bottom, cocking on the side of the house. Then when they take them to the workplace, because they haven't set the environment right, it's inevitable the dog cuts off a sheep or does something a little bit wrong. Then they go and belt the dog so it ends up thinking he's getting pummelled for working.

'By the time I go near sheep, my dogs know full well I'm boss. If he goes in and cuts off a sheep or something, I ignore it for a while.'

People make a big mistake by not ensuring their dogs are civilised: 'I can tell when someone gets out of their car and walks over to the yard whether their dog will work properly. If the dog's giggling all over them, jumping and straining the chain and being a pinhead, then I know they've got very little chance of having success in the sheepyards.'

According to Neil there is no such thing as a dog trainer, only a 'situation creator'. He maintains that shepherding dogs such as kelpies, collies, some Smithfields and some coolies don't have to be trained. 'All you have to do is create a situation where they'll work just as they would in the wild. Then, if they look like going clockwise around their sheep or cattle, you give them an appropriate order like "get over", "go left", whatever. If you are consistent enough, they will correlate that command with that action. Therefore they won't treat the learning process as an imposition—and note I said learning, not training.

'For most of us, however, it's "get here", "go there", "do that". Too often, the workplace for a dog is like a bloody torture chamber.'

As for picking your future champion out of the litter, there is no formula. 'Just pick the one you like most,' says Neil. 'Then you'll be prepared to put the work into it.'

To be any good, though, it has to have instinct to go around stock and receptiveness to commands. It must be able to take orders, because eventually you'll break the dog from only going around stock to do other things that are against its natural instinct. 'Once we grasp that dogs need to be allowed to develop their natural instincts, then we are halfway home.'

A good dog also needs intelligence, as well as a good memory. There's basically no difference, Neil believes, between kelpies and border collies, and indeed both are crossbreds from the same basic source. The kelpie, however, seems not to have as good a memory as the collie. While a collie will remember a lesson from the day before, the kelpie needs to go through it again. However, collies tend to lack initiative and independence. 'It always will be a kelpie that does the legendary feat like retrieving five runaway cattle that escaped to the mountains,' says Neil.

But whatever the breed, your chances of getting a decent pup are increased, Neil says, if you go to an established breeder who also successfully trains and trials dogs. And yes, of those 50 dogs with him on the Queensland trip, about 36 pups and young dogs are for sale.

Basic care of the dog involves tying it up short so it doesn't fall off the ute or get snagged around objects. And he's particularly heavy on 'Gold Coasters': 'You try going to the Gold Coast with a couple of hundred thousand dollars and see if you want to work after that,' he says in explanation that a working dog should be tied up whenever it is not actually working.

But back to the school in progress in sheepyards in some far-off town. You might see Neil with his tight mob of quiet sheep running clockwise around them and a pup on the opposite side doing the same. When Neil switches direction, so does the pup. He corners the sheep and points to demonstrate that the pup will move opposite to the way pointed. It's all to reinforce that wolf instinct buried in the brain of every shepherding dog. He demonstrates how to link these natural characteristics in with commands which will eventually lead the mature dog to work counter to his instinct.

Then it's time for the psychology of livestock to be explored and, for this exercise, Neil paints up a quiet mob of sheep in different colours to demonstrate the role of the leader of the mob. By using gentle dogs, it can be seen that the leader through the gate is nearly always the same one.

'Then we put in a rough dog and immediately he'll chop up the order, knock over the leader, and turn him into a tailender—totally changing the psychology of the mob. Because the tailenders then start going through the gate, they don't know how to lead, consequently they get halfway through the gate, turn, and before long you get a row of bums in your gateway.'

People then try to shift them with tougher dogs: 'They try and shift them with force, but you don't untangle a ball of string by yanking at it, do you? So I let them make a great mess in the yard and everything goes wrong. Then I go in with my dogs and unravel them straightaway, simply because they are receptive to commands and they get into position. It's not the sheep that are wrong, it's because the dogs are not in position.'

After problem-solving sessions on matters like dogs being 'too fast'— 'That's rubbish. You want a dog that's fast. The problem is it's working too close'—they tackle a few other sacred cows. 'Teaching a dog to sit is the ruination of a dog,' says Neil. It eventually means they give up trying to head off the 'antelope' because they can never get to them.

There are lessons on backing, mustering a big mob, casting, and teaching how to push stock away. The final exercise involves people being paired up as 'dog' and 'handler', trying to work sheep. Besides being entertaining, it helps participants to understand things from the dog's point of view.

'Above all, the schools teach people where to stand and when to keep their mouths shut,' says Neil. It sounds like advice for more than just dog handlers.

ACCORDING TO DAD

Wendy Treloar, Cummins, South Australia

Boots was a barker, a biter and a marvellous watchdog—but not much good at anything else. He only *thought* he was a sheepdog. Our cats lived in trees. But he was loyal—he loved all our family and slept beneath his master's bedroom window. He would always be at the back door to greet us each morning with a smile. But he was not even half-decent as a sheepdog.

My father, a pioneer of the district, always had good dogs, so we always had to justify Boots's consumption of dog food and his sheer existence—especially as my Dad had Nicky, a dog who could do everything that was asked of him. Everything. Dad continually compared his dog with ours. He forgot how much training was required to achieve such perfection—and that it was all the actual shouting involved that taught his daughters how to swear.

Nicky knew, according to Dad, whether or not he was going to town (good clothes) or around the farm (old clothes). Our dog, Boots, leapt onto anything that moved, no matter what it was wearing. He *loved* barking all the way through towns, stirring up the town dogs. He thrived on going to footy practice too, on the back of the farm ute—plenty of noise and action. But everyone kept their distance.

Nicky, according to Dad, 'slept at my feet and knew a mile from home when it was time to sit up.' Boots *never* stayed 'down'. He hung over either side of the ute, around corners, and leaned, as far as was possible, into the driver's face, where he puffed and dribbled. His frantic galloping from side to side one day caused him to be sucked out by a passing road train. Neighbours recognised the wounded, snarling and mortified dog by his bristling neck hairs and quickly devised a foolproof 'dog retrieval' scheme whereby they grabbed, lifted and threw, then shut their car boot simultaneously.

Boots wasn't born fierce. He just was never friendly to strangers. After an illness and a visit to a vet when a pup, he reacted violently to anyone who appeared as though they may be aiming a thermometer at his rear end.

Dad's dog, according to Dad, *never* attacked chooks. Boots did. He loved chasing and playing with chickens if the chance arose. Boots was caught 'red-handed' one day with a dead chicken, so we tried an old remedy. 'Tie a dead chook around their necks and they'll never touch poultry again,' they had said. Ha! We did that and he ate the chook.

According to Dad, Nicky followed him around the paddock during seeding, only pausing to rest when the combine was filled at headlands. Boots, when weary, slowed to a walk right in front of the wheel, making us stop. He then rode on the wide old tractor seat, eyes closed, paws and head on the driver's lap. His breath and body odours were hard to take—but it was in the days before tractor-cabs and radios and air-conditioning, and it was better than no company at all during the long tractor hours.

According to Dad, Nicky obeyed his commands and knew what meant what. Boots didn't. 'Right back' to Boots meant get up on the back of the ute. 'Around' to Boots meant run around anywhere. 'Trough' meant a swim, never mind about showing the sheep where water was.

According to Dad, his dog mustered at just the right distance. Boots couldn't stand that. We called him 'ALB' (aggressive little bugger) as he worked so close to the mob the sheep thought he was one of them. We called Boots 'Smoko' too, as it was only at shearing time he was really good at anything—*food*. He loved hot toasties. He eyed the old shearer called Tog and, pressing close, begged him to part with some of his food.

Nicky, according to Dad, knew his place in the shearing shed: 'Never on the board and only in the shed at penning-up time.' Boots didn't. He roamed. It was *his* territory and if forced to defend it, he did. Whenever Boots was needed for penning up, he would be stalking the shearers' dogs and claiming and staking out his patch. And he never worked for the boss's missus.

Dad's dog never bit anyone. Boots did. Often. Never savagely, but as a warning. When it became unsafe for neighbours to get out of their car and conversations had to be shouted from half-wound-down windows, we had to consign Boots to the great salt patch.

When Dad retired, *his* dog was put to stud at the kennels where he was bred and lived in stately dignity to an old age. He couldn't have come to our place. He was always bashed up by our bitzers.

Dad still lives nearby. He reminds us frequently of how bad our dogs are. None of ours would have saved our lives as Nicky did his when the sugar gum fell and pinned him to the bulldozer. Nicky licked him and kept him conscious until Dad got free and found help.

The older the old farmers get, the better their dogs were!

ONLY ORNAMENTAL

Joyce Shiner, Albany, Western Australia

On a bleak July morning in 1940, we heard the convoy moving out under cover of darkness, just as they had come. For more than a week the white-gum ridge above the homestead had concealed a battalion of soldiers from the Northam Military Training camp.

It was said to be a survival exercise and all week long small parties of khaki-clad men had straggled around the district trying to live off the land. They were hungry and readily accepted what food donations we made. Garden vegetables were consumed on the spot. Fresh-laid eggs and Keep-eggs also failed to reach camp, judging by the piles of eggshells behind the trees outside the orchard fence. The rabbits were also temporarily eradicated, leaving paddocks looking as though a major battle had already taken place where the warrens had been ripped open with shovels and bare hands.

The last time I saw them, they'd come stumbling up the path like a bunch of weary schoolboys, khaki shirts and baggy shorts, their thick woollen socks hanging over heavy army boot-tops. They were following the little Scottish sergeant, who was being towed along at a rather undignified rate by a big yellow dog on a length of frayed binder twine. As they scuffled into a semicircle around the basket of wet clothes I was pegging on the line, Scotty said, 'We've come to say goodbye t'ya. An' me and the lads thought we'd like to show our appreciation of your generosity by offering you our mascot.'

I looked at the dog, a handsome, noble-looking creature, but I said, 'It's a sheepdog we need.'

'Tut, tut,' said Scotty. 'Not too loud, or he'll bring all the ruddy sheep in the district and we'll be had for sheep-stealing.'

'What's his name?' I asked, trying to ignore his tomfoolery.

'Teddy,' they chorused, but the dog was too absorbed in the activities of some hens scratching under a carob-bean tree to recognise his name.

'He doesn't look much like a sheepdog,' I observed. 'Looks more like a poultry retriever to me.'

'Well, lady,' said Scotty, 'ye could set the dog t'mind the bairn and bring in the sheep y'sel'.'

There was a shuffling of boots as Scotty went on: 'Well, chaps, it looks like the firing squad for our faithful friend.'

'You mean shoot him?' I asked, thinking to myself that he might be just what Bly needed to bring in the cow at milking time, as Peggy was one of those exasperating animals that seemed to have to graze all the way home. The clan was beginning to break up, so Scotty said, 'I'll tell y'what, lady—we'll leave the dog with y' until y' good man gets in and we'll come back tonight and see what *he* sez.'

I brought the collar and chain from our last beloved sheepdog and Scotty fastened the collar around Teddy's neck, leaving him chained to an old fig tree near the back door.

When Bly rode in that evening, I heard him snorting as he dismounted: 'What the devil is this! Who does it belong to?' he asked.

'He's supposed to be good with sheep,' I said lamely.

'Looks more like a blasted Alsatian to me,' he scoffed.

I recounted the story briefly as he handed the bridle reins to me and walked toward the dog. Teddy wrinkled his nose, showing strong, white teeth and looking very ugly. We offered him food and water but he ignored it. I told Bly that the soldiers were coming back that night to see whether or not we wanted the dog, but he scoffed: 'That's what *you* think.'

At the end of the second day, the dog still refused to eat and, as it seemed there was no getting near him, Bly said, 'We can't keep the poor brute chained up forever. We'll have to think of something.'

A little later he came from the house carrying the rifle. At first I thought he meant to shoot the dog, but he cocked the rifle and handed it to me, saying, 'Now I'm going to walk straight up to the hound and let him loose. He can go to Timbuktu as far as I'm concerned, but if he turns on me, let him have a bullet anywhere you can . . . I'll finish him off.'

It wasn't easy to keep the rifle steady, even though I rested it against the verandah post. Bly walked matter-of-factly to the dog, who had his eye on me. Bly dropped the chain from the collar and the dog bounded over to me! We fondled him and called him a good dog, then he went careering around in circles and back to us again and again. Bly emptied the bullet from the rifle saying, 'He's all right. It was only fear.'

He put the gun away and I continued with preparations for tea, while the dog went scampering around the orchard. When the dog returned a few minutes later, he dropped one of my best laying hens at Bly's feet, but before he could get angry, a handy hint came to mind—one we had been storing for just such an occasion. Taking the dead bird by the legs and the dog by the collar, Bly administered a token beating. Feathers went in all directions, while the dog yelped and writhed, then capitulated with his four feet in the air.

Teddy proved to be utterly useless with sheep and despite Bly's painstaking attempts at training him to bring home the cow, he would desert and make for the house.

Early one morning Bly came to the bedroom searching for bullets in the drawer. 'I'm going to give that mongrel hound a lesson in obedience,' he said. 'I'll shout "come behind" and if he doesn't, I'll fire a shot into the dirt just ahead of him. Don't look so worried, I couldn't hit a moving object if I tried.'

I must have dozed off, for presently there was a lot of scratching and scrambling on the polished lino in the passage, and the next instant the whimpering hundred pounds of dog landed on top of me, flapping his ears and spraying blood everywhere, trying to get under the covers. I was still trying to get him off the bed without waking the baby when Bly strode in demanding, 'Where's that fool of a dog?'

'I think you've killed him,' I wailed.

'Nonsense,' he declared. 'I merely did as I said I would.'

Then, when he took a look at the dog, lying as still as death at my back with his head on the pillow, he went quiet. We got the flaccid body onto the bedside mat and dragged him out into the daylight.

'He's still breathing,' Bly said. We started to search for the wound and found, to our surprise, that all that blood had come from a minute hole in the tip of one ear. Bly insisted it could only have been made by a grain of sand sprayed up by the bullet.

As soon as Bly's back was turned, Teddy came to life.

He wasn't even a good watchdog, but he certainly was loyal and very ornamental, and he never even looked sideways at another fowl. Bly reckoned the new roll of barbed wire, left where they had cut the fence, was the army's way of saying 'thank you'.

TRAINING THE OFFSPRING

Marjorie Noll, Ballina, New South Wales

When I was a small child in Victoria, we lived on a sheep property owned by my father. Our working dog, Sally, a beautiful sable kelpie, was also the mother of all our dogs.

She usually had two pups, and my father trained them by attaching them to Sally with straps when they were about six months old. Sally would walk along, moving the sheep. The pups on the straps would do the same as Sally, and every now and then she would lick the pups—I'm sure telling them they were doing well. After two weeks they would be out on their own and really worked well.

My father could always sell these pups if we did not want extra dogs, and was always complimented on their being well trained.

WASHAWAY WONDER

Peter Mercer, Euroa, Victoria

There is great benefit from breaking in a young dog by always using the same commands, the same signals and insisting that it does what it is told from the start.

In the late 1930s I was pleased to be given the job of jackeroo on a beautiful property in western Victoria. It was quite large and in a lovely red-gum area. Several permanent creeks ran through wide, deep valleys which had well-grassed, gently sloping sides.

The manager was a very experienced man and good with sheepdogs. As a young man he had worked with Mr Walter Field, a well-known breeder of good dogs and a successful trials man. We made inquiries in the district and soon heard of a chap who was breeding Field-type dogs. They were of medium size with quite long hair and prick ears, all black except for a little white bib on the chest. We decided on an alert and friendly young male pup and called him Rod.

When he got going and was under some control, I was instructed to see that he always came around behind me. When I held out my right arm and said 'go back', he was to go to the right hand side of the mob. If I held out my left arm and said 'get over', he was to go to the left side of the mob. He was always expected to turn the mob and then return to me the way he had gone out. If he 'crossed his cast'—that is, going from my right across in front of me to the left of the mob (or the other way about)—he would be spoken to severely. I stuck closely to these rules and he developed into a beautiful dog that I could use to bring home to the shed or yards any mob without the slightest worry.

One day we had mustered about 900 young ewes and were travelling home with them along one of the broad valleys when I stopped to block a rabbit in a hollow log. Looking up I saw that the mob had gone around the head of a small but steep-sided washaway and was heading back to cross the creek again down below to the right. I said to my dog, 'Go back', and off he went. However, he found he could not easily cross the washaway, so went up to the head of it and then worked his way down the right hand side of the mob, quickly shifting the ewes away from the steep edges as he went, turned them in the direction of home when he got to the head of the mob down near the creek and came slowly back to me.

Over the last 50 odd years I've seen many dogs at work and feel quite sure that a very large proportion of them would have taken the easy way—gone past the head of the gully, crossed their cast and raced down the left side of the mob, thereby pushing the sheep towards the creek and quite probably making them splash unnecessarily through it.

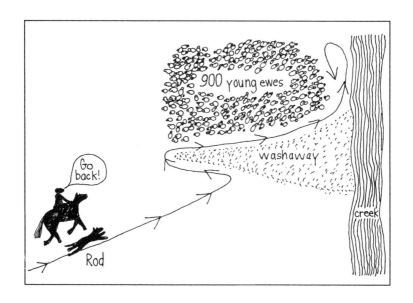

'WATCH AND LEARN'

Peter Murphy, Mildura, Victoria

During 1985 I was studying at a Victorian agricultural college where dogs played an integral part in the management of sheep and cattle.

One of the farm staff who was renowned for his dog breeding and training would often sell the progeny to students. In most cases they were students who had absolutely no use for a working dog, but fulfilment of the agricultural image required a dog to stand in the back of a ute. I knew a couple of blokes who had bought these dogs and witnessed the world of new interests owning a dog opened to them. Among these interests was the old favourite, sheepdog trials.

It was at one of these trials that two college lads, clad in the appropriate bush gear, dogs by side, were questioned by Ted, a so-called expert in the field.

33

'Are you blokes entering those dogs in the trials?' he queried.

'No, mate. We've just come to watch the event,' they replied.

'Probably just as well because those dogs look pretty useless to me. Take that one, his eyes are too close together, back legs are bowed, front legs are too short,' and so he continued until he had exhausted every fault that could hinder the performance of the dogs.

With their pride shattered, the lads were convinced there was no future for their dogs. Through sheer embarrassment they hid them and returned to catch a glimpse of the master at work with his perfect dog. Patiently they waited until finally Ted stood forward with his dog. It was his turn. A flock of sheep was released in the distance as the judge explained the rules.

'Not a problem,' was the confident reply from Ted.

One mighty whistle and the dog was off. Seeing the young lads nearby, Ted turned to them, smiled and said, 'Watch and learn.'

The two *were* watching and couldn't believe what they were seeing. The dog was running straight for the middle of the flock, certain to cause absolute chaos. When Ted turned around, he too saw what was happening and quickly tried to remember the command that would rectify the situation and save face in front of the students. Ted cupped his hands around his mouth and, as loud as he could, yelled, 'Split them.'

There were roars of laughter from the crowd and then Ted's ultimate humiliation—disqualification.

The lads returned to the college, their pride restored, to gleefully tell the story of the great sheepdog expert. As the story floated around it was exaggerated to the extent that Ted's commands also included 'Leave those three' and 'Kill that one.'

NO, YOU GO FIRST

Charles and Moira Warburton, Lyndhurst, New South Wales

The usual procedure on a rice farm when checking the level of the water in the rice paddies was to send the sheepdog up ahead to scare off the snakes. These would be lying in the sun on the grassed rice banks, waiting to catch frogs.

Randy, our working kelpie, soon woke up to the system. Certainly he would start off in front of us, but then invariably he would leap into the paddy and kindly let us lead. We would always have to do his dirty work—scaring off snakes and disposing of any within reach of the irrigation shovel.

For seven or eight years we tried many times to correct the procedure but when Randy got that faraway look in his eyes, we knew our efforts were useless.

HEELING THE RUNAWAY

Daphne Bannerman, Macleay River, New South Wales

When my elder daughter was born, we had a blue heeler dog. While being a very good dog with the cows, he was also very good with her.

From the day she came home from the hospital, the minute she cried, he would bark and carry on. I always knew when she was crying if I was outside. He had a track worn around the house.

When she learned to walk, he followed her everywhere, but the minute I called her and she started to run away, he would knock her over and wait until I got to her.

SMUG SUZIE

Liz Bishop, Laggan, New South Wales

As soon as she saw me I knew we were not going to get along. It was obvious she thought I was intruding and should get no respect from her.

In the beginning I hoped I would overcome her attitude. I complimented her, gave her lots of affection and generally went out of my way to become her friend, but to no avail. She never overcame her contempt for me. I was from the city and she was of the country—and no way was she going to let me forget it.

We started to work together, along with Nippy and Lassie who had decided if the boss thought I was all right then I couldn't be too bad. On a typical day we might have to bring in a mob of sheep for drenching or crutching. We would pack lunch, put the dogs in the back of the Landrover and set off on a bumpy gate-opening trip.

Being in charge made me feel quite important, but Suzie just knew I had to be brought back to size. I'd open the door of the Landrover and send the dogs off. 'Go back—far back,' I'd say, and two streaks of enthusiasm would race away. Suzie would jump down and slowly make off at her own pace, giving me a withering glance over her shoulder. Eventually the mob would arrive with Suzie in charge. She would just gently hold them together, no mad dashing about and yapping. She knew her job and did it well—without any help from me.

One day when I had the mob to myself, the boss being away, I decided to drench them in the old race which was held together by bits of wire and several poles. I had put them through there before, so saw no problems. But I didn't take Suzie into account, did I? It was her moment of glory. I was totally at her mercy. I would get the mob into the race and she would promptly put them back out. I roared. I yelled. I told her to get in the Landrover, to go home—just get out of my day. The non-barking Suzie turned into a yapping, growling, snarling monster—not directed at me. She was just telling the mob that I wasn't the boss and not to be fooled—she would save them.

It wasn't long before bedlam reigned supreme—scattered sheep, shattered nerves. Then, feeling she had achieved what she had set out to do, Suzie went and put herself under the Landrover in the shade. I'll swear she laughed at me for the next hour, smug beyond words.

The boss had to shoot Suzie later because she had cancer. I wept to think that one of the personalities I loved in my life had gone.

MOVE OVER!

Shirley Low, Port Lincoln, South Australia

Ringer, that was his name—this large, sleek, black kangaroo dog. A top dog he was, when 'roos and emus were causing such devastation in crops. He was indeed the 'ringer'.

Years of hunting and tramping over the hills had built a very close rapport between him and his master. When I became the third party in this arrangement following our marriage, another side of Ringer emerged.

If we walked side by side, Ringer was never content to walk alongside his boss, but always pushed his way between us as if to say, 'He was mine first!'

Just a dog? Sometimes one wonders.

WHY BOTHER ABOUT HER?

Cheryl Lockhart, Wedderburn, Victoria

Sam, our kelpie-retriever cross, tends to be a very possessive dog. He usually lies on his mat beside the kitchen table, near Dad's chair.

Once Dad finishes his second cup of tea, clanks the cup back on its saucer, slides his chair back and says, 'Righto, better do something,' Sam is promptly up on his feet and whining (we call it talking as it is a very loud 'Aaauurr-ar-ar' deep in his throat) for Dad to get going.

As soon as Dad stands up, Sam takes off into the lobby, ready to fly outside. Much to Sam's chagrin, though, Dad always gives Mum a goodbye kiss and hug. Talk about jealous—Sam comes rushing back in, barking and jumping all over Mum and Dad as if to say, 'Hey, come on, Boss! Why bother about her? Let's go!'

As always, Sam gets his own way, trotting out before Dad with his tail and head high in the air.

BOXER

Rod McIntyre, Pambula, New South Wales

An old cockie once told me
That he liked to pick the runt,
I had no better theory then
So I thought I'd take a punt.
He was the smallest of the litter
From Dad's kelpie bitch called Jen,
By old Cobber who was really
Working at his prime back then.

Well he grew into a useful dog
In a funny sort of way,
Although he had this tendency
To muck around and stray.
He'd go off chasing rabbits,
Lead me almost to despair,
Yet when I really needed him
He was always there.

And he seldom did the wrong thing,
Like split the mob in half
Or push them too hard up the hills,
And he often made us laugh
How he'd take his share of credit
When the job was finally done,
Although Cobber had done all the work
While he'd had all the fun.

Yet . . . he had one tasteless habit.
He used to mount the lambs
And other creatures, if they'd stay still,
Though he wouldn't take on the rams.
And oh—how he'd embarrass me
When the ladies were about,
I used to have to lock him up
And hope he wouldn't get out.

I became a bloody laughing stock,
I could see the people snigger,
And although I tried to hush it up,
I found it hard to figure.
Till this sheila up and asked me
As I went walking past her,
Was it true what they were saying
That dogs take off their master?

Now he's not the type of dog
That you'd take to any show,
The distractions there would be too great,
If you ever let him go—
And if I put him in a sheepdog trial
I'm scared that we would find
He'd give a whole new meaning to the phrase
'Push up', from behind.

PART 3

CROPPING COUNTRY

Where paddocks wave and rustle like green-gold taffeta, a dog can have a heap of fun. When the machines move in to cut and tie the fabric into knots, comb it into windrows, and to extract the grain, a dog with time on its paws can run down a fox, deliver a message or even 'drive' the ute.

With the humans safely tucked up in their air-conditioned tractors or headers, or delivering grain to the silos, dogs can enjoy unfettered bliss. They lie around in the shade watching everyone else work, or peel away to visit an obliging friend or two.

Because their farms are multi-enterprise operations, these dogs have to be versatile too. They can sniff out a lost hat, move pigs, or do some pretty fancy mustering in difficult conditions.

There are dangers, though—big, unforgiving machines, snakes, baits, argumentative farmers and even . . . low-flying aircraft. The dogs in cropping country are a gallant lot indeed.

MIND YOUR MANNERS

Denis Adams, Apsley, Victoria

Dad's Uncle Ralph has become a legend in our family. He was a drover in the 1920s and we always delighted in hearing his stories.

His most popular route was up along the Coorong with 'coasty' sheep collected from the south-east which he would take to the districts further north. After feeding them gently along the grassiest roads for a while, they'd make a splendid recovery. Then he'd take them back to their homes. Once it was discovered that Coast Disease was simply a deficiency of trace elements, Ralph's favourite job ceased to exist. He'd loved travelling along the Coorong. It was teeming with fish and wildlife then, and Ralph was a campfire connoisseur long before the Bush Tucker Man got it on the act.

Sometimes he hired sidekicks. Few were satisfactory, though, and none was half as loyal and dependable as his sheepdogs. Ralph loved his dogs. They never got on the grog, never demanded money, never argued or shirked their duty, no matter how tired and hungry they were. They also had better manners than some of the people Ralph met.

You hear of drovers cutting fences or opening farm gates to sneak extra feed for their stock. It was not Ralph's way, however. He got on well with most landowners. Sometimes he took farm dogs with him to train. He was able to help farmers out in many ways and usually they were appreciative. Better being asked in for a yarn and a cuppa than being hounded out of the district.

There was always the odd person, though, that no-one could get along with. One of the nastiest specimens Ralph ever encountered was a newcomer to one of his favourite wheat-farming districts. He was a man so lacking in bush etiquette that he didn't even say, 'G'day.' He came charging into Ralph's camp in his buggy, scattering dogs to the four winds and almost skittling Ralph. Then he began maligning all sheep and all drovers, concluding his attack with threats of physical violence and legal action if just one of Ralph's sheep got into his wheat. Not only was he concerned for his wheat crop, he warned Ralph in no uncertain terms to keep his sheep moving past his farm. Apparently all the roadside grass was his too.

Ralph was too flabbergasted to make a suitable reply before the aggressive cocky had whipped his horse up and headed back to his farm. 'That fellow could do with a lesson in manners,' Ralph spluttered at last to his dogs. They were just as offended as their boss and were looking disdainfully at the vanishing buggy.

There is a close, almost psychic bond between most drovers and their dogs. Not many farmers have their dogs with them night and day, seven days a week. Ralph's dogs were a sort of extension of his personality. They knew almost by instinct exactly what he required of them without a word or gesture from him.

That morning the dogs got the sheep moving with more vim and vigour than usual. The sheep hardly had time for a bite of grass on their way to the forbidden wheat crop. By the time they arrived, the wheat cocky had his large family drawn up in battle formation, armed with sticks and stones and backed up by a motley mob of dogs. 'Keep them sheep moving!' the farmer shouted as he and his small army of kids and dogs moved along just inside their boundary.

The fence was in a shocking state. Fair enough to be on hand lest any sheep push through. Not knowing Ralph or his dogs, the farmer was not to know that normally some of the dogs would have stayed between the sheep and such a rickety fence. There was no excuse for his verbal attack, however, or for his possessive attitude to the roadside grass. Pointedly ignoring all the fuss, Ralph let the horses pulling his little wagon stop for a spell while, with studied nonchalance, he leaned back in the seat. His dogs, taking their cue from him, also decided to take a rest.

Sheep are only stupid when it suits them. Within seconds they had summed up the situation. Soon they were pushing through the fence in a hundred different places, skipping and bucking light-heartedly as they ran rings around the opposition, grabbing great mouthfuls of the young crop. There was pandemonium from the farmer, his wife, and all their kids. They yelled and screamed, ran this way and that, waving their sticks, throwing their stones, jumping up and down and thrashing their arms about, vainly trying to turn the invasion of the woolly monsters. Their dogs had cleared out for home, thinking the sticks and stones were meant for them.

Before long the farmer and his family had all collapsed exhausted, leaving their crop to the mercy of the sheep. All the farmer could do was glower his hatred at Ralph, who shook his head sadly, like a parent forced to punish a naughty child. It had all been so unnecessary. Not that any damage had been done. If anything, the crop would stool out better now.

Ralph gave his dogs the nod. Soon all the sheep were back where they belonged, feeding along well clear of the fence—exactly where they would have been all the time, had the farmer not antagonised Ralph.

There was neither physical violence nor legal action from the farmer. It had all been hot air. Ralph's only problem was living with his dogs for the next day or so. They were a bit swollen-headed for a while after they'd shown off in front of the farmer.

NO TROUBLE FOR PATCH

Prue Boswell, St George, Queensland

This is a true story about my brother's dog Patch. She was a black and white kelpie bitch and one of the best. My story goes back twenty

45

years or more to when I was about seventeen years old. My father had asked me to go and bring in the killers. In those days it was all stock horses, no bikes, and of course no day's mustering was complete without half a dozen or more accompanying dogs.

I caught the old night horse and whistled Patch. She was the only dog who would work for me. The other dogs would only work for their owners. We had to ride about half a mile to the paddock where the killers were and it just so happened that this particular paddock had recently been pulled. For those of you who may not know what I am talking about, this simply means that two large bulldozers with a monstrously heavy chain attached between them had driven through the scrub pulling the timber down in their wake. Later the timber would be raked into rows and burnt, leaving a clear piece of land for crop planting.

Well, it was a really hot afternoon in the middle of summer and all the timber was lying on the ground. After about an hour and a half of sheer exasperation, I rode home without the killers, nearly in tears. The sheep just went everywhere—over logs, under logs, through logs, you name it, there they went. Dad, of course, wasn't very pleased when I turned up minus the sheep and, as it turned out, minus the dog.

It must have been about dusk a good two hours later when Dad called out to me, 'Come and have a look at this.' The sheep were in the yard and Patch was lying in the gateway, waiting for somebody to come and close the gate.

BUMPY LEAP TO STARDOM

Wendy Treloar, Cummins, South Australia

There can't be too many dogs in the world that have been hit on the head by an aircraft flying by. When our eldest son Peter bartered a box of seedling trees he had raised for a kelpie pup from a neighbour, we were not to know that Baldric, as he became known, would achieve such unusual fame.

Baldric is one of those hyperactive types that loves footy practice, flying over fences and jumping onto anything. Consequently he scores more rides on trucks than the other dogs in the family, simply because he can leap so high. He soars up from paddocks, chasing after birds which he races for miles.

Baldric was all set to compete against my other sons' dogs in a home-style obedience and sheepdog trial, but the event was totally upstaged when Baldric became too famous to compete in anything. Before this terribly important test of the worth of the various dogs— and accompanying ego-boost to the successful owner—took place, the sons had a job to do in the paddock.

The aerial sprayer had been called in and Peter and the two other boys, John and Michael, had to act as markers for the plane. As the plane zoomed in, Baldric did his usual leaping, nipping act as it went overhead. Suddenly, the pilot was heard to mutter over the two-way radio: 'I think I've hit your bloody dog.'

Peter had heard a thump and when he looked across, there was Baldric, prone—out cold in the crop. John couldn't leave his mark but yelled out to Peter, 'Pick up the gun. We'd better put him out of his misery', not believing for a minute that the dog could have survived the thump they had heard.

Feeling miserable and wondering how on earth he would manage without his now special mate and good working sheepdog, Peter also kept marking the runs until the plane had completed the paddock. Then they both raced back to try to find the dog.

Baldric had already come around and was staggering, with a definite sideways tilt, toward the ute for which he aimed, leapt at and missed, getting another thump in the process. Peter lifted him up onto the back where, apart from his eyes sticking out quite noticeably, he appeared unharmed. He must have leapt and been hit by a wheel, but not hard enough to kill him.

Apart from short-term memory loss, he is back to leaping for birds, but absolutely hates the sound of planes. He barks frantically when one comes too close, but he now stays right next to Peter's legs when marking for agricultural spray planes. The pilot, by the way, was very pleased to know the dog was alive.

So, after a cartoon in the local paper depicting Baldric as the Red Baron, as well as a photograph and story, the planned farm dog trial seemed a bit tame and the other competitors slunk off miffed. No-one, it seemed, could compete with such a performance.

IN A STATE OF SHOCK

Malcolm Seymour, Miling, Western Australia

My black and tan kelpie was eleven months old at the time of this story and was spending a lot of time with me as part of his training. During the day, between spells on the header and trips to the silo with the wheat trucks, he would sleep on the passenger-side floor of the utility.

Harvesting a long, narrow, sand-plain paddock next to a shire road one day, I noticed as I came around the top corner that the header steering was not normal. One of the back tyres was half flat due to straw stuck in the valve. Since it was too flat to carry on with, I had to walk about one kilometre to the other end of the paddock where the truck and ute were parked next to a gate leading onto the road. I drove the utility, which had the compressor on the tray, back to the header to blow the tyre up again.

That being done, I was then faced with the problem of returning the ute to the other end of the paddock and another long walk. Because the paddock was clear, I decided to point the ute straight at the truck, put it in low-range first gear, and let it get there on its own. I tied the steering wheel to the seat springs and started it off slowly back down the paddock.

Carrying on with the header, I kept one eye on the progress of the ute to ensure I was near the truck when it arrived. As I went past I saw that the dog, who had been asleep on the floor, had woken and jumped up onto the driver's seat to see what was happening. I was getting close to the truck with a header bin nearly full of wheat when I noticed that a car had pulled in off the road and a salesman was standing waiting for the ute to arrive so he could tell the driver all about his product.

I stopped at the truck and left the header unloading to walk over to the ute which was just arriving. The dog was sitting in the driver's seat, front paws on the steering wheel, being watched by the salesman, who had just realised the dog was apparently in full control. Opening the door, I pushed the gears out and turned the engine off. I casually remarked to the surprised onlooker that, although the dog drove quite well, he wasn't heavy enough to work the clutch, so I had to start and stop the ute for him. Conscious of the header unloading, I quickly found out what product the salesman was selling, decided we didn't need any, hopped back on the header and carried on harvesting.

The salesman, who was a stranger to the district, appeared to be suffering from mild shock as he slowly drove off. I have often wondered since whether he ever mentioned to anyone about the smart dogs in our district, or if he wakes up in the early hours and lies awake worrying if he really did see a dog driving the ute that day.

A NOSE FOR FLOPPY HATS

Joan Judd, Wycheproof, Victoria

We were in the middle of haymaking, so I decided to take lunch out to my husband, who was on the rake. While he ate his lunch, I offered to do a round or two. It had been a few years since I had raked hay, so he gave me a quick refresher course. 'There's nothing to it,' he said. 'Just keep the front wheel of the tractor beside the windrow.'

It was hot and sunny so he offered me his green floppy hat as there is no cabin on the old Fordson. It felt a bit big, but as it was a still day, I thought it would do the job. However, I had hardly got started properly when a sudden gust of wind whipped the hat off—only for it to disappear into the newly raked windrow. It took some time to pull up as the hat blew off right on a corner and I was concentrating on keeping the front wheel on the inside of the windrow, as instructed, while getting the rake around the corner.

My husband and I spend ages walking up and down the few chains of windrow, peering, throwing and kicking the hay, but to no avail. 'Not to worry—surely it's not that valuable,' said I nonchalantly. My husband replied that some poor cow might choke on it. He then hopped onto the tractor and went up and down, again and again, slowly raking and turning over the hay with me peering intently— only to eventually give up.

'Why don't you go home and bring Mitch back,' my husband suggested. 'He's always sniffing out birds and rabbits. He might find it.'

I thought it was a pretty remote chance but as I had nothing urgent to do, thought I would give it a go. I duly returned to the paddock with Mitch and another of my husband's hats. I shoved the second hat at the startled dog's nose and told him to 'fetch'.

I think he thought it was a good game, running up and down after me along this line of hay. On our third trip down, he suddenly stopped, jumped over the hay to the left, jumped back to the right, sniffed the top of the windrow and started scratching at it. I enthusiastically helped him and a few inches down from the top was the old, green, floppy hat.

I was amazed and my husband was suitably impressed when the dog and I drove over to the tractor to show him.

EARNING HER KEEP

Joyce Chandler, Ceduna, South Australia

We picked her up from the neighbours down the road. She was a small brown kelpie pup and we named her Brownie, for obvious reasons. She was a good all-round farm dog—travelling on the front of the motorbike for sheep work when needed.

What was unusual about Brownie, and it is a story we remember with humour, occurred back in the days when harvesting involved the bagging of wheat. It was then loaded onto trucks to be driven the long miles to the port where it was stacked ready for shipping to overseas markets.

Brownie would always insist on riding on top of the load, wind whistling through her hair as she enjoyed the view perched high on top of the bags. When we arrived at the weighbridge, no amount of calling would get Brownie off the load and she would inevitably be weighed in with the bagged wheat.

However, when weighing out after the wheat had been lumped off the truck, she could never be found—thereby always giving us a higher net weight and a few more shillings for our load. When we were ready to leave the port, the perverse creature would hop up into the cabin of the truck and sleep all the way home on the floor. It would be interesting to know how much extra she earned for us over the years.

BUSH REMEDY

Joyce Shiner, Albany, Western Australia

In 1940 my husband Bly bought a little red cloud kelpie pup at a sheep sale in Northam. He carried her fifteen miles home in his greatcoat pocket after having missed the train. We named her Greta and she became a great worker and family pet. She was one of those dogs that would bring the sheep along behind a horse, or a slow-moving vehicle of any kind, and she would never leave an animal behind.

When I contracted German measles my brother-in-law's niece, Rita Neve, came to Bakers Hill to help keep house and care for the baby. It was shearing time and our lovely little kelpie suddenly began to take fits. We thought she may have been poisoned, and all kinds of remedies were suggested such as cutting the tip off an ear to make her bleed, giving her a bit more strychnine, large quantities of warm milk, salt water and so on—but still she suffered paralysing convulsions.

Rita asked if she might try a remedy she had read about in the *Western Mail* which had worked when they had tried it on their own sheepdog. Rita was a big, strong young woman and she found it

51

no trouble to pick up the dog and swing it around and around by the hind legs. This caused the dog to vomit up what looked like a poison bait—and after a few minutes the fits ceased.

Greta was back to her old self by the next morning and anxious to be back at work among the sheep. She continued to serve us faithfully until her death at nine years of age.

CUT OFF AT THE BLOODLINE

Frank Bawden, Tumby Bay, South Australia

My father, who had been a farmer all his life and a bit of a wag, became fascinated by the working dogs at the Tumby Bay sheepdog trials.

He decided that he would like to buy a dog and go into breeding good dogs. He had it all worked out. He told us—a family of six boys and a girl—that he thought he would charge a $5 service fee and take his choice of the pups for allowing outside bitches to come to his dog.

He eventually made his purchase of a fine border collie dog at the trials that year. The owner said that Dad could collect Spot in a few weeks. When he was finally collected, Spot proved to be a good sheepdog, but a better playmate for the boys. After a wrestling game with Spot one day, young brother James came rushing in to inform the old man, 'Dad, Dad, your dog's got no nuts.'

Dad didn't miss a beat and calmly informed us that he'd still take the service fee but would have to overlook his choice of the pups! It seems that gelding a dog was common to stop people obtaining the bloodline.

WORKING OVERTIME

Irene Arnold, Tambellup, Western Australia

Our family was watching the television program 'Countrywide'. Skipper, our red kelpie, was lying at our feet.

A close-up of a dog working sheep appeared on the screen and immediately caught his attention. Then, as some sheep went to break away, Skipper rushed forward to head them off.

You should have witnessed the look on his face as he came from behind the television set wondering where the sheep had gone.

META THE MESSENGER

Jean Ferres, Macclesfield, Victoria

My father used to walk lambs five miles from Kallista to Emerald to put them on the Puffing Billy train to market. His kelpie, Meta, always helped him. They used to pass my father's brother's farm in Emerald and on the way home would always drop in for a chat. The dog got very used to this routine.

One day my father was sowing oats on his farm at Kallista. Huge flocks of crows kept flying in to eat the seed. He shot at them to deter them, but then ran out of ammunition.

He decided to write a note to his brother in Emerald asking him to send him more. He attached it to Meta's collar and sent her off. It was a good five miles there, but in due course she returned with the ammunition. Luckily it had been rolled in a waterproof cover as Meta had crossed a creek on the way.

NO WAY DO WE PART!

Elsie Dunn, Macgregor, Australian Capital Territory

My father was a farmer at Majura in New South Wales, but we had to move when Dad's land was taken up by the government in 1900 to help form Canberra.

I was five when we bought land near Boorowa, between Canberra and Binalong, to re-establish our mixed farm. We grew wheat, oats, barley and lucerne. Dad also ran a lot of sheep, a few cattle, 32 bullocks for his team which were changed about each day, and Clydesdale horses for the wagon and farm work. We each had a saddle or stock horse and there were several for sulky and buggy work. We also bred pigs.

At the age of fourteen, I was asked by Dad to drive 52 pigs about two and a half miles across our paddock, then across the end of the wheat paddock, across a grazing field, through a gate, across the main road and through the gate of the man who had bought them.

I set off early, riding my pony and taking my ever-faithful fox hound, Patch. He was a tall, sturdy and strong dog who was always with me. It was a difficult task keeping the pigs along the track. Without Patch I would never have managed. It took a couple of hours to get to our gate on the main road. Nearby was a huge dam and the hot, tired pigs immediately headed for this and wallowed in it blissfully.

I saw with dismay that along the road a drover was bringing a large flock of sheep. I rode along the fence and asked if he could hold his sheep until I had got my mob of pigs across the road. He called a couple of kelpies to his aid and soon had the sheep stopped. I rode back to the dam, which by now was full of wet and muddy pigs over which Patch was standing watch. I told him to get around them, so in he dived. He swam back and forward around the pigs, snapping and barking, while I swung a stockwhip and rode close to the dam's edge. Between us we got them out.

I opened the boundary gate while Patch stopped the pigs from returning to the dam. I then opened the gate on the other side of the road and we rushed them across and into the other field where the new owner was waiting—although he never offered to help.

The drover came along when the road was free. He must have been impressed by our performance as he offered to buy both my dog and horse.

'No way do we ever part!' I told him, nevertheless feeling quite elated.

Later that night he dropped in to see my father and told him how well I had done a very difficult task. He again offered a good price for the dog and horse, which was very flattering, but we took great delight in rejecting it.

GRINNING FROM EAR TO EAR

Val Pate, Renmark, South Australia

When we were first married my husband owned a nondescript red kelpie called Sailor. He was a constant companion as well as a workmate on our partly developed property at Mingenew in Western Australia, some miles from the nearest neighbour. He was also somewhat of a lady-killer.

In mid-January one year, we were doing some contract harvesting about five miles from our home for a neighbour. Just after lunch during the hottest part of the day, we took a load of grain into the local siding, leaving Sailor with the tractor and header. We considered it would be kinder and cooler than taking him in the hot truck with us.

On our return Sailor was missing. We thought he had taken umbrage at being left and had returned home. When we discovered he wasn't at home, we tracked him for about eight miles along the road heading north into town until nightfall prevented us going further.

Next morning we headed into town 22 miles away and asked around if anyone had seen him. No luck. We proceeded on to visit my parents, nineteen miles north of town, to be greeted by a furious father and a very contented Sailor grinning from ear to ear.

The night before, Father had locked, so he thought, his bitch in the shearing shed in solitary confinement for the duration of her heat—only to be greeted in the morning by two happy dogs lying peacefully side by side.

Sailor had been with us three weeks earlier when we had all had Christmas with my parents. He had not seen the young 'lady' in the interim, but had been quite prepared to walk 48 miles in the heat, somehow knowing the timing would be right. And to think we had been feeling sorry for him.

EVENTFUL ENCOUNTERS

Jeff Eime, Port Lincoln, South Australia

I am a retired wheat and wool grower. In my many years in the industry, both in the lower north and on Eyre Peninsula, I bred border collies. I found them very intelligent and faithful. One of these was Rip, who, in his working life with me, had several eventful encounters with wildlife.

During harvest one year I went out reaping early to finish off a small area that took between ten and fifteen minutes for each lap. Rip was following the header out to one side, putting his nose under heaps of straw and chaff left the day before from the machine. I was just about around for the first time when up jumped a big fox. I saw the fight begin and, as the header moved past, thought the fox, like many before it, had no chance.

When I returned about ten or so minutes later, I came over a slight rise around a corner of the paddock. I could not believe my eyes. There was the fox, mounted on Rip, with his front paws clasped tightly around Rip's hindquarters in the mating position. Both the dog and the fox had their tongues hanging well out and were puffing. There was some blood over them. When I called out, 'Get him, Rip!', he spun around. The fox, still gripping him, came around as well.

They were both near exhaustion, so I stopped the header and took a shovel off the machine to go and strike the fox. I hadn't quite reached them when the fox let go and tried to run off. It stumbled and Rip grabbed his throat and finished him off. I have often wondered if others have seen similar acts of cunning by foxes trying to overpower dogs.

Foxes weren't the only wildlife in our paddocks. One morning I sent Rip to round up the rams and ration sheep that grazed in a small paddock near the homestead. He went in the right direction but could not jump through the cyclone fence like he usually did, so I helped him. He went a few yards and looked back at me. I sensed something was wrong so I went to him and noticed he was having trouble walking. I took him back to the house where he just lay down—obviously he was a very sick dog.

I rang the vet and went into town with Rip lying motionless on the seat. By the time the vet saw him, Rip was completely paralysed. The vet suggested putting him down.

'Not on your life,' I protested. 'Not my Rip.'

The vet gave him little hope, but gave him an injection of antivenene and handed me some pills to give him every so often. I had a heavy heart as I took him home and put him in a stone shed that had doors. I made a bed for him out of bags and lay him out flat. He couldn't move any part of his body, not even his tail or ears. We could look into his eyes and see life, but that was all. His jaws and tongue wouldn't move, so we had to lift his head up to pour liquids down his throat with his vitamin tablets and a bit of mashed-up food. We kept a good eye on him, talking and patting him whenever we could spare time from farm duties. This went on for about three weeks.

One evening when covering him for the night, I noticed his heart was beating very unevenly. I went to bed thinking Rip would die overnight, but next morning he was still with us. His heart was beating more evenly. Then one morning when I went in and spoke to him, the tip of his tail moved a little. It was the first sign of life in three weeks. Every morning after, I noticed small improvements. First his tail started to wag, then his ears moved. Then the jaws started moving, and he could drink. We had won, but there was still a long way to go.

Eventually he started dragging himself around the floor, so we made a portable sling for him. It was a frame on castors that we hooked a bag into, then put him in it. His legs could just reach the ground. After the first five minutes in it he was exhausted, so we just did a little at a time. Later he pushed it outside. He seemed to be getting stronger and was now looking more like a healthy dog even though he still could not walk.

Sometimes we used to carry him to other sheds where we were working. One day my son, who was filling the ute with petrol, yelled out to me, 'Look at Rip!' There he was, standing up alongside my son. That was after ten weeks of tender care and encouragement. Before he was ill he had always seemed to understand what we were saying, so perhaps all the talking we had done, telling him to hang on, had helped.

He was once again able to come along with us mustering sheep, and he seemed to be looking forward to working again. Some weeks later he seemed very much alive and as I had a flock of 400 sheep needing to be moved to a back paddock, I thought I would give him a go. The sheep were about 500 yards away, around a dam near home, so I sent Rip around them, keeping my other two dogs with me. The tail wagged, the eyes shone and off he went. He couldn't get there fast enough. He rounded the flock and brought them up to me—but the exertion had made him very tired.

I praised his effort, which seemed to please him, and then I told him to sit where he was until the ute came to pick him up later. The other dogs and I were going to take the mob out the back. We moved off, looking back when we got to a rise and there, about 900 yards away, Rip was still sitting. It took us an hour to travel the mile and a half to the paddock and my son arrived soon after with Rip in the back of his ute. Rip jumped out and gave me a lick. My son had picked him up right where he had been told to sit an hour earlier.

As I said before, Rip always seemed to know what we were saying to him. I'll finish by telling you of an incident that always makes us laugh. If perhaps one of us had to go away for a few hours, he would greet us on our return and we would ask him where everyone was, mentioning a name or two. He would promptly turn around and lead us to whoever it was we wanted to see.

One day I was on the long-drop toilet near the shearing shed with the door shut. All of a sudden—bang, it flew back against my leg, giving me a hell of a shock. There was Rip with, I think, the biggest smile on his face I have ever seen, and my son behind him was having a good laugh too. One of my sons had asked Rip where I was . . .

58

PART 4

BLIGHT'S BLOCK

When the call went out nationally for tributes to working dogs, numerous large packets of wonderful stories started arriving from a place called Narrogin in Western Australia. When I subsequently discovered that Narrogin, on the edge of the wheatbelt, south-east of Perth, had been officially dubbed Sheepdog Country by its citizens, it seemed imperative to pay a visit and meet Geoffrey Blight, the person responsible for that avalanche of dog stories.

Just in case I was under any misapprehension about this being the land of the sheepdog, I was met at my lodgings by the ebullient Blight at 6.30 am in a ute loaded down with twelve working dogs of all shapes and sizes, including one that looked very much like a dingo. So began a most informative and entertaining visit . . .

THE STORYTELLER OF SHEEPDOG COUNTRY: A PROFILE OF GEOFFREY BLIGHT

Angela Goode

Geoffrey Blight, 53, is round, jolly and whiskered, a farmer, mulesing contractor, philanthropist, entertainer and writer. He is the driving force in the Narrogin shire to publicise the contributions of working dogs far and wide. It is a task he tackles with almost envangelistic zeal. He wants to see signs and a large sculpture in the town proclaiming to all that this is indeed Sheepdog Country.

Pride in the achievements of the district's dogs is certainly justified. From a tiny local working sheepdog club founded in 1983, two of its seven members have hit the heights. Last year Doug Connup won the Australian Sheepdog Challenge Series, which was broadcast on ABC television on 'A Dog's Life', with Glenromian Dinny, a dog bred by Byn Dinning. This year, Phil Slade won the second Challenge of 'A Dog's Life'.

Geoffrey Blight's own dog, Broc, first alerted him to the extraordinary abilities of dogs. Broc, who lived to the age of nineteen, was half-dingo, the result of a mating with an obliging kelpie at the famous Haddon Rig property in New South Wales: 'He became a legend on the hundreds of farms we worked on,' says Blight. 'He had a way of coping with everything. He was the most popular animal I have ever known.' Broc became so famous on Blight's mulesing rounds that even today people bow their heads in respect.

Blight had the body stuffed and mounted. While most sheep farmers usually hate dingoes with a vengeance, Blight is different. The dingo, he says, is able to be trained, is highly intelligent and also has a greater ability than most dogs to read a human mind. One of his stories—'A Northern Territory Kelpie'—reveals some of the talents he has observed. These talents are shared by many kelpies, a fact that, according to Blight, is hardly surprising since many have a dose of dingo in their genes.

So, in Narrogin on the morning of my visit, I climbed into the ute and embarked on a day of total 'indogtrination'. First we visited Old Bill, whose story—'Not the Best Dog in Highbury'—as told to Geoff Blight, appeared in *More Great Working Dog Stories*. It was a story of great poignancy about the night 50 years earlier when Bill returned home unannounced during war leave to find his dog was there to meet him at the railway station when the train pulled in at midnight.

The existence of a telepathic bond between dogs and humans is something that Geoff Blight is convinced about. He has seen evidence of it countless times during his voluntary work with handicapped children, when one of the team of dogs he takes to entertain the children befriends the loneliest and most afflicted child and makes it respond. 'Look at Sam there. He spends his whole life just telling people he likes them,' says Blight. 'Where in technology can you find a machine that tells people it likes them? Dogs will sit for hours with crippled children that other people are frightened of.'

To further demonstrate his dogs' talents Geoff Blight has, on a number of festive occasions, driven sheep and a variety of other animals through the main streets of Perth. The parades were ostensibly to publicise the Royal Show or help impart the true meaning of Christmas, but leading the merry throng of ducks, geese, goats and sheep and wearing a pet chook on his hat, Geoffrey Blight had a heart bursting with pride that his dogs were able to keep their concentration amid a noisy lunchtime crowd of 20,000 people.

On our travels that day we also visited Ken Atherton, president of the working sheepdog club. Ken had some young pups he wanted to put around a mob of sheep so Geoff could take his pick. There in the watery morning light, the five little workers and their mother loped around the sheep. Before long we were enclosed in the mob with no way of escape since the pups had obeyed their instinct to return the prey to the head wolf.

After cups of tea inside the house, we departed with a little blue kelpie bitch added to the load on the ute. She had an interesting free-flowing style and showed potential as a trial dog, so Geoff Blight was going to start her on her way. Although he hasn't had the same success as fellow club members, Geoff Blight still enjoys the challenge of training and working dogs to a high level.

His great pleasure at present, however, comes from working in the feedlots where wethers are held before being shipped to the Middle East. While a dog trial hinges on a dog's finesse with three sheep, loading trucks and moving 40,000 headstrong wethers through the yards takes not only finesse but also extraordinary stamina and courage—for dogs and handler.

Blight leaves Narrogin on ship-loading days at 2 am for a 4.30 start. He and his three rotating teams of four dogs don't knock off until about 8.30 at night, and sometimes ten-thirty. 'It's just another challenge,' says Blight. 'Up until I went to the shipping job, the biggest mob I'd moved with one dog was 5,000 sheep. The job is teaching me how far I can test the bond with my dogs. But I can tell you, the more I see of men, the more I like dogs.'

We finished our day in Sheepdog Country by driving over to Geoff's farm where the eight or so dogs he hadn't been able to fit onto the ute that morning rattled their chains with ecstasy. It was time for their run. If you have never seen twenty or more dogs taken for exercise at once, I can tell you it is a stirring sight. A seething mass of bodies, which included two yellow dogs a bit like Broc, rushed from tree to tree before taking off across a paddock.

One may indeed wonder when this man—who has also been a shearer, a racehorse trainer, stud sheep breeder and is the father of five sons—ever gets time to produce even one dog story, let alone the hundreds in his folders produced since only 1986. Suffice it to say, if Geoffrey Blight does not wake up until 3.30 am, he considers he has 'slept in'. He writes in the quiet of pre-dawn the stories he has heard the day before in the yards, at a trial, in the street, or around the mulesing cradles. Many of these he tells at schools and community groups. He has also released a cassette tape, *Broc Sheepdog Country*, of his stories and poems to raise money for cancer research.

Geoffrey Blight remembers with affection the storytelling tradition he grew up with. As a small boy, he stayed up all one night listening to the old men of the district yarning as they kept vigil over a bushfire, watching for outbreaks. In the main street of Narrogin, there would always be knots of people standing around talking. They are not there any more. People now rush past in cars and are too busy even for a chat. He regrets that technology and television in particular have interfered with that storytelling art. Geoffrey Blight is doing what he can to keep the tradition alive.

I SEE ROVER

Geoffrey Blight, Narrogin, Western Australia

'I see Rover, Rover sees me.' As a five-year-old boy these were the first words I learnt to read and understand, as any child would have done if they'd attended a state school in Western Australia in 1944. To me they had a special meaning. I knew Rover. He was part of our family, a cattle dog and pet. A massive brown and black kelpie-type dog with a white chest and blaze, he had been a member of the family since my parents' marriage in 1937.

Many things made the dog I knew special—his gentle handling of the milkers, his dedication to keeping the garden free of cheeky hens, his babysitting my little sister. Everyone seemed to know Rover but, above all, he was said to have saved my life. Following the birth of my older sister and myself, Mum made a practice of leaving us, either in the pram or on a rug on the grass outside, in the company of Rover. Should either of us cry or move, he could be counted on to bark or attract my mother's attention. Many early photographs that go beyond my memory bear witness to this, showing us sitting with, or embracing, the big dog.

It was when I was able to walk and really get around that one day Mum made the frightening discovery that I was missing and could not be found anywhere. Our small dairy farm was on a winding little road on the north side of Mt Shadforth, near Denmark. We were only chains from all manner of dangers—forests of impregnable thickets, running creeks, pigs and horses, Guernsey bulls.

The alarm was raised and neighbours were summoned to help but, as time passed, I was not found on the farm. A creek ran to the north of the house and it was believed I may have fallen in. Nobody had thought I might have crossed it by following the road. I hadn't been seen on the road.

The search of the creek proved fruitless, several more hours passed and I still couldn't be found. By now everyone was nervous. The only bright spot was that Rover was missing also. This was important—with Rover I had a chance, without him the outlook was very grim.

The day was drawing on with more and more help being called. It was by sheer luck that a young lad, riding his bike a long way from the search area, saw something move in the bracken adjoining a forest reserve. He stopped, but it had vanished. Then he saw it again—it was a dog's tail moving slowly through the bracken away from the road and into the thick forest. He whistled and there came a bark. It wasn't his dog. He whistled again, but still it didn't come. He hadn't been told about Rover but he knew I was missing, so he decided he'd take a look.

It was a very excited young man who pushed his bike feverishly into my parents' farm bearing a toddler under his arm, followed by a big dog. The lad told how he had found me carrying a billy only yards from the wattle thicket, where vision was down to only inches, and there were numerous creeks and swamps. My mother offered thanks to the Almighty for our safe return. I showed no ill-effects from my adventure whatsoever.

It was this incident, more than any other, which made Dad very proud of Rover. As the dog grew old and his time was near, Dad decided he could only replace him with the best dog that money could buy. He answered an advertisement for a guaranteed, Queensland blood, champion stock, trained blue heeler. A supreme cattle dog which was to cost a month's wages and replace the reliable old mongrel who had been part of the first twelve years of marriage and family. Dad knew the value of a good dog. I was living proof of that. He was going to have the best.

Arriving home from school one day, I found we had our new dog. Up until then, my after-school chores were to bring in the milkers and help with the milking. Our small farm boasted several little paddocks both sides of the narrow, winding road. To get the milkers, I would call the dog, go with him and open and close the gates and follow them home. When I opened the gate old Rover would take three steps into the paddock, bark loudly and sit himself down. The cows would immediately stop grazing or rise from where they sat and amble quietly past the sitting dog toward home. To keep control of the situation and to prevent loitering, the old dog usually made a habit of nipping the heels of the last cow or heifer through the gate.

Being a bit of an adventurer, I used to like to get a ride home. I would make haste and beat the slow-moving old dog to open the gate and try and get seated on the nearest quiet cow before he barked. There were only six in the herd I was not prepared to mount and I always made sure I didn't get the one that was going to be last out of the gate. The practice came to an abrupt end one day when Dad caught my sister and me sitting astride the same cow, Old Lady— strolling up the road, oblivious to the danger we faced if a vehicle should come along. With a solid slap on the butt, we were told it was not permitted.

Back to the day of the new dog: Dad told me he would get the cows in so he could try out his new acquisition. He was all excited with this dog. He had dreamed of an aristocrat, a true blue blood, bred from centuries of champions. He had spent as much on him as he had on any animal he had ever owned.

With me standing behind the gate, old Rover confined to the house yard, Dad gave the order and the young dog flew into action. Straight onto the heel of the nearest cow, then to the next and the next. Before Dad could stop him, the cows—with startled bellows, tails straight up in the air, the air full of flying wet dung—had rushed straight through the back fence, over the creek and into the swamp. My father's roar of outrage seemed only to spur the dog on as he flew from heel to heel or swung on any tail within reach. No matter how we tried, the cows would not leave the swamp and risk the dog, who Dad was persisting with—he was also trying to save face with Mum, who had not been at all happy with the price that Dad had paid.

Dark closed in. I was sent to bring the lantern so we could see. The dog continued his chasing while Dad bellowed and cursed the jungle of bog, scrub and reeds. I arrived with the lantern just as a number of very loud 'Come here' commands brought to heel the devilish-looking young dog, tail wagging and bearing a dead fox nearly as/big as himself in his jaws. This proved just too much. The pure rage of my father as he kicked the air and cursed the 'dirty rotten BBB' was alarming. But he was totally unable to either catch or humiliate the energetic blue dog, who seemed to be enjoying the whole charade immensely.

We didn't get many cows out that night. Things were pretty strained in the house when we ate tea, everyone being careful not to talk about the new dog. I think Dad was having second thoughts about his would-be champion.

We did get the cows milked next morning but things warmed up again when the heeler almost caught the neighbour's daughter as she pedalled her bike frantically past the front gate. She wasn't so lucky that afternoon when the heeler, who by now had had some practice, caught her and tipped her upside down in the thick scrub on the road's edge, with her bike landing on top of her.

Dad's humiliation was complete when he went to put a rope on the old gelding to run the upset girl home. The now over-excited and uncatchable dog flew in and locked his jaw on the cart horse's heel, sending the horse galloping round and round the paddock with the champion, the blue blood, the best dog that money could buy, yap-yapping at his heels.

I was surprised when the school bus stopped to drop my sister and me off. Rover was there to meet us, as was his usual habit, when he should have been shut in the house yard away from the new dog—who wasn't to be seen.

I don't know what happened to our new dog, but I know when I was told to use Rover to get the milkers in that night, four of Dad's top pedigree Guernseys had the end of their tail bitten off. I think the bloke who sold Dad the dog probably thought he would be safer if he took it back.

Dad was always to have a dog, mostly good ones but nothing spectacular. He was content to settle for just ordinary, inexpensive pups that reminded him of Rover and who could be forgiven if things didn't always turn out right.

I remember best old Rover on a Saturday night when Dad and Mum, rug over their knees, sat tightly together on a cart seat. We children, on a mattress beneath them, would be cuddled up to the big warm bulk of Rover as the old gelding plodded through the cold, dark air to a dance or the pictures.

I remember him as together we travelled the creek's favourite gilgie holes, and his joyous bark and high-tailed carriage as he raced with me up and down the long lines of vegetables in our market garden. I remember his protective snarl if danger threatened, or beast trespassed on our path.

Strong, too, among the memories are those of my mother crying as we arrived home from school and Rover wasn't there. The words 'I see Rover' were no longer a reality, just a memory of a wonderful childhood with a dog. As time dragged me forward into youth and manhood, to other dogs and other places, I would often repeat these words to myself—'I see Rover, Rover sees me'—as I sought the dog of my dreams among the adverts for champions, the expensive blue bloods and the unwanted mongrels. But never did I find one that could wear that coveted title among dogs of 'Rover'.

TRIALLING SHEEPDOGS

Geoffrey Blight, Narrogin, Western Australia

So often I have heard the comment, 'Trialling sheepdogs is far removed from the realities of sheep farming.' Unfortunately, after several years of trialling, I must agree.

Trialling sheepdogs is a good sport and very educational in teaching communication between dog and master, but it falls short by miles in demonstrating what support a top sheepdog can give in the real sheep world, where labour is very expensive, time is precious, hours are long, climate varied and sheep are most unpredictable.

Probably the major difference between a trial dog and one that is used to earn a living is the fact that in a trial the master does nothing to support the dog. In sheep farming and handling the master is continually working and the dog is supporting, quite often uncommanded and out of sight of the master. In a trial the dog is supposedly told everything it should do, which makes the trial a test of the master's sheep sense. But farm work needs a dog with initiative and commonsense, anticipation, endurance, strength and patience. It must also be able to cope with unpredictable situations and interference.

Not that a trial dog can't be a good farm dog, but I now believe the very best farm dogs are actually hindered by the restrictions on their movements and instincts that the discipline of trialling places on them. Heading sheep probably comprises five per cent of farm sheep work, yet is 75 per cent of trialling. Cover and cast are very important to both, but in farming a vehicle is used to help dogs gather sheep and check the paddock. Barking is frowned on in trialling but is essential to farm work. Most farm work consists of *driving* sheep. Most trialling consists of *drawing* sheep. A trial requires only fifteen minutes of concentration and fitness. Many farm jobs can last hours, if not days. A dog that over-concentrates tires quickly and will eventually quit.

No doubt the skill, or lack of it, of a dog is highlighted in trialling. His biddability becomes obvious, but not necessarily his loyalty, endurance and adaptability.

Every farmer knows there is a time in sheep handling when a dog might have to bite, even to save his life. (You can't bluff *all* sheep *all* of the time). A dog must be able to convey his superiority over sheep when tested. If he doesn't he will soon become a weak dog in a tight spot. But biting as a habit is undesirable and damaging, so a dog who only does it when he *has* to is the ultimate. How dogs work in the company of other dogs and men is a major factor in farming but not evident in trialling. Cunning is an important part of a farm dog's make-up.

No doubt the sheep trialling sport is a testing ground for sheepdog breeds in the same way car-racing might test the rubber used on a truck tyre. Ninety per cent of sheepdog triallers are old shearers and most know the difference between the sport and the job. Most of them have a favourite dog, but it's *always* the one that does the best farm work.

A SHOT OF WHISKEY

Geoffrey Blight, Narrogin, Western Australia

Back in the 1960s when I was much younger, I was working at an almost insane pace mulesing lambs seven days a week and well into the nights, because in those days no-one else would do it. I suddenly found I'd lost my sheepdog. To get by, I had been using my father's, but that was causing friction.

We had been mulesing for a Scotsman at Williams and he had a dog that was a biter. It actually killed four lambs the first day we were there. He was far too rough for me, but that doesn't mean he wasn't still there twelve years later. After he'd had some of his teeth kicked out, he actually worked sheep pretty well.

On that farm one day, I happened to be asked to shoot a dog that was blamed for much of the rough stuff and therefore had to be left tied up. I could see it was a yellow collie, a very pretty young dog, that had cut a channel round and round at the end of his chain, till he had nearly buried himself. What they had to say about him didn't impress me—he wasn't the sort of dog I wanted—so I agreed to get rid of him for them as he was said to be hopeless with sheep.

Shooting a dog is a job that sometimes has to be done and is often kinder than seeing an animal ill-treated. But I didn't have the gun with me so I ended up taking the dog all the way home, hooking it to the tank-stand until I could get around to the task.

Somehow, being tired, I forgot about him, and he was still there next morning. Being so pretty he had attracted the attention of my wife and my mother, who immediately suggested that, as I needed a dog, I should give him a try. I told them how bad and useless he was supposed to be, but that apparently wasn't sufficient excuse, so to please them all I actually took him down to the yards and let him go.

Well, I could spend all day telling you what farmers get wrong about their sheepdogs, and with Whiskey, as he was named, the Scotsman certainly was way out. He was what you call a good heading dog with a lot of cover and a fair amount of eye. He appeared to have none of the faults I was led to believe he had. No doubt an older dog had been influencing him and probably getting him into trouble. Very few farmers draw sheep toward themselves or go in front of the mob—most prefer to drive from behind, usually in a vehicle, tooting the horn every few yards and revving the motor to keep them going—so Whiskey's skills had probably not been recognised. I was quite taken with the dog and decided he was worth a try—anyway, I had nothing to lose.

He was probably the easiest dog I have ever trained. I went working at the farm he'd come from about a week later and he was already working far better than his former mate, who was still intent on chewing lambs to pieces. It was there I soon found out why Whiskey had not done well for his former owner. Every time he made a move, the other dog would attack him in jealousy. Whiskey, being no coward, would make a fight of it. This eventually led to 'the ripper' dog getting put on the chain and his owners, who were very good people, coming to realise why they had been so unsuccessful with Whiskey.

But I had one problem with Whiskey—he was too easy to make friends with. However, I was delighted that he got on with two Aboriginal workers I had with me and helped restore their confidence with dogs after their experience with 'the ripper', who'd bitten them too often. Everywhere I went people wanted to play with him because he was so attractive, and it started to ruin him at work. He started looking for pats. I wanted a dog no-one would be able to take again, so I started to teach Whiskey to bare his teeth and growl every time somebody stroked him. It wasn't hard to do and he did it to a T—and we were back in business, with him improving every outing.

I suppose I must have bragged about how clever I was, teaching him to growl and bare his teeth when stroked, because my young son soon woke up to it and used to show people, even though I scolded him. I soon found that every time there were people around, all the little ones would get Whiskey and cart him around to some unsuspecting mum and ask her if she would like to pat the dog. On touching him, only to have him bare his teeth and growl, the mums would usually go into orbit. On landing, they'd demand that their child, who by then was usually cuddling the dog, 'get away from it'. The kids would just laugh and demonstrate all over again what I had taught the dog, usually with Whiskey furiously wagging his tail.

Whiskey was a very useful sheepdog, particularly in the mustering of ewes and lambs where indeed he had some wonderful tricks. When faced with a bunch of breakaway lambs, he would head the front runaway and stop it, even by making it fall over. Then he would stand perfectly still for several seconds until the bunch halted, which it usually did. At this point, rather than try to cover the lambs, he would walk casually back toward the main flock and the runaway lambs invariably followed, walking all around him.

He was also a master at yarding lambs. Near the portable yards, when they would start to circle the flock rapidly threatening a break, he would go to the head and, rather than stop them, he would increase their speed as they neared the opening into the yards. He would then deviate, straight into the yards, with the lambs hot on his heels. By jumping the back fence before circling rapidly to the tail of the pursuing flock, he'd trap them neatly in the yards. This is a trick light-coloured dogs seem to do very well. I regret it was before the advent of the video.

Unfortunately, Whiskey's career came to a sudden halt in the early 1970s. He went mowing hay with one of my sons and when a rabbit appeared suddenly, he pursued it straight into the path of the mower. His hamstring was injured and as he was unable to run again, he lived on as a housedog.

His injury was a blow, but it was the day after Whiskey's accident that I was forced to take a gangling, ugly red kelpie with an undershot jaw from the pen where he had spent his first nine months, and use him to muster sheep. Little did I know, at the time, that this would be the beginning of a nineteen-year association with a dog that I later named Broc. Together we worked more sheep than most others would in Australia's sheep history. This dog is still regarded with awe in and around our district, which many have dubbed Broc's Sheepdog Country.

SHOWING THE ARISTOCRATS HOW IT'S DONE

Geoffrey Blight, Narrogin, Western Australia

Many are the men who have been brought down to earth by skiting about their great sheepdogs. In half a century on farms in Western Australia I've seen plenty come a cropper. When it comes to dogs, we're all in a class of our own.

One of the most memorable occasions was in the early seventies, out in 'wild west' Williams. I was a mulesing contractor and we had the job of doing about 3,000 lambs for a recently arrived English squire who came from generations of best British stock and knew the value of a good sheepdog. This had led him to buy the best (said to be state champion, in fact) sheepdog money could buy at the time. He was a beautiful border collie, trained to the whistle. The dog was about as obedient as I've ever seen.

His new owner was very proud of him. So much so that on our second day of mulesing, we were told by the English gentleman that a friend was bringing some British aristocracy, in Australia on holidays, to see the dog work. To this end, he had left a mob of 1,400 ewes and lambs to be mustered when the visitors arrived. He asked us to keep our kelpie, Broc, out of the way in case he interfered. Broc was locked in the car even though it was unnecessary. We did it to please the boss.

My crew for that day was a very strong eighteen-year-old girl named Judy, who was catching the lambs, and three of my sons, aged from twelve years down to six, doing the earmarking, castration, tagging, etc. The little six-year-old was dressed in a plastic urea bag and had to stand on half a 44-gallon drum. He was vaccinating and releasing the lambs. We were averaging about 1,200 a day, although our best day was nearly double that. By the time the four black cars, including two Mercs, drove in we were well and truly covered in the usual mess.

The visitors included a Lord and his Lady who farmed 6,000

acres just out of London, and also one of Western Australia's biggest sheep farmers, who was their host—all coming to see the best sheepdog in Western Australia. They never came near us, much to my boys' disappointment. We were well used to doing the tourist special (castration with our teeth), which usually left the visitors with a very gruesome picture of the Aussie sheep farmer.

Even though we didn't stop, the whole crew was all eyes as the boss, with his dandy little cap and whistle, was followed by a washed and, I'm sure, scented border collie. His guided his visitors out into the adjoining paddock and, after all the pleasantries, sat down, then cast his very obedient sheepdog. He guided him with well-rehearsed blasts on the whistle, stopping and starting him to perfection. For a while it was all admiration. The big mob bunched and came up close to the yards where twenty people were standing admiring his skill and effort.

But these were ewes in 'wild west' Williams and the dog was new. They weren't about to make it easy for him. As the boss waved, whistled and sat the dog, first one lamb made a bolt, then another, then swoosh—they were gone. The dog was still rising and sitting to his orders, totally unable to hold the mob. They did it all again, and again, and again . . . each time losing them faster than the time before.

The whistle was now forgotten and the bellowing had begun. The guests were even asked to spread out around the sheep and help. Alas, all in vain. The sheep completely had their measure. Nearly an hour was wasted with the sheep not one bit closer. It was a very frustrated boss who had to give it away. I guess to save face, he brought his visitors over to see us since we were very nearly finished the flock we had been working on.

With a twinkle in their eyes, my sons went straight into turning the well-dressed visitors off tailing lambs. While I made certain I had the odd testicle still hanging from my chin, the boys were pumping out five lambs a minute with red bottoms, tags, earmarks, vaccination and drench.

The ladies weren't keen on watching and a couple of them had found Broc in the car and were talking to him. We broke our routine to refill the pen. My six-year-old, who was letting the lambs go and was covered in blood, jumped down, strutted over to the car and opened the door to let Broc out. He turned, pointed in the direction of the flock and, imitating his 'betters', shouted 'Way back, Dingo, you old bastard,' making the ladies flinch with his gusto. Broc, who had been watching the whole episode, strutted off at his usual gait towards the flock. We went on working, forgetting about him.

It was about ten minutes later when the guests were about to leave, having heard many excuses as to why the Champion had been unable to pen the sheep, that the two ladies who had been far more interested in watching Broc than lambs getting cut about suddenly became very excited and pointed at the flock coming in. It isn't hard to know why a dog who musters ewes and lambs every day might know something that a dog who is told how to muster three wethers in a trial might not. In his casual manner, Broc had ambled out around the big flock. Using his voice with great skill, he had the flock pushing up to the yards where now there were no people in the way. An open gate led to a few remaining lambs. The bolters of the flock, sensing escape, charged straight into the pens.

The twenty visitors just stood gaping in awe at the ridiculous ease with which Broc put in those sheep. He then sat in the gateway waiting for a very proud, six-year-old, blood-covered Australian boy to go and close the gate. The boy patted the 'old bastard' he was intent on calling 'Dingo' that day.

When one of the visitors said something to one of the older boys about how 'the dog could do anything', the lad replied that he still wasn't very good with the drenching gun, but they were working on it.

That was a long day and we had a lot of laughs about the look on the boss's face and his excuses. I also clearly remember reaching home well after dark that night and untangling a sleeping ball of dirty six-year-old boy, curled up in the lap of a big yellow dog on the back seat of the car, and having a great sense of pride in that hairy brute the boys occasionally called 'Dingo'.

DUDS

Geoffrey Blight, Narrogin, Western Australia

Anyone who breeds stock for sale has unsaleable culls or 'duds'. They have to be got rid of in the best and most humane way possible to make room for fresh stock. I had been breeding sheepdogs for a few years and selling about forty dogs a year. A week before Christmas is a time you often take stock of things. Wanting to cut down work in the holiday season, you don't want any unwanted stock to look after.

I had two dogs that were over a year old that nobody wanted. One was a kelpie runt and too small, the other a very rough-coated border collie and very ugly. They hadn't attracted any interest whatsoever and were costing money to feed—so they had to go. But when I went to get bullets I found my sons had taken the two packets I'd had, not even leaving me a single round.

When I tackled Mike, my eldest son, he wanted to know what I wanted them for so urgently. After I told him, he said if I looked in his ute I might find a couple of bullets to get me out of trouble, and get rid of the unwanted dogs. Sure enough, I found two, lying among the rubbish of the glove box. I decided I'd dispose of the dogs immediately while I knew where the ammunition was. It didn't happen, though, as neither bullet would fire. I pointed the single shot .22 and only heard . . . click.

That night I had a call from a chap wanting a dog. His dog had been killed accidentally, so he was impatient to replace him. A woman rang next day wanting a dog as a Christmas present for her husband: could he come by and pick one out? I had several very nice pups and didn't think I would have trouble supplying something suitable.

However, when the first chap arrived, he wanted an older dog that he could start immediately. I tried to tell him the eighteen-week-old pups would work but he wasn't convinced. I mentioned I only had a couple of one-year-old dogs that probably weren't what he wanted, but he insisted on having a look. It's crazy how some people select a dog, but this chap wanted the ugly dud the minute he saw him. He was just so much like a good dog he used to have, he had to be a good dog too. I suddenly found I had a cheque for two hundred dollars in my hand and only one dog to shoot.

I had to wait for the second chap to arrive the next morning before I could go to town and get supplies, including bullets. The chap turned out to be really fussy, and it didn't look like I had a dog to suit him. Pups from an Australian champion weren't quite it: too much eye. Brothers to a state yard champion weren't it either: too much bite. A top New Zealand Huntaway pup: too boisterous, too much bark. Then he spotted the runt. 'What's that one?' he asked.

'One that didn't grow,' I told him. 'He's too small.'

' Too small be damned. The best dog I ever had was smaller than that. Will he work?' the chap asked.

I wasn't sure but there didn't seem to be any reason he shouldn't. So I let him out onto the small flock we had been testing the dogs on.

The dog hadn't even reached the sheep when the bloke decided that was 'his dog'. Even I was surprised at how keen the little fellow was. I wondered later if it had anything to do with me trying to shoot him two days earlier with a dud bullet.

So it was Christmas Eve and I had another two hundred dollars in my hand and no dogs to shoot. I had even suggested to the bloke a hundred and fifty for the runt was enough. He decided, seeing I'd kept him over a year, that two hundred was a very cheap dog. Blimey, I wish it was always that easy.

But that's not the end of the story. On Christmas Day I was bragging to my sons about the sheer luck of the dud bullets and being able to sell the two culls that the other forty customers hadn't wanted. I even had the dud bullets still in my pocket, so I put one in the old single shot to show Mike, pointed at the sky and . . . BANG.

PUTTING A STINK
ON SOCIALISING

Geoffrey Blight, Narrogin, Western Australia

Simon is an ordinary farm lad on a dairy in south-west Western Australia. To help get the cows in, he got himself a lovely blue heeler. He was very careful to get one with a really kind nature as he felt little would be gained by having a savage pet—although he did have friends who took delight in owning such dogs.

Cloudy was, as his name suggests, almost a crimson blue, and very lovable. As Simon gradually got him interested in the cows he found he was often distracted by visitors—they always made such a fuss of him that Simon soon realised it was spoiling him completely.

At the shed one day, Cloudy was working away exceptionally well when Simon spotted some children coming to play with the dog. It really annoyed him. They had been doing this far too often and he was getting nowhere. Suddenly he had a thought. Grabbing Cloudy, he deliberately dunked him in the large pile of fresh cow manure that always built up at the end of the dairy. He made sure Cloudy was well covered with it.

It must have been very confusing for Cloudy when suddenly the children rejected him and didn't allow him to jump up. They left quite quickly. A very disappointed Cloudy went back to work, much to Simon's delight. From then on, as soon as Simon saw anyone coming, he would make every effort to find some fresh manure and dunk Cloudy's front feet in it.

It took Cloudy a while to get the idea, but with visitors it worked immediately. Now if you go and see Simon, you'll spot the very quiet heeler just sitting and waiting his boss's pleasure. He no longer needs 'to put his foot in it' to make himself unpopular with visitors.

A 'NORTHERN TERRITORY KELPIE'

Geoffrey Blight, Narrogin, Western Australia

Annie was the first dingo I owned. She came from Central Australia via a truck driver who dropped her off at a friend's wildlife park.

As she crossed the Western Australian border she had to become a 'Northern Territory kelpie' in order to get around state laws which attempt to prevent ownership of a dingo or dingo cross dog. Bureaucracy ignores the fact that a large percentage of working dogs in Australia are already dingo crosses. However, this was a fact about which I was not confident when I was younger. After an association of over nineteen years with my big ginger kelpie, Broc, I decided I owed it to him to investigate his heritage.

I had tried to find books or information that could tell me more about dingoes, but nowhere was there anything about the possibility of dingoes making working sheepdogs. I had heard stories and spoken to men who said they had owned dingoes or dingo crosses. In the end I decided to get myself a dingo and test out my own theories.

It wasn't easy and I waited a long time before Annie turned up. Many people had tried to own dingoes as pets but most had difficulties with the Agricultural Protection Board. Someone usually made a complaint about the dingo getting into a neighbour's chooks or the like, and they were confiscated or destroyed.

I noticed immediately that there were many clear similarities between my kelpies and Annie. So I started training her as a sheepdog. She was friendly, very attractive and intelligent.

The first big shock I got was when I released her into an open paddock to see if she would cast. After sending two border collies around the flock, I let her go. She took off in hot pursuit but the collies got around the sheep first. She didn't waste time. Instead she cut straight across the backs of the running flock to reach the collies. It was the best bit of high-speed backing I have ever witnessed.

She proved all my suspicions—especially with her ability to read my thoughts. She wasn't as good as the sheepdogs I had—no doubt because they came from 400 years of rigorous selection—but to me there was no question that these dogs were very much a part of the kelpie history.

She often gave me heart attacks when she took things into her own hands. I became very wary of using her in public. Although she worked sheep, she did bite sometimes and I would have to discipline her. She was also very good at climbing out of her pen.

There were some incidents that I remember well. On one occasion a government stock inspector was looking at our sheep when Annie got out. I wasn't around and the farm hands panicked that she might get into trouble. They saw her trot past the yards where the stock inspector was.

As she disappeared over the road, the workman set out to find me or my son Mike. He realised the department would love to have evidence of stock damage. It would solve their problems of dealing with my dingo venture and the publicity it had gained when I displayed her at the Perth Royal Show.

When the workman found me I rushed down to where Annie had last been seen. There, standing near the gate, was the inspector. In the paddock were over a thousand weaners moving slowly up to the yards with Annie trotting along behind. I soon got her out of sight.

Some months later she climbed out again. On that day I had to attend my mother's funeral some 250 kilometres away. I was upset and impatient to leave when I noticed her standing in the paddock over the road from my house. When I tried calling her, she wouldn't come. I got angry and went after her, only to find she kept retreating across the paddock.

I couldn't get near her. I went back home and released some of her sheepdog mates for a run, thinking she would join them. The little rotter didn't. She just stayed over the road and continued to retreat if I approached, or came back toward me if I turned to walk home. I was getting very annoyed. I had to leave and no way was I going to leave her loose with no-one around for two days.

So I got the ute and went after her but she even outran that. Halfway across the paddock I realised she was going to beat me to the next paddock. This wasn't mine, so I stopped and returned home . . . for the rifle. It seemed the stories I had heard about dingoes going wild might indeed be true. I had never had this kind of trouble with her before. I certainly didn't want to shoot her, but I was running late and out of ideas. When I came out with the rifle she was back near the ute. As I approached she seemed to read me and took off down the exact same line she'd followed each time before.

I jumped in the ute and pursued as fast as the paddock's rough surface would allow, noticing that she was occasionally looking back to see where I was. There was a small group of trees right in the far corner and she was heading for it, flat-out. I thought she would just jump through the fence and keep going, and I tried to get the rifle ready to get a shot.

Suddenly, without warning, as she reached the trees she stopped, turned and sat. I couldn't believe it. As I drove right up to her, I could see her lip curling, which was her way of talking to me.

What was even more surprising, right beside her, jammed between two small trees, was a woolly hogget. It couldn't get out. I don't know whether Annie had chased it in there or what had happened, but it was unharmed and I let it go. Meanwhile Annie had jumped up on the ute and was ready for a lift home. I suddenly realised how close I had come to shooting her, believing she had gone wild.

I have seen several films and read the stories of dogs that wanted to tell their owners something important. Even after 40 years of working nearly every day with dogs, I had thought many such stories were probably mostly fictional. However, on that day, a very sad one due to the loss of Mum, I was confronted with evidence I can never dismiss. A plain ordinary desert dingo went to quite a deal of trouble— and risk—to attract me to something it felt I should know about.

SEEING-EWE DOG

Geoffrey Blight, Narrogin, Western Australia

People often ask me what is the cleverest thing I've ever seen a dog do. No doubt some of the dog acts in circuses are extraordinary, but they are taught to the dog. I have also seen some very good working dogs doing great things under command. However, my soft spot was always for the intelligent dog working out the solution to a problem on its own. Very few dogs get such an opportunity and very few people believe a dog has that ability.

The most intelligent dog—although not necessarily the hardest worker—I ever encountered was Elbon Park Gus AA259, a Scottish merle shorthaired border collie. The incident that brought me to that conclusion occurred on a property just east of Narrogin in the late eighties. We had mustered a flock of ewes and lambs into portable yards but one ewe, totally blind, had separated from the flock and was left half a mile away, continually walking in a tight circle.

The only way to shift such sheep is to catch them and return them to the flock where they survive by following sound and smell. When a flock becomes infected with pink eye, temporary blindness can cause trouble and even make sheep work dangerous if a big wether takes fright and charges into you. I have known a farmer to be hospitalised through such an encounter.

Anyway, Gus spotted this sheep and as he was never happy leaving a sheep anywhere, off he went. The men and I watched with interest, believing he would certainly fail since the sheep couldn't see him. But we underestimated old Gus.

After he realised that normal tactics weren't going to steer the sheep, Gus gradually got in closer and closer. He moved first to one side and then the other, letting the sheep bump into him so it would turn. Gus never gave up. We had to go on with the mulesing and tailing, so for some time we forgot about Gus—until one of the men drew our attention to the fact that Gus was still at it and had halved the distance into the yards.

So for the next half hour we watched as we worked, and to this day how I wished I could have filmed old Gus. Realising that to make progress he had to keep touching the sheep, he continually put himself in a position where the blind ewe walked into him before he could eventually walk it into the yards. The ewe followed in the same way it obviously did to survive in the flock. It took him a while but he did it without any commands or assistance whatsoever.

I have never seen another dog move a sheep in such a fashion. I doubt that many believe a dog capable of solving such a problem, part of which was understanding the sheep was not like normal sheep and couldn't see him.

ENDURANCE

Geoffrey Blight, Narrogin, Western Australia

I know there are many stories about the endurance of a good working dog, but often it is hard to measure these feats in concrete terms. However, in 1964 we got a good indication of the endurance of one of my kelpies when I did some contract ploughing for a chap in the north-eastern wheatbelt.

Using an International A554 tractor we drove in transport gear (I guess about 16 mph) for 22 miles and ploughed for a straight 36½ hours at 6½ mph before returning home. It was over 39 unbroken hours, except for refuelling, nature stops and meals. It was approximately 240 miles or 380 kilometres. Throughout this whole time the sheepdog, Sally, never dropped behind the tractor. She arrived home looking exactly as she had left.

I must point out that the kelpie, who might have had some labrador in her, had made a habit for two years of running with the working tractors. Catching field mice, she was probably as fit as a dog could be. I don't recall her being anything but lean, and she was none too great at working stock. Her demise came in 1965, when she was following a bulldozer in virgin bush and picked up a dingo bait laid by the Agricultural Protection Board.

TUCKERBAG TAILS

Geoffrey Blight, Narrogin, Western Australia

The most common way of counting lambs at tailing time is to count the pile of severed tails. Frequently there is a bit of argument about how many tails the dogs ate. Farmers have strange rules. If their sheepdog pinches a tail, that's fine. But if you're the contractor and your dog has one, he's at best likely to score a broken rib.

Yet the most successful working dog food I have ever used is unskinned lambs' tails. Dogs need to get used to them, but they certainly thrive on them. I now regularly feed over twenty dogs every day during tailing season on them.

The best dog I ever had on the job in the early years of mulesing was Broc. He lived on lambs' tails from May till November for sixteen years. On average he ate about nineteen as we started the day and another twenty at about 4.30 in the afternoon.

We had a lot of years of watching and counting his eating habits. Although there was always an open bag of pellets left for him in the garage, he rarely touched them while the tails were coming off.

In the early years I used to worry about the wool blocking him up but now, with the luxury of hindsight and experience, I realise that the wool was probably the secret to his long working life. Bowel cancer is a common killer of dogs and nature has a way of combating it. Modern pet foods ignore the fact that in their native state dogs were meant to consume prey with either wool, fur or feathers still attached to it. I have never had a dog suffer damage from the consumption of wool.

The dogs that eat the tails straight out are not a problem—let them have their fill. The ones that want to suck on the juicy end are a damned nuisance. They will spread hundreds around all over the place if you don't watch them. So will the dogs that think it's a good idea to bury some. In order to see how many a dog would remove if left unhindered, we sometimes did a count, and noted that they're capable of disappearing with well over a hundred before tiring of the novelty.

That would be a hundred I don't get paid for, so I ensure the dogs don't get stuck into the tails until after they have been counted!

THE BEST SEATS FOR THE BEST WORKERS

Geoffrey Blight, Narrogin, Western Australia

In all my years of going contracting on sheep properties in the southern part of Western Australia, I have always made a habit of giving the best seats to the best workers. In other words, the dogs rode in the front and the men on the back of the ute.

For many years I only had one dog and we usually travelled in a car pulling a trailer. This generally allowed the three human workers ample room in the car with the dog.

In later years I started using a one-ton ute with dog boxes on the back so a team of dogs could go with us. The dog boxes were extremely well built and comfortable. There were four compartments on each side of the tray and their doors could only be opened when the drop sides of the tray were down, which was good insurance against a door rattling open.

Fitting up to four people in the cab was a very tight squeeze indeed. When we did try it we would arrive at our destination with all sorts of cramps. One of the lads working for us at the time decided that, as there were only four dogs on board, he'd throw an old mattress in one compartment and get in the dog box.

This certainly helped the space problems a lot. However, the lad was so comfortable—he was even able to sleep for the one and a half hours it took to get to the job—that the workers started fighting over whose turn it was to get in the dog box. In next to no time I had two workers stretched out in the box, which often led to one dog having to sit on the front seat.

When I arrived at the job, farmers never really got used to seeing me alight from the cab with a dog or two, then walk around and drop the sides of the dog box to let out the men.

A WORDLESS LESSON

Geoffrey Blight, Narrogin, Western Australia

Some years ago, I was asked to give the Children's Talk during the Sunday morning service at the local Narrogin Uniting Church. Our church is well attended with a considerable number of small children who participate until the Children's Talk, after which they branch off to their Sunday School. The time allocated for such talks is three minutes, although we have had some lasting many times as long, which weren't popular. As it was my first time, I was told to be sure and keep it short.

Being near Easter, I was informed that the thought for the day was the need for affection, loyalty and sacrifice in life. These are things I have often claimed I have learnt more about from a sheep-dog than from some human beings. Therefore I decided I would take Broc, my sixteen-year-old kelpie, along as a prop, since kids are a tough audience.

Immaculately dressed in collar and tie, Broc walked into church close behind my wife and me and sat himself on the pew facing forward, with all the dignity of any other member of the congregation. Already he had the attention of every child in church. Half an hour later I was asked to come forward and give the children's address.

Old Broc followed me to the front where the Pastor had invited the children to come and sit. The dog sat on the carpet immediately in front of me. The children, immediately very curious, came forward and eyed off the well-dressed dog. While I began a deliberate search in all my pockets for notes I didn't really have, I relied on my intuition for what might happen next. Sure enough, I wasn't wrong.

A very small child, too young to have any inhibitions, suddenly wobbled forward and embraced the old dog, who responded quietly. Within seconds, every child in front of me became part of a tangled mass of patting, affectionate children, responding to a very near deaf sheepdog, who welcomed each in his own manner.

Needless to say, all the children were oblivious to my continuing search for the speech notes. The congregation was amused at the turn of events. My three minutes ran out very quickly. I quietly apologised for having forgotten my notes and explained that I'd intended to tell the children of the wonderful rewards of loving one another—though on this occasion, I would have to leave that message to my dog to deliver.

As the children untangled themselves and filed off to Sunday School, the Minister said he doubted if anyone present would ever forget the 'wordless lesson' which had been delivered that morning, given in affection by an old sheepdog.

BOB THE UNBEATABLE

Geoffrey Blight, Narrogin, Western Australia

Bob was a border collie that was said to be well bred. I paid $400 for him when he was about nine months old. I badly needed a dog to replace Broc and thought Bob was a quick solution, but he fell a long way short of the mark.

A big dog, he was supposed to have been trained, but whatever training he'd had was very limited. He had a bit of a cast at a speed that usually left a third of the sheep behind, and he loved to jump fences in the yards. That was about all there was to Bob. Compared to Broc he was as 'thick as a brick'.

Far too much eye made him very hard to get to respond to commands as he would stand and stare and stare . . . usually until you tossed something at him, at which point he would go flat-out at what he thought you wanted. He had two speeds—stop and flat-out. It was irritating, but in those days I believed a good trainer could change such things. I had as much to learn as Bob. Having owned only four dogs in 40 years had not given me much dog training experience.

I was told I shouldn't have bought him by someone who'd had him on trial. He called him a gutless wonder as he had showed a tendency to run off and crawl under the ute for this fellow. What he didn't tell me was that he had accidently hit him with a large stick he had thrown, cutting his eye as a result, an injury still visible at close inspection.

I tried to teach Bob to trial, and ended up with sheep going around and around and around until we were all exhausted, but finally one day I penned. It was the first time I ever had and I got a score of one. Meanwhile we had sorted Bob out in yard work and he had a couple of useful moves. He'd bark and he'd push or crawl through anywhere, no matter how the sheep might belt him around. I soon realised Bob was not going to be anything marvellous, though, so I started to get other pups, some even more useless, hoping for another Broc.

My trialling career was going well if making my mates laugh had anything to do with it. I often used to wonder how, after working so many sheep in my day, I could not seem to come to terms with the three-sheep trial, never seeming to get steady enough to look in control. I became known for my shouting at the dog in exasperation, something I rarely ever did away from the trial ground. I would get disqualified for everything in the book: walking backwards, patting my dog. Even if they didn't disqualify me, I'd end up running the sheep ragged by trying to get a dog up close, just as I had always worked them in the pressure of contracting.

I soon started to wonder whether I had any talent at all and whether I could make a dog do anything other than by accident. The thing that bugged me most was that several of the triallers became friends and I worked contract for them on their farms. My dogs would have guts and moves that made their trial dogs look weak. Many times they couldn't even yard a flock of ewes and lambs and my 'mad bastards' would do it with style, even with them being in the way. This had gone unnoticed and had led to me being given every conceivable bit of advice, much of which just frustrated me and made me even more impatient and hopeless.

Bob was always my masterpiece. I'd enter him in all three sections: novice, improvers and open. Strangely enough, he was usually so exhausted by the time the open came around that this was usually his best run, nearly always lasting fifteen minutes—of not quite catching up with three wethers.

We didn't have many utility trials in those days, where a dog has to work yards, but they held a big one at Muresk College to coincide with the Americas Cup Challenge in Fremantle. We were even lucky enough to have some American participants. It was held at night because it was January and very hot. I only had one dog I could enter: Bob. He wasn't much, but I really wanted to have a go against what could be argued as many of the best yard and field dogs in the world.

My run was on the third night and there had been some brilliant trialling. I'd been brushing up Bob as much as I could, and during the day he had been doing all the work of bringing in and taking away sheep for the trial—strangely, being as good or better at this than most of the dogs. Off the trial ground, neither he nor I were hyped up. We were just working and nothing ever went wrong. I'd had 40 years of this and I guess I did it well. But in trialling, you wouldn't believe what I could make happen.

The sheep were very big wethers. Many were stags that had horns due to late or faulty castration. They were also half-woolled, which sometimes makes them very hard to trial in smaller numbers as they tend not to be able to see the dog and panic when he is behind them. They are very apt to stand up and fight the dog, as I was to find out.

When my time came I started off well. Bob was behaving beautifully (for Bob). Blimey, I was in with a chance even. As we made the cast, the draw, the yards and so on, everything was on track. My excitement was rising . . . then disaster.

I was clearing the very tightly packed race and a big stag with long curly horns suddenly decided he was going to have Bob. The race was very narrow and didn't allow a dog to jump clear. Bob tried to duck under the charging stag as was his habit, but the long curly horns gathered Bob's hind legs, not only turning him up but dragging him heavily along the entire fence of the race. It was sickening and I made a jump at the sheep in the hope of helping Bob get clear. The sheep stopped and Bob fell clear, yelping.

I stood there looking down at Bob, wondering what to do. He stood up and, without looking at me, charged straight back down the race at the horny predator. Not giving it time to turn, he was under it and, with a snap, had it and the race cleared. I realised that the crowd had spontaneously applauded the dog's effort.

I could see Bob's back leg was up high from the ground. He could be hurt, I thought. To touch him meant disqualification—and we were being applauded for the first time in our career. Maybe I was just thick too, but I kept going with Bob, who was still working keenly on three legs. Out in the field we didn't do too badly but Bob was battling. Our final score left us one place out of the final, but I was happy as I left the ground with a badly limping dog.

Men were heard to comment on the guts of the dog, never having seen a dog take such a bad knock and get up and go on. Not bad for a gutless wonder, I thought.

When we got to the vet and had Bob X-rayed, I felt sick. His leg was broken in two places and his hip ball broken off . . . and I'd kept going. I felt terrible. They fixed Bob up. It cost a fortune, and I gave him away to a chap who had light work and asked for him.

Bob was the most expensive dog I ever owned. He was as thick as a brick, yet in a few short seconds on that ground that night, he showed the world something that is the envy of all dog men: guts and loyalty. And he did it for me. When half the dogs in the final failed by being forced to retreat from fighting sheep, I was not surprised to hear people recalling Bob's effort. Whether I learnt something I needed to know from that, or whether it impressed my mates, I was given some rather brilliant old dogs that had finished their trialling days. They became very popular with children in hospitals and schools where we shared our bond in all sorts of displays.

Bob was not the best dog I've ever had—far from it—but when the chips were down he gave his all. I remember that 'thick bastard' with much affection.

A DRIVE THROUGH PERTH

Geoffrey Blight, Narrogin, Western Australia

Farmers are always trying to find ways of describing the brilliance of their sheepdogs and I am no better. When the yarns are being told, you've got to come up with something!

It was a boast I must have made a thousand times that finally got me into trouble. As a contractor handling sheep practically every day I always had a dog—for most of the time only one, although that has changed in recent years. When talking Dogs I would often say that mine were 'good enough to drive sheep down Perth's main street'. This was always a convincing boast, but in the mid-eighties a reporter from the *Sunday Times* asked me if I'd ever tried it. I said I hadn't, but as I was doing some sheepdog publicity for the Royal Agricultural Society, I made the statement that I was giving it some thought. This statement appeared in the *Times* and everyone seemed to get interested.

The Agricultural Society and Perth City Council asked me if I could. My best mate, who is one of Australia's best sheepdog triallers, told me how a top trialler had done it seventeen years earlier. So what the hell! Why not? I was always trying to show off my dogs, but as a new worker in the sport of sheepdog trialling, I wasn't doing too well. I was far more acquainted with the pressure of angry farmers, stupid dogs and mean sheep on the farms where I worked.

Saying I would was a mistake. The first thing that happened was the animal libbers went mad and wrote to the Society and the Council urging them not to let this 'idiot' with 'marauding' dogs and 'disorientated sheep' onto their streets. They claimed that sheep would be killed running under the feet of the public. I thought this would be the end of the idea, however the instigators urged me on and I decided to let people judge for themselves.

Commonsense had it that if I was to drive sheep through Perth, I would have to walk in front and show the way. As the time drew nearer I decided I'd use five dogs and about 25 sheep so that I could cover most situations, especially as at one part of the trip I would be walking within ten feet of oncoming traffic doing 70 kph. I had found out that the earlier drive I had been told about had involved only seven wethers and one dog, and that the sheep had escaped soon after the press shot had been taken. My mate told me this only two days before the event, which really took the wind out of my sails. But I believed that I had dogs that I could rely on— they'd had plenty of experience coping when things went wrong, as they often did on the farm.

On the day the first thing that had me in a panic was the crowd. Blimey, I hadn't thought too much about the people side of the thing. Then there were the TV crews ducking and diving in and out of the sheep like my neighbours' mongrel sheepdogs. The streets were to be cleared by the police, but that amounted to only a couple of officers on bikes who weren't always able to prevent cars coming from carparks and side streets and turning up in the middle of things. As I hadn't been keen to be on my own, my daughter-in-law and two grandchildren came along to help.

When the policeman waved me on my way, I can remember wishing then that I had old Broc—the four border collies and one kelpie I had were showing obvious nervousness. But with Regal working backwards in the front, Merle on the left, Nigger on the right, Steve pushing the rear and Gus troubleshooting, we were off on the most anxious two and a half kilometres I have ever walked. But those mongrel dogs didn't let me down as very quickly they realised their jobs—despite considerable starting, stopping and attempted breakaways early, they rose to the occasion far better than I did.

Even though Merle swiped an unsuspecting little girl's ice-cream from off the cone as she stared at the sheep, and Gus stuck his head in the occasional bin, we made it in front of some 20,000 onlookers, but not without a price. Being warm, the bitumen road played havoc with the dogs' feet and Nigger, who had had to do most of the covering, was bleeding from all four feet, but was still giving it his best shot.

It was well into the drive when my nerves settled and I thought again of that boast I had made a thousand times—'good enough to drive sheep through Perth'—and old Broc, about whom the boast had usually been made. He was still alive at the time, in his nineteenth year, so I bought him a paper and let him see it on television.

PLEASE, LADY, THERE'S NOBODY ELSE

Geoffrey Blight, Narrogin, Western Australia

Jenny lay quietly in the dark, her husband Phillip sleeping peacefully at her side. An eerie silence surrounded everything. Faint beams of moonlight stretched gently across the room. The small red digits read 2 am.

Rolling over, Jenny stared into a dark corner, unable to dismiss from her mind the events of the last four days. Her thoughts wandered to the old, near-white collie dog sitting outside. For four days it had refused to eat. Its sad eyes haunted her. She had tried so hard to make friends and have it eat, but to no avail. What would become of Sally-Anne? How the dog missed the man who had brought her here.

It had all started four days earlier, with that 9 am phone call, after Phillip had gone seeding. She had answered the phone with her usual 'Hello', and was shocked at the violent coughing which assailed her ears. The heavy breathing and gasping made her wonder if anyone was going to talk. Finally, a very weak and strained voice mumbled a series of disjointed statements: 'Dog . . . back . . . bought.'

Trying to make sense of the call, Jenny asked who she was speaking to, but the man's voice immediately broke into another violent coughing fit, which seemed to go on forever. Then she heard the faint voice again: 'Jim . . . sorry . . . sick . . . hospital.' Then, 'back' and 'dog'.

By now Jenny was totally confused and said she didn't understand, could he ring back later? Then came the five words that now haunted her: 'Please, lady, there's nobody else.' The sentence she could never forget, from a man called Jim.

It was these words that sent a shock through her. Initially she had thought the man might be drunk, but now she wasn't sure. In a daze, she mumbled, 'All right', not knowing what it meant, but Phillip could sort it out later.

After replacing the phone, she made herself a cuppa and thought about the call. Perhaps it was a bloke who'd bought a sheepdog off Phillip, messed it up, and now wanted his money back. Probably for booze by the sound of it, but it wasn't worth worrying about. She wasn't a great dog lover like Phillip. They always seemed to be the centre of attention around the farm. She felt jealous of the way Phillip always seemed to idolise them. He should try getting them to clean his house and sit here, miles from anywhere.

At times she was so lonely she would cry. The children were all away at boarding school—a farmer's wife, the great life! Well, you can have it, thought Jenny.

The noise of an approaching vehicle, mid-afternoon, cheered her up after a very dismal morning. Perhaps Phillip was home early, was her first thought, or maybe Gwen had popped over from next door . . . but the unmuffled spluttering and jerking of the motor told her it was neither. As it stopped in front of the house, it brought back memories of the dreadful sound of coughing on the phone some six hours earlier, which, till now, she'd forgotten. Peeping out the window, she saw a twenty-year-old rusty ute. The grey paint was all but gone and the rust holes gaped in the guards. She could not see who was driving and felt a twinge of fear. It was probably someone wanting petrol—better keep out of sight.

She sat quietly, hoping to hear the vehicle start up and leave, but there was not a sound, nothing happened. After nervously waiting nearly fifteen minutes, she decided to take another peep. Whoever it was may have been stealing something.

Just as she was about to open the door, someone knocked on it, weak and low. She jumped then stood paralysed as she heard that sound again, the coughing and spluttering. It sent shudders through her. Slowly stepping forward, she gingerly opened the door. 'Yes?' she asked—then gagged. It was the smell that hit her first, a dreadful, decaying smell. He sagged down by the door in another fit of coughing, unshaven and utterly filthy. Horrified, she stepped back, almost tripping over the dog that had quietly moved up behind her and was sniffing her dress.

The gasping body called, 'Sit, Sally-Anne.' It cringed.

At first Jenny thought it was Sally, but Sally had died ten years earlier. Sally was one dog she had liked. My God, it did look like Sally. 'Sorry,' she whispered, and put out her hand to the frightened old dog.

Looking again at the figure trying to rise, Jenny could now see his face. She'd never seen anything so ravaged and tormented. The eyes were glazed and staring at her, just like the dog's. Good God! What on earth . . . the man's nearly dead, she thought as he tried to speak. Help, her mind screamed, then she put both hands forward as the man slid further down the wall in a gasping fit. The phone, she had to phone for help.

The sergeant's quiet voice came through to her. 'Jenny, just sit down, I'm on my way. We'll handle it. Do you know who he is?'

The waiting seemed to go on for hours. She tried to give the man a sip of water and sit him more comfortably, but he was so filthy. There was blood and spittle all down his front. He kept trying to talk. 'Dog . . . back . . . hospital,' which only confused her more.

The dog was not one Phillip had sold recently. It was far too old. Yet the man had called it Sally-Anne. It looked so sad and frightened. She hadn't moved an inch since being told to 'sit'.

Finally Jenny heard the sirens, then saw the police car followed by the ambulance. The problem was no longer hers.

She tried to place the dog in the ambulance, which brought a weak protest from the man, so she kept a firm hold on the frightened dog. The ambulance sped away. Jenny told the sergeant everything she knew about the man, which wasn't much.

That had all happened four days earlier. They now knew Jim was a hermit who had a caravan in the coastal bush 200 kilometres away. He'd rarely been seen for years. Phillip also recognised the similarity between the dog and their first dog, Sally. He said it must be her pup as he'd sold a litter thirteen odd years ago. A shearer called Jim had taken one, but they hadn't seen him since.

The police found his caravan in poor shape. Four chooks were the only sign of life. It appeared Jim had had a family break-up some twelve years earlier. She wondered if they would find his family, for he was very sick. The doctors said that he had no will to live.

In a coma, he'd called for Sally-Anne, but they hadn't been able to locate anyone by that name. Jenny realised she had not told the police she had heard him call the dog Sally-Anne. She must tell the sergeant . . .

The moonlight looked so soft and gentle. She felt the wet warmth of her tears as she remembered his words, 'Please, lady, there's nobody else.'

It began so low, so sad, she almost missed it. Then she heard it again. The howl of a dog, a very lonely, old dog. A dog who had not eaten in four days. A dog in mourning.

Jenny rolled over, her sobs coming freely. She buried her face deep in the pillow and began the wait for the call that she now knew, with morning, would come.

PART 5

HIGH COUNTRY

Where the earth heaves up in stony surges leaving behind valleys streaked with silver, the call is for dogs and people with tough bodies, iron stamina and strong character.

In the high country human contact is sparse, so livestock are touchy. Scrub is dense and there are plenty of places to hide. Terrain is rough. The weather is unpredictable—quiet days with limpid sunshine turn vicious, with driving, freezing winds and fog and snow and rain.

Dogs and handlers need all their guile, for the potential for tragedy is great.

A MOUNTAIN MAN AND HIS SHAGGY DOGS: A PROFILE OF RUSTY CONNELLY

Angela Goode

Above the Beloka Valley in the Benambra district of the Victorian high country, Rusty Connelly lives the life that has made a legend of mountain cattlemen. Every year before the snows arrive, he has to bring his cattle down off leasehold country 4,500 feet up in the Alpine National Park. His leasehold adjoins Tom Groggin station, that sacred site of folklore immortalised by Banjo Paterson in *The Man from Snowy River* in 1895. This was where Jack Riley did his epic ride up Leatherbarrel Creek, which feeds into the River Murray.

With his home-bred Australian stock horses and four dogs, 55-year-old Rusty, who has been in the high country all his life, heads off up the mountains for three or four days at a time. High up in the Great Dividing Range among the snow gums, running streams, rocks and fallen logs, Rusty Connelly couldn't muster his cattle unless he had a team of good dogs. 'You've got to use dogs in the mountains,' he says. 'It's scrubby, rough and steep. Some of it is one-in-one gradient. In fact, good dogs are even more essential up here than good horses.'

The dogs which accompany him belie their looks. They are, in Rusty's words, 'not a pretty sight and they make terrible pets'. They are as shaggy as the shedding bark on the eucalypts and as tough as the terrain. They are Smithfield–kelpie cross dogs that Rusty specially breeds for his alpine cattle run. These whiskery, hairy dogs have brownish black, tan and greyish coats extending from their ears to their paws and to their naturally stumped tails. On the run they look like a moving shagpile carpet with beady black eyes—anything but a super-efficient mustering machine.

'They are hard-working dogs,' says Rusty. 'Great at finding cattle in this rough country. And they are faithful, hardy and tireless. They are so tough, they sleep quite happily out in the snow. But they are not sociable dogs. They don't like being petted or fussed over.'

So off they go—Rusty, with his Akubra on the red head that gave him his name, oilskin, chaps, warm sweater and thick socks, sitting deeply in his stock saddle, with pack horses and dogs—picking their way over wombat holes and rocks to scour 10,000 acres for his Herefords. When he gets to the hut where he'll camp, he spells his team, checks his holding yards and prepares for the following day's muster.

At dawn he takes two dogs and leaves two behind. As he searches for cattle tracks in the dense scrub, he also keeps a close eye on his dogs. They'll tell him when there are cattle nearby. Their noses, poking through that shaggy mat, sniff the air and if the scent is promising, the dogs walk in its direction.

They cast wide and flush out animals toward the horseman. Some Smithfield cross dogs, Rusty says, are forceful and give the beasts a quick nip, but mostly they work quietly. If they do bark, it is with a relatively soft voice.

Rusty remembers with fondness many great dogs over the years, but especially Biff, who could track and scent cattle and handle up to 100 head on his own.

In the old days, before times got tough, Rusty had his two sons to help with the muster. These days one works at the copper mine at Benambra and the other is a mechanic in the town. He does 90 per cent of the stockwork on his own, just bringing in casual workers at branding and weaning time.

Rusty and the others who graze the alpine runs are not just battling a failing rural economy, they are struggling to retain their alpine leaseholds. Claims that the cattle are damaging the mountains are nonsense, say Rusty and other members of the Mountain Cattlemen's Association.

'Log trucks and four-wheel-drive vehicles do far more damage and bring in weeds. Cattle don't do damage, and they help with fire control by keeping the grasses down. If anything, the mountains are understocked.'

He rides away among the broad-leaf peppermint, the black sally in the creeks and the snow gums twisting on the slopes. The shaggy dogs that will help move about 200 cattle into the lower country in the next few weeks lope behind him, sniffing the leaf-scented air for work waiting to be done.

UP ON THE SEAGULL BEAT

Peter Chillwell, Harvey, Western Australia

Having been a shepherd in the high country of New Zealand's South Island, I reckon mustering sheep in Australia is easy. Being at 7,500 feet on the 'seagull' beat in the Awatere Valley with no motorbikes or four-wheel-drives really tests out your shepherding skills. I was one of a team of four or five shepherds on Middle Hurst station to 'bark up' the side of the mountain in the tussock country. We had to get up at 2.30 am, have breakfast, collect our teams of dogs and be climbing by 4.00 am.

It's a long way up to the seagull beat and damn steep too. Some of New Zealand's most popular tourist lookouts nestle in the land the shepherd walks daily. Although sheep rarely get up above the 6,000 feet mark, I sometimes had to go up to nearly 9,000 feet looking for strays. So you certainly need a good head for heights. Often a helicopter is used to take men and dogs up to a high plateau where they will be dropped off to start their mustering, way up in the clouds.

I was new to the game and like many in that position, I was keen to impress my older and wiser workmates. We were mustering a station on a day of immensely thick fog. We flew in above the incredibly thick murk that lay like a custard over the mountains, leaving only the peaks above 6,000 feet jutting out in all their magnificent rugged glory.

The pilot put us down on a wide ledge which was actually level with the fog's upper surface. It was so thick you couldn't see more than a few feet into it, so it was apparent we would have to wait until it lifted before we could get our bearings and start work.

With nothing to sit on, my mustering mate just squatted uncomfortably. I decided it would be much more comfortable to sit on the ledge and dangle my feet over the edge just above the impregnable fog—despite advice that it would be wise to keep away from the edge. I had already worked a few weeks in the high country so felt very confident—even cocky. I wasn't scared of slipping a few feet down a shingle slide. However, I hadn't been up on a seagull beat before. My bloody dogs wouldn't come near me as I sat there waiting—kicking stones off the edge to fall into the blanket below my feet.

When mountain fog lifts, it can do so very quickly. I can still feel my stomach heaving as I sat there in my foolhardiness, showing off, and looking down . . . and down . . . and down. I became paralysed with fear as I suddenly realised that there I was perched, wriggling around on my bottom, on a very unstable ledge a thousand feet above absolutely nothing.

I remember now with sweaty palms the incredible fear that overtook me as I lay back and ever so carefully brought my feet onto more solid rock—slowly retreating to where my dogs sat with sombre, know-all looks on their faces.

Another day I was the man high on the slope. This time there was no fog, but because it was so steep I could hardly see the next bloke below me. There weren't many sheep right up at the top— there never are, just small bunches here and there.

I had a team of four dogs, all Huntaways—Chum, Nell, Bruce and Ruff. Some days you needed even more dogs if you wanted to get off the hill by mid-afternoon. I sent a few little lots down to the next man and was checking out the crags, bluffs and knolls. Crikey, it's beautiful up there—it was worth doing the job just for the view. In one particularly steep part I was looking out over one of the many sheer drops. Right below me, between 70 and 100 feet down, I spotted a small bunch of sheep crowded on a ledge.

All four dogs were looking over the edge. They'd seen the sheep and were waiting to see which one I would give the word to. It looked safe enough. There was quite a wide track leading down to the ledge and on down the slope, so I thought I would let Chum go. He was the keenest and liked to get the nod. However, when I said, 'Chum, come out,' I thought he'd cast out down the track to them, but the silly idiot went straight over the top before I could stop him.

I'm sure I could see him looking up at me as if to say, 'Blimy, Boss, you ask a bit of us poor dogs,' as he floated down, legs spread-eagled, ears flapping like a parachute. I was sure he was a dead dog.

But he got it right. He landed slap-bang in the middle of those big woolly wethers, sending them scattering after breaking his fall. Completely undaunted, Chum soon had them back together, off the ledge and on their way down the mountain.

On the mountains, like in the Australian outback, there's not much between you and the stars. I didn't work in the high country long, but long enough to learn its ways. I witnessed the human effort, the beauty, the skills of the dogs—and the tragedies. It took just one tragedy, the death of Chum, for me to decide to give the mountains away and try my hand where the land was a bit flatter.

Chum was just an ordinary Huntaway. He was no national champion, but he was my best dog. We spent a lot of time together up there in that mountainous country and he never let me down. He was always keen as mustard and the dog in my team that had to do the tricky work. Up there, you sometimes don't get the chance to do things twice. You do it right the first time—or you're dead. The mountains have claimed a long list of men and dogs who didn't get a second shot at the job.

I was shepherding up the Growler Creek near Mesapotamia station. Things were not going too badly. I'd 'barked out' several small bunches of merino wethers, but there were half a dozen stuck on a very narrow ledge overlooking a sheer drop.

With the ledge narrowing to as little as six inches in places, there wasn't room to get past them. Besides, the ledge had no exit path, so I decided it was far too dangerous. I'd leave them there and move on. A well-known New Zealand high country proverb was in my mind: 'It's better to have a live straggler than catch a dead sheep.'

Just then the boss flew past me in his Cessna and circled to let me know he'd seen the sheep that I had supposedly missed. Shepherds aren't supposed to leave sheep—only bad shepherds do, and they get known. I had a good name and since I wanted to keep it, I went back.

The job was tricky, so I had to pick Chum. I couldn't even get across to the ledge, but even if I could have, it was only going to put me in the path of the wethers when they came out. It was simply too narrow, so I stayed where I thought I would be able to see what was going on. When I sent Chum, it took a while to steer him over onto the opposite slope and bluff. Finally he spotted the sheep. The only hope he had was to drive them along the ledge to where he could pass and then push them back out. His approach was stealthy but the sheep moved quickly along the ledge and out of my sight. Chum followed and then he was on his own.

For five minutes I waited, hoping to see the sheep reappear with Chum behind them. As the minutes passed I knew Chum was in trouble.

Suddenly they came into view much further around the bluff on a much narrower ledge—a thousand feet over pure nothing. Chum was past the sheep but they had turned on him and were coming at him. There were six big woolly mongrels, all of them four times Chum's weight. Chum obviously wasn't the first dog they'd seen. That's why they had retreated onto that inaccessible ledge—I bet they had escaped a dog before.

Chum had nowhere to go. The sheep knew that and I guess Chum did too. There wasn't a thing I could do but watch. He did his best. He barked and stood his ground. But a big merino rig knew he had him cornered and charged. Chum met the charge as best he could but it wasn't good enough. The rig belted him that hard, he went straight over the edge.

I went down a shingle slide I normally wouldn't have dared tackle, hopelessly calling to Chum as if some miracle could save him. I cursed the sheep, the mountains, even God—but I was wasting my time. Chum hadn't a chance.

I just sat there for a long time, hours, dampening the shingle, remembering. Finally, when I knew I had to think of getting in off the mountain, I built a mound of stones over the mutilated body of my Chum.

I got back to camp hours after the others, but no-one said a word. No-one said, 'Where have you been?' or 'What happened to you?' They could count. They had counted a mate's dogs before. They knew. They let me be. The story would be told in good time.

It wasn't the last day I shepherded sheep on the mountains, but I knew, everyone knew, that I'd be moving on.

Station bosses in New Zealand can be pretty fussy about the men they employ to shepherd their flocks. I found this out when I applied for a job at Gray's Hills in McKenzie country.

In order to ensure that one weak, lazy or gutless shepherd doesn't blow a whole muster by leaving sheep behind or knocking them up, they have a novel job specification. They insist that all their shepherds are smokers who 'roll their own'. Gray's Hills is a 70,000-acre dead-flat spread and these unconventional rules have evolved over the years to protect the flock.

Because the country is so flat, shepherds are always tempted to push the sheep too hard. This makes a lot of extra work collecting the sheep that can't take the pace. If he's on 'rollies', a bloke has to stop or dismount from his horse and search his pockets for the 'makings'. While his dogs take a quick camp under the nearest tussock, he has to go through the whole ritual of gauging the right amount of tobacco, getting the paper right and completing the task with an experienced lick. And don't underestimate how much longer it takes to light a rollie, especially in New Zealand's climate. Even the weakest of sheep has a fair chance of keeping up with the mob.

I was told to be sure to be seen rolling my smokes if I wanted the job, and to keep it. It was the only time in my life I had to resort to such primitive satisfaction for my addiction. Exasperation with my DIY fags meant I probably gave the sheep on that station the easiest walk home—and my dogs the slackest time in their working lives.

LEFT IN THE DARK

Les Brooks, Barraba, New South Wales

After spending 60 years in Sydney, I came to Barraba to become a wool grower and cattle breeder. One day I had to do repairs along the boundary fence, so set off with my motorbike and border collie, Sonnee. I found a large hole in the fence in the south-east corner of the property and set to work on the necessary repairs.

The repairs took me ages. It was only when I had finished that I realised how late in the day it was. It was so dark that I had to feel for my tools on the ground. I couldn't even see my hand out in front of me. I turned around and started to walk back to my motorbike but found, to my horror, that it was so dark, I had no idea where it was.

Realising the seriousness of the situation—I had never been to that part of the property before—I felt that my only hope of getting out of there was to call Sonnee. It was one of those dense black nights—no moon, cloudy sky—and bitterly cold for we were at 2,000 feet in the New England area in the month of August.

I called out to Sonnee but nothing happened. Then I called a little louder. Nothing. Then, feeling the panic rising, I called at the top of my voice. I was relieved to hear a rustle in the bushes and feel him brush my legs. I knelt down, put my arm around his neck and said, 'Sonnee, I'm lost.' I then asked him to take me back to the motorbike.

He immediately set off and I followed the sound of him rustling the bushes. Sure enough, he led me straight back to the bike. I knew we were there by the smell of petrol which had been leaking from the carburettor.

I patted Sonnee, thanked him for leading me back to the bike and said, 'Now, my boy, you'll have to take me back to the homestead.' For that was my next problem. When I started the bike the headlights immediately came on, but although the track through the heavily timbered ironbark could be found easily in daylight, it was impossible to recognise at night. Everything looked the same. So once again I was totally lost.

Sonnee had already taken off, so again I had to call out to him but, as before, I had to call out three times and at the top of my voice. Then came the familiar rustle of the bushes and the brushing against my legs. Once again I got down on my knees, but this time I put both arms around his neck and said, 'Sonnee, I'm really lost. Take me back to the homestead.'

So off he went, but this time he only went a few yards before he stopped, turned around and looked back to see if I was still following. He did this all the way back to the homestead—even at the public roadway where normally, during the day, he would try to beat me back to the homestead over the last 1.5 kilometres. This time he kept stopping, looking back and ensuring I was still following.

I got home, cold but safe and eternally thankful to Sonnee. I quite forgive him for not being the world's greatest worker.

A GUTSY LITTLE AUSSIE

Stuart Leigh, Heyfield, Victoria

We need to go back to the late fifties and into the mountain country of eastern Victoria for the story of Rupert. Those were the post-myxomatosis years. Myxo went through the district in the summer of 1951–52, spreading by contact. As there were no mosquitoes to carry the virus, the build-up of rabbits had begun again.

The country was rough and the paddocks were covered with fallen, ringbarked snow gums, a haven for rabbits. The prime method of eradication was fumigation of the burrows. The fumigant was larvicide, and a pack of dogs was required to flush rabbits out of logs and scrub and into their burrows.

The pack consisted of dogs other people did not want and ranged in number from four or five up to as many as ten. Over the years it contained a multitude of differing breeds, mainly hunting dogs— Irish wolf hounds, whippets, greyhounds, deer hounds and many others. Then along came Rupert, an Australian terrier weighing no more than a couple of kilos, hairy, with Bob Menzies eyebrows, docked tail and bristles around his mouth. His gait was offset— that is, his back legs tracked to one side, similar to a truck with a broken rear spring centre bolt. This gave the impression that he never quite went in the direction he was aiming for. He was definitely no beauty, but was most certainly the leader of the pack.

The pack was housed in a half-acre enclosure, surrounded by six-foot wire netting slung between black sallee trees, with a post here and there for support. The kennels consisted of several square, riveted steel water tanks of 1920s vintage seen around many farms. Sleeping arrangements were strictly regimented, with the same clique sharing a kennel and not going outside their allotted place. Except for Rupert.

He was accepted by any clique at any time and spent his nights in the kennel of his choice.

A working day for Rupert would begin with him being first out of the enclosure when the gate was opened, but never participating in the general free-for-all created by the yelping, barking mass of dogs celebrating their freedom. Instead, he came dutifully to heel, ready for action. The mode of transport was tractor and trailer, the latter loaded with shovels, mattocks, fumigant and lunch. There was no room for dogs. With the first turn of the tractor engine there would be a wild forward scrambling of dogs—but not Rupert. He would follow closely behind the rear wheels of the trailer, trotting along with his offset rear legs.

Once in the paddock he was in his element, running to a log or a squat and yelping to the others that here was a rabbit. He was everywhere—into hollow logs, burrows, stumps—tail wagging, barking furiously and always looking to the others for support. A fully grown buck rabbit was almost bigger than Rupert, and the few times he was able to catch one, he had great difficulty in subduing his quarry. Mostly, of course, he would flush out the rabbits and the pack would tear off after the victim with Rupert a long, long way in the rear.

If one of the other dogs caught the rabbit, Rupert would pester the captor until he gave up his kill and Rupert would proudly bear the victim back to the camp as if it was his own achievement.

If things were a bit quiet with nothing much to chase, Rupert would suddenly jump up and dash off, yelping and carrying on, and the rest of the pack would follow with great excitement. After covering 100 yards or so, he would stop short, turn around and trot back, very pleased with himself for having organised a successful wild goose chase.

Rupert had somehow acquired a cat's 'nine lives' survival facility and over the years had many escapes. The technique of fumigating was to cut back the mouth of the burrow with a mattock or a shovel, squirt the fumigant into the burrow, then seal the entrance with soil, stamping it firmly with the boot. On one occasion during smoko, the crew was sitting around the fire when Rupert was noted as missing. A hurried search located some muffled barking and, after a few quick shovelsful of dirt were removed, out came Rupert. He was a very sick little dog, gasping for breath, eyes watering, but still grinning. He flopped under the trailer for half an hour then was off again, right as rain.

Another time the entrance of a burrow was being cut back. Rupert, who had gone unseen down the burrow, decided to resurface. The descending mattock caught him flush on his head and opened up a big wound from ear to ear across his scalp. Back to base, out with needles, catgut and disinfectant, and we sewed him up. Within 24 hours, an unbowed and 'ready for anything' Rupert was back on the job.

One October there was a very big flood in the river which bisected the property. An early morning inspection revealed twenty or more sheep marooned on a nearby island with the water levels still rising. Poor Rupert, who happened to be with us, was thrown into the torrent upstream of the island—it seemed to be a good idea at the time. We thought he would swim to the island and chase the sheep into shallow water on the other side.

Unfortunately, we had misjudged the strength of the current. He missed the island and was last seen disappearing downstream very quickly, his head bobbing up and down in the pressure waves created by the torrent. An unsuccessful search on horseback followed for several miles until the river fell away through a chasm and down some 50 feet.

During the long six- or seven-mile ride home, there was time to contemplate the situation, and that 'good idea' suddenly seemed cruel and unnecessary. However, each day brings a new dawn, and next morning, there on the back doorstep, never a place he would ordinarily be seen, was a very hungry and bedraggled small dog.

The story of Rupert would not be complete without mention of his love-life. It took some time to discover the full extent of this other world of his. As the pack was strictly a 'male only' society, he had to take advantage of every opportunity that presented itself to guarantee his genes for posterity.

He made several attempts with the cattle bitches from time to time, but these were unsuccessful because of the height disparity. It was not until several reports were received from neighbours describing litters of pups with bristly hair and short legs that Rupert's lustful activities were revealed. It was discovered that, when especially tempted, he could scramble up the wire netting of the enclosure and tumble down the other side to be off to his latest flame. He would roam far and wide on these sojourns, making one regular excursion of sixteen miles there and back to satisfy his passion. The neighbours even used him as an early warning system because he would arrive, ready for action, before they realised their bitch was due on heat.

All good things must come to an end and even in his last chase, he showed courage and tenacity. One of his very bad habits eventually led to his demise. He took great delight in chasing the horses whenever he was free and especially if there was an audience. His final horse chase went unnoticed until a whimpering was heard and observation revealed Rupert crawling up the driveway to the homestead. His injuries were massive—a broken leg, broken ribs and a split in the skull revealing his brain.

He had dragged himself 300 yards in that condition and had to be put down. But after all these years and dozens of working dogs later, the most memorable of them all is still Rupert, a gutsy little Aussie.

AT YOUR SERVICE

John Harland, Mount Hope, New South Wales

A few years ago our neighbour, who lived ten miles to the south of us, had a good red kelpie named Digger.

This particular day the neighbour and Digger had been out all day mustering. They arrived home after a hard day's work just before sundown. After feeding Digger, the neighbour went inside. Digger went to bed on his favourite mat.

Next morning bright and early Digger was still on his mat and eager to go to work. Unknown to the neighbour at the time, this is what had happened that night. After the neighbour went inside, Digger must have sniffed the night air and headed out, because just after sundown Digger was noticed at our dog yard. I went out to tie him up, but he was gone.

Another neighbour rang later that night to see if I knew who owned a big red kelpie dog because this dog was over there with his bitch. This neighbour lives another fives miles to the north of us. When he went outside to tie him up, Digger was gone.

Overall Digger must have covered at least 30 miles that night to find his lady love. But he was back home in time for work next morning.

LOOK, UP IN THE SKY . . .

Mavis Summerell, Bega, New South Wales

In the early 1930s during the Depression, we owned a small black and white cattle dog, Flop, who was almost human. We spoke to him like a person.

We were lucky to have a job paying 30 pounds a month which we could have lived on if we had actually got the money. Because the boss was feeling it hard too, we only got five pounds each month and two sheep for meat. We supplemented this income by trapping rabbits for their skins and often we had to eat them to survive. Lots of families had no other meat source.

We often lost traps but the dogs all learnt to scent the rabbit or fox or whatever it was that had taken off with them. Flop became adept at finding anything. If a possum had taken it, he'd scent it to a tree. One day it was a huge goanna with a trap on up a tree.

We were very puzzled, however, when he started scenting down the hill and then looked up in the air whinging and whining. My husband said he thought Flop was going mad.

About a week later one of our neighbours asked if we had lost a trap: 'There is an eagle flying around here with a trap on it,' he said. We realised then what Flop had been trying to tell us.

BRIGHT AMBER

Lesley Klan, Rathdowney, Queensland

We were mustering cattle in the foothills of the McPherson Ranges. It is very hilly country with quite a bit of lantana growing. At the time of mustering, the grass was high due to an overabundant rainfall season.

I had driven some cattle down a ridge alongside Amber, my four-year-old kelpie with a dash of border collie. We left them and went on further in search of more. On our return, the cattle were nowhere to be seen. I didn't know whether they had gone down into the gully for a drink or continued along the ridge.

As Amber was looking hot due to the high humidity, I sent her down into the gully for a swim. Having done this she came back up to me. I continued along the ridge but Amber disappeared. I called but she didn't come.

On reaching the end of the ridge, about a quarter of a mile along, I looked down onto clear country where the cattle congregate before being pushed into the yards. There was Amber with the missing cattle. She must have seen them while she was swimming and therefore decided she would go back and take them down.

This is but one example of her mustering expertise.

CLAWS LIKE A WOMBAT

Bruce Rodgers, Merriwa, New South Wales

Our son picked Max up as a pup while he was a jackeroo on Gunbar station in the Riverina. When he went off to work in the US, Max was left with us along with a brown mare that had not long been broken in.

As a working dog Max, who was jet black with mad, staring eyes, got about three points out of a hundred; but he was a hell of a character. Energy abounded—you couldn't wear him down, but his energies were all at the wrong time and place.

One of the things our son had taught Max when he was a pup was to hop up on the pommel of the saddle. He became clever at it. You only had to look at Max and he would be up on the saddle with you.

Although we didn't get much work out of Max, we had the brown mare going quite well at this stage, although she was still pretty touchy. She had just learnt to stand at a gate while you leaned over and opened it.

And that was when Max performed his most woeful deed. The mare was stationary—Max thought he was a little tired, so he decided to jump onboard. I saw that look in his eye all too late.

'No, Max! No! Get away you black animal!'

There was no stopping him. He didn't quite make the saddle and had to claw his way up the mare's shoulder. The mare took off. Through the gate—head down, ears back, me yelling and Max clawing on for dear life. He had claws like a wombat. No amount of pushing and swiping would free him. Half a mile we went like this—a terrified mare, a more terrified rider, and a black dog enjoying the whole business.

Max was at last despatched from the saddle at 30 miles an hour. He was not only exuberant, but also very tough. He bounced three times and got up running—and barked at the horse's heels for good measure.

'If I live, I'm going to kill you, Max,' I said between gasps for air and through clenched teeth while we galloped on flat-out.

Well, I didn't kill him and a relationship persisted with that dog for a long time. Whenever you felt like throttling him, he would come up and look at you lovingly with those starey eyes and offer you his paw to shake hands. That always broke me right up. So Max would save himself from a hiding and everyone would go away in stitches.

MOUNTAIN SAVIOUR

Margaret Weston, Nimmitabel, New South Wales

A good working dog is a wonderful asset, but if he also happens to be your best mate and saviour, then he's priceless.

My story is set back in the 1950s, high in the Snowy Mountains above Jindabyne. Our neighbours used to lease land in the mountains where they grazed sheep during summer, a practice not allowed these days—which still raises the hackles of many mountain people.

At the time my brother Jimmy was a boy of twelve, and so proud when our parents agreed that he could go to the mountains and help with the muster. He felt really grown-up being part of such an assignment. My father's best dog, Ring, was to be his helpmate as Ring was reputed to have more brains than Jimmy and knew twice as much about everything.

Our mother, a descendant of the Pendergasts who were pioneers of the mountain, had prepared Jimmy for the trip and warned him of the dangers that he might encounter, and how to overcome them. However, during a heavy fog Jimmy lost his bearings, became completely disoriented and failed to rendezvous with the other musterers. Ring stayed by his side and Jimmy said his presence gave him confidence and subdued his immediate panic.

At nightfall they sought out a hollow log and both crawled in. Although the temperature dropped dramatically that night, Ring's body kept Jimmy warm. Jimmy said his short life flashed before him. He could imagine his father wailing, 'Mary, I've got ten more kids, but only one dog as good as that one.' Jimmy was my twin brother and one of eleven children in the family.

Next morning the majestic mountains were bathed in sunshine and Jimmy was rescued after an all-night search on foot and horseback.

Ring was revered in our family after this incident and was assured of a pampered retirement. My mother always believed he saved Jimmy's life by providing body warmth throughout that freezing night in the mountains.

PART 6

BACK OF BEYOND

Far from the bitumen and streetlights lives a breed of dogs and people who share the qualities of our pioneers. They survive without mollycoddling, without doctors or vets, without shops and theatres.

Some, like Gundars Simsons, find the transition to the blackblocks a startling culture shock—but a dog helped strip away his naivety. Others, like Aboriginal jilleroo Jannial Thunguttie Kamilaroi, reveal the close relationship formed between dogs and people when human company is scarce.

Through such close bonds, a dog will risk its life to save its master, as did the Arnolds' pig dog in Queensland. They'll also run miles to get help for a stricken friend, like Old Don of St Kilda. They learn to work in an equal partnership, like Copper the rabbit dog. And Jim Stephens's dog seems to have spent a lot of time acutely observing its master.

Trucks and two-way radios are vital links to the outside world. Travelling dog Mate understands technology, while Linda was transported far from home. Frank, however, with his light-hearted approach to work, found a truck dog's life his only means of survival—but for how long?

DOG'S-EYE VIEW

Jim Stephens, Northampton, Western Australia

He's pathetic. Absolutely pathetic. Without me he would never survive.

He has no fur, or at least very little. He has to put some on before going out of the house. His feet are so big he cannot avoid a blob of sheep manure. He is so slow at running, and no wonder—he tries it on his back legs. I've tried it and it's hopeless.

He seems defenceless. His teeth are so blunt, and another thing—his teeth aren't even real. I saw him one night when we chased a fox: no upper teeth—just like a sheep!

His ears are useless. They are small, round and can't swivel to pick up a sound. His nose is always dry—no wonder he can't smell. Sometimes he gets a moist nose, but then he doesn't seem well.

His eyes are poor, even with those bits of glass in front of them. He's also very fussy—he won't eat rotting sheep. He nearly chucks up from the smell of my breath after I've had a good feast. Then when I roll for a bit of extra perfume, he does a strange sort of dance and bans me from the ute. Still on smells—his female even has to buy the scent to let him know she's on heat. They've really lost the plot those two.

It's quite obvious he completely lacks ability to express his affection. In the ute I often lick his face and hands, but he has never once licked my face. And as for having any pride of ownership—he's a wimp. He'll let anyone into his territory, and no wonder—he's got no idea about marking out his plot, and is totally lazy even about ute wheels.

He's too scared to fight, doesn't understand the pleasures of a good scratch and has no appreciation of my attempts to beautify his garden with bones. So, I do the best I can to brighten this poor creature's life a little. I smile at him and laugh at his jokes, and when he's sad I try to be sympathetic. If I didn't stay with him, who would?

OLD DON OF ST KILDA

Beryl Thomas, Toowoomba, Queensland

My childhood was spent on St Kilda, my parents' property twenty miles north of Roma in western Queensland. Sheepdogs were part of our life. They lived in kennels under the pepper trees, chained up when they weren't working in the paddocks or the sheepyards. They were kelpie-collie crosses mostly, some red, some black and white, some a mixture, with names like Snip and Don and Treacle, Lassie and Laddie. The dogs changed but the names were recycled.

Old Don was one of the red ones. At that time, in the early 1940s, my father rode a horse called Derry, a big chestnut. Don always trotted alongside. The three of them were very much a team. If Don was very tired or the burrs bad, he would be taken up on the pommel of the saddle, for there were no motorbikes then.

On this particular day, my father went off in the morning with Derry and Don to check the dams. He rode past the windmill and the woolshed and my mother waved to him from the verandah of the house. We children were all away then—one brother in the RAAF and my other two brothers and I were at boarding schools near the coast. It was a lonely life for my mother and a busy time for my father because of course during wartime there was little extra help available.

Mother used to write all the news from home in letters describing everything in detail for us. The events of this day—a day we still discuss at family reunions—were recorded with special care and have been repeated often, because this is the day Old Don became a hero.

Dad always came home for a hot dinner in the middle of the day, but he was sometimes held up, so my mother was not unduly concerned by his lateness that day. She was surprised, though, when Old Don came home by himself and barked at the bottom of the back steps. An occasional dog was sent home in disgrace, but never Old Don. He stayed close by my mother, whimpering and barking.

Clearly, all was not well. Although my mother had driven a sulky as a country schoolteacher and as a young wife, in all her 90 years she never did learn to drive a car. She called the nearest neighbour on the phone, a party line with five families connected. The neighbour was over in half an hour with his widowed mother, who had been a nurse. They drove out across the paddocks following Don, who led them to my father, lying injured and in great pain in a steep gully.

Derry had tripped and fallen forward as he was going up the side of the gully and Dad's foot had been caught between the stirrup and the bank. Many bones in his foot and leg had been broken when the horse had struggled free and scrambled out of the gully. Derry was lame, but he set out for home and arrived very late that day. Don was determined to stay with my father. Apparently it had taken some persuading by my father to convince Don to leave him and go home, but persuade him he did and off Don had gone, as fast as he could, straight to my mother. Had he not done this, a search party would have had enormous difficulty locating my father—it may have taken days.

My father recovered after first aid from the neighbour and a bumpy ride home, followed by many weeks in hospital. He went on riding horses and working sheepdogs for a very long time after that. He lived to be ninety-one.

My nephew lives on St Kilda now and the sheep have long been replaced by cattle. There are no sheepdogs under the pepper trees now. No more rattling chains and wagging tails. Just the ghosts of the Snips and Treacles, Lassies and Laddies and fond memories of Old Don.

THE GETTING OF WISDOM

Gundars Simsons, Devoit, Tasmania

Charlie was a weather-beaten farmer of indeterminate age who was instrumental in my development from being a soft, young, city-bred schoolteacher to a human being with the first glimmerings of wisdom.

I had been posted to Australia's southernmost school, on Bruny Island to the south of Hobart. It was a community which time had passed by, and I felt somewhat dislocated. There I was, newly graduated from college, thinking I was pretty clever. I was also well used to the comforts and excitement of city life—but here I was appointed to this extraordinarily remote rural region.

Charlie and his family took me under their wing. He had twelve children and many of them were associated with my school. From Charlie and his sons I learnt how to farm, use a chainsaw, split fence posts, slaughter, butcher, build fences and drive farm machinery. These rough diamonds exposed me to many important human values which were quite new to me.

I associate the time I first began to understand these tight-knit locals with the day I borrowed Charlie's sheepdog Patch to drive a small flock of 33 Polwarth ewes to a nearby farm. I was accompanied by the farmer who had purchased the flock from me and assured him that, with a good dog, the task would be simple.

Patch was an extremely well-behaved working border collie. However, as we got started it semed to be me who was running from side to side in a lather, barking commands at Patch, who simply cocked his head to look calmly into my eyes as he walked quietly along behind the flock. It was as if he were saying, with that wise dog look, 'What *are* you doing, city boy?'

I knew he could and would work and I knew from previous observation that I was using the correct commands. As I stopped a moment to catch my breath and look into the dog's disbelieving eyes, I contemplated the problem. Could it be that my tone of voice and lack of colourful adjectives were confusing the poor animal, who was more used to rougher treatment?

In desperation and frustration, I yelled in my gruffest impersonation of Charlie's hoarse tones, 'Get back, you bloody mongrel bitch,' at which Patch sprang into immediate action. I kept up this voice impersonation and relieved Patch from his schizophrenic confusion. The sheep sprang into immediate action, recognising at last some real and purposeful authority.

FROM THE LAB TO THE LAND

Bill Clissold, Maryborough, Queensland

The first time I set eyes on him, he was a half-starved, half-grown dog which had been collected from a pound in a Sydney suburb. He had been picked up as a stray running the streets and had been brought to the veterinary research farm where I was employed as a stockman. He was to be used in an experiment to develop a tick serum.

I took an instant liking to this miserable-looking black kelpie with a white chest—a trait from a border collie somewhere back in his breeding—and couldn't bear the thought of him being stuck in the laboratory and then being killed when the experiment was finished. When I asked the vets if I could have him to make a working dog out of him, they laughed so much I thought they would all have a fit.

A few months later, though, I was the one laughing. Sam, which was what I called him, grew into the best dog I have ever owned—

the most intelligent dog ever to look through a collar. The vets watched in awe as his talents revealed themselves.

Although at first he was terrified of sheep and cattle, he became a strong and fearless workmate, unafraid of any beast on four legs, no matter how wild it was. With sheep he was gentle, working equally well in yard and paddock. But let a steer break from the mob or turn on him and he could bring it to its knees by grabbing hold of its nostrils.

He would block a lane while I opened the gate and after the stock were through he would push the gate shut by standing on his back feet and pushing with his front ones. I could leave a mob of sheep with him while I rode home for lunch and when I returned, perhaps an hour later, he would still be shepherding them. He would allow them to spread out a little in order to feed and then turn them back into the bunch. I could go on for ages about his exploits, both during our time at the vet station and in the years we worked at other places.

He did his last job for me when I was on a stud farm. One afternoon I sent him to bring up the milking cow and calf, which he promptly did. But then he came up to me, looked into my face and lay down by my feet. He was clearly unwell and I took him to town that afternoon to a vet. He was operated on that evening and it was found that he had a large growth in his stomach. Although he must have been in a lot of pain and aching like hell, not once did he show any sign of discomfort until that last day. He didn't survive the operation and died that night.

Although I no longer work with stock, I'm sure I could never be lucky enough to find another dog like Sam. He certainly would have been wasting his talents in that laboratory.

WELCOME HOME!

Ethel Batten, Dubbo East, New South Wales

Bonnie is a black kelpie with a loving nature—and she thinks she is almost human.

When she was about ten months old I was away from home for two weeks in hospital. Upon my return her joy was ecstatic. She showed her loving welcome and her pleasure at seeing me by racing around me and about the gardens and trees, tail tucked under, ears up, eyes bright, tongue lolling from a big toothy grin.

On her last lap under the grapevines she paused to snatch off a bunch of grapes and placed them on my foot. It was truly a marvellous welcome home from a loving friend. It made me cry!

LITTLE GIRL OF THE BUSH

Jannial Thunguttie Kamilaroi, Ashford, New South Wales

Since my old cat had mothered a variety of baby animals, I presented her with the two pups my friend and I had been promised. Their mother had been killed when they were one week old.

Beershee (meaning 'wild cat'—all my animals and birds get Aboriginal names), a grey, white and black tabby, sniffed around the tiny puppies, licked them and then pushed them towards her teats. They became hers to raise with her odd assortment of other babies. She had three kittens, the two pups, two rabbit babies and one baby guinea pig. She was an amazing old cat.

My pup, Bami (meaning 'little girl'), was a little Australian silky/Sydney silky/wirehaired terrier. When she was six months old we moved out onto a farm called Yurialawa, which was about 21 kilometres out of town. I went there to work as a jilleroo/caretaker/gardener.

From time to time when I was not needed to work, I would find Bami missing. I would call and call and look everywhere but I could never find her. Finally the manager's wife came over and told me not to worry about her. She was with her husband. 'He loves your little dog,' she said. 'Have a look when he comes back and see where she is.'

She obviously did enjoy his company too, because there she was

121

in his saddlebag on the horse. Other times she would be up front on the saddle or at the back on the rump. Or sitting on the seat of the tractor. Or up alongside him in his truck. I soon learnt that whenever Bami was missing, she was always with him.

I also had a little orphaned goat brought to me to hand rear. He had kicked up a terrible stink when my boss took Bami with him— so my boss took Daryal the goat with him too. I had been looking everywhere that day for the little goat so I could give him his bottle, but could not find him.

I went to the manager's home thinking he may somehow have got out of the gate and gone down there, as he often used to follow me there when I went to do gardening. But the manager's wife said she had not seen him. We were both puzzling over it when her husband came toward us on his horse. To our surprise he had the goat kid over the saddle in front and Bami sitting at the back on the horse's rump. His wife and I were laughing so loudly we nearly split our sides. Bami and Daryal used to team up with working dogs when they rounded up sheep and cattle. They were quite a sight. During a bad drought later on, I had to find Daryal another home. That farm was sold when the owner got very ill and I moved on.

Three farms later I was rounding up the sheep on foot and a Suffolk ram knocked me to the ground and would not let me up. I called the working dogs to help me but they did not come. But Bami did, and she ran between his legs and grabbed hold of his testicles with her teeth and hung on for dear life. He turned around and around trying to shake her off him. He jumped and pushed back onto the rails of the sheepyards. No way could he get rid of her. I got up off the ground and laughed until I cried. Shaking with laughter, I shut the gate of the yards on the ram and called Bami. She let go and came to me. The ram never gave me trouble again.

About three months later the boss sold some old ewes and the stock truck came to pick them up. We had drafted off what we had wanted but then this same Suffolk ram somehow got into the yards and no way could we get him out. Not even the stock truck driver and his dogs could budge him. We tried the other dogs too, with no success.

'I know how to fix that ram,' I said, and called Bami. Well, you should have seen the look on his face—and did he move!

Jim, my boss, was amazed. 'Have you ever seen anything like it?' he said. 'That little dog is the only one that can manage that ram.'

The truck driver said he had seen all sorts of dogs work but nothing like Bami. He wanted to buy her, but not for anything was she for sale. Bami could work goats, cattle, sheep, horses, pigs, poultry, wild ducks on the dams—and even children!

She lived until she was fourteen years old. I think she fretted for me when I unexpectedly had to go into hospital for nine weeks with a leg ulcer. I was a bit upset when I found out the boss at that time did not bury her but just threw her body out into the bush. When I came back I found it and buried her where she could see the sun going down over the hills.

THE FORTUNES OF FESTIVAL FRANK

Pauline Smart, Port Augusta, South Australia

I used to suspect that it was only the good dogs that met an early death. Since knowing Frank I am convinced this is so.

Frank was given to my husband at ten weeks of age as a replacement for a dog that had died from snakebite—a *good* dog, of course. Frank was pure black, had an undershot jaw and an unquenchable spirit. As time went by he developed a light-hearted approach to life and work that no amount of discipline could discourage. It wasn't that he was idle—it was just that he didn't feel as though he should take things too seriously. However, he had also developed an uncanny ability to realise when to display just enough talent to keep him from that celestial paddock where all sheep have wings.

One day my husband was trying to draft some ewes ready to truck and was running late, largely because Frank was his offsider. Ears pricked, snout pointed skyward and tail up jauntily, Frank would rush about barking at the birds, showing no interest in the sheep. It was looking as though he had finally Gold Coasted it once too often.

The heat, the dust and the tempers were all rising as the truck pulled up and the driver got out. He jumped the fence to lend a hand, but from somewhere up behind the sheep he could hear a continuous yapping and catch glimpses of a very enthusiastic black dog. A thick haze of dust obscured the total picture. Once the sheep were loaded, the truckie commented, 'Not a bad dog you've got there.'

A whistle brought Frank, expecting praise, bouncing up into my husband's arms—and greatly appreciating the weight being taken off his feet.

Without a word my husband walked over to the truck, opened the door and put Frank in. 'He's yours,' he said, throwing in Frank's chain for good measure.

The truckie was a bit suspicious of the haste with which Frank was being given away, but my husband muttered something about needing a paddock dog rather than a yard dog—and that the jackeroo also needed a bit of exercise. The last I saw of Frank, he had his paws on the dashboard, ears pricked, eyes bright, tail wagging, and he was grinning widely at his new associate, happily unaware of the consequences had he not opted for a career change.

A few years later we were helping in the yards at my in-laws' property a couple of hundred kilometres away when a truck pulled up to load some weaners. I recognised the driver, and there was absolutely no mistaking the black dog with the pointed snout and the festival attitude. He was still barking at birds and didn't seem to have developed a more thoughtful outlook on life at all.

We asked the truckie how Frank was progressing and he said, not suprisingly, that he nearly hadn't kept him. But it seemed that every time he had serious doubts about his continued association with Frank, the dog would miraculously deliver a performance worthy of survival at least.

The time to pay up registration fees had come and Frank's future was hanging in the balance. His output had lately been very ordinary and it looked as though his apprenticeship would be terminated. But while the truckie was away on a trip his wife had gone ahead and paid the fee.

Maybe one day Frank will turn out to be a good working dog, or maybe one day his luck will just run out. In the meantime Frank is sporting a shiny new registration disc and can continue to pursue his life of pleasure with just the right amount of shrewd judgment thrown in.

COUNTING THE SHOTS

Paul Holst, Ravenshoe, Queensland

Pete was a rabbit shooter camped out in the never-never about 80 miles north-west of Bourke. I met him when I was out that way doing a bit of fencing in the early 1960s. Pete's spotlight was mounted on a frame on the dashboard of a bashed-up Landrover with no doors, no windscreen and no roof. It had a rack made from old water pipes and bush saplings on which the rabbits hung. His rifle with 'scope stood in a rack handy to his left hand.

I conned him into taking me with him one night. It was very uncomfortable. I had to sit in the back, but there were two very good reasons for this. The first was that when I went to sit in the passenger's seat, Copper, who was big and black, was already there. The huge bared fangs and the warning growl convinced me that it would be unwise to insist. Secondly, Pete said the dog had to sit up front to be able to work properly. I thought he was having me on, but I clambered into the back with my hurt feelings and we drove off.

We followed a vague track for a few miles before turning off and going bush. Pete turned on the spotlight, which he operated with one hand while steering with the other. We came to a small flat surrounded by tea-trees and dotted with rabbits. Eight shots rang out in quick succession and eight rabbits died.

Copper, who seemed to be part Doberman and part ridgeback, sat upright and alert, watching the scene intently. Pete switched off the spot and turned on a small work-light hanging from the rack. He then turned to the dog. 'Okay, Copper, go get 'em,' he said.

The dog disappeared into the darkness and Pete reloaded the rifle. Copper returned with a rabbit held gently by the loose belly skin and dropped it at Pete's feet. Eight times he did this without another word of command. He then jumped back on his seat.

Pete gutted the rabbits and paired them by slitting the leg of one and threading the leg of another through the slit. He then hung them on the rack. We set off again and Pete was mumbling something that I couldn't quite hear. It turned out he was talking to his 'dawg'— in fact he did most of his talking to the dog.

We worked on until about midnight, then stopped to boil the billy and have a feed of cold mutton and spuds washed down with black tea. Pete rolled a smoke and cleaned the lens of his 'scope. It seemed an appropriate time to ask how Copper knew exactly how many rabbits to collect when he stopped shooting.

The look I got would have withered a crowbar. 'He counts the bloody shots of course. He's not stoopid!'

'But what if you miss one?' I asked.

'I tell 'im.'

'Oh right, sure,' I said, mindful that he was a big man and it was a long walk back to camp.

We set off again and at the next stop Pete shot seven rabbits, then fired an extra shot into the butt of a tree. He turned to Copper. 'I missed one, mate. Go get 'em.'

Seven times that dog returned with a rabbit. He didn't hesitate at six and he didn't go looking for eight.

At sunrise we were back at the camp and Pete stacked the rabbits in the freezer which stood about 100 yards away because of the noise from the diesel motor. I fried some eggs and bacon and we were having breakfast when the fortnightly truck arrived from Bourke to pick up Pete's rabbits. The truckie joined us for a cuppa.

I was yarning to the driver and telling him about Copper. 'He's the smartest dog I've ever seen. If I hadn't seen it with my own eyes, I'd never have believed it,' I said.

'Yeah, well I never seen it, and I reckon no dog can count,' he said.

'But you're only a bloody truckie and that dawg is smarter than any truckie I ever met,' rasped Pete. 'Would ya believe me if I told ya that there dawg can tell the time by the clock?'

'I wouldn't believe no rabbit shooter unless I seen it with me own eyes,' the truckie said.

'Righto then, I'll give ya a demo. It's time someone put ya tail between ya legs. If Copper can't tell the time I'll load that truck by meself. If he can, you load it. Now watcha got ta say?'

The truckie grinned. 'You're on!'

Pete disappeared into his tent and came out with a battered old alarm clock. He wound it up and set it by his watch. Copper was asleep under Pete's vehicle and Pete called him over. The dog sat up in front of him.

'Now, Copper,' he said, 'I want you to *lie down* here and keep your eye on the clock. I have to go over to the freezer and count the rabbits because this bloke is going to be loading them by himself and ya can't trust a bloody truckie. You *stay* here until exactly twenty past eight, then come on over.'

The clock showed five past eight. Pete put it on the ground in front of Copper and walked off over to the freezer. The dog stared at the clock with pricked ears as it ticked away.

The truckie looked at me and scratched his head. 'I reckon Pete's been out in the scrub with the rabbits for too long. He's slipped a cog for sure.'

I said nothing. We poured ourselves another mug of tea, rolled a smoke and watched the minutes tick by. Copper lay on his belly, head on paws, in front of the clock. He was tired and seemed to be dozing with eyes half closed. The clock showed nineteen minutes past eight.

The truckie was feeling relaxed. 'By Gawd, I'm gonna enjoy watching while that silly bugger loads them bunnies,' he said with a laugh. 'Serves 'im right for skitin' an' bullshittin' about his bloody dawg.'

The big hand reached the twenty-minute mark. Copper jumped to his feet and bounded across the flat to the freezer like a bloke running late for his bus.

The truckie gaped and gasped—'Gawd! I don't believe it!'

'You'd better believe it,' I said. 'You've seen it, haven't you?'

The truckie got to his feet and moved off to the truck, muttering to himself and shaking his head. He drove over to the freezer. Pete and Copper were walking back and Pete gave a cheery smile and raised his hat as they passed. He got a puzzled look in reply.

Pete went into his tent and came out with a bottle of Bundy rum. 'I reckon that's worth a drink,' he said with eyes that laughed.

The rum helped revive me after the long night, so I got the courage to ask whether Copper really could tell the time—or was he pulling a swiftie somewhere, which was what I suspected.

Pete looked at me really hard and then grinned. 'You're not stupid, are ya?' And he paused.

'All right, young fella, if ya promise not to let on to that truckie, I'll let ya in on it.

'Remember all that spiel I gave 'im when I got the clock? He really only got the "lie down" and the "stay" outa all that.'

Then Pete took a whistle from his pocket and blew it. Not a sound came from it but Copper, who had been asleep under the vehicle, jumped to his feet and came running. The penny slowly dropped.

127

'You bloody old fraud! That's one of those high-frequency whistles that are inaudible to our ears but dogs can hear like a bugle blast. That truckie will shoot you if he finds out!

'But what about that counting act—how do you rig that?'

Pete turned serious again. 'That's the Gawd's truth, young fella,' he said earnestly. 'He really does count and he is the smartest dog in the country.'

LOVELY LINDA

Emmie Cripps, Northampton, Western Australia

Years ago, in the late 1940s, we bought a pure-bred border collie pup from a breeder in Northam in Western Australia. Her grandmother, The Horwood's Linda, was a champion sheepdog at the Royal Agricultural Show of Western Australia and was the winner of the annual sheepdog trials on more than one occasion. Like her grandmother she was a sable colour, not the usual black and white type. Her ancestors were from Scotland.

This very intelligent wee pup arrived by train at Northampton after being some two days in transit. She had been transferred no less than three times before arriving here, shut in a small box with slats and a tin inside for water. My husband and our young son went to pick her up. Once home, having been removed from the box and nursed by son Geoffrey, we gave her a good drink of water and later milk on and off for the first day as we felt giving hard food such as meat may be too much after so many hours of starvation.

Once she had recovered, she was put on a leash and taken for walks around the house and the paddock close to the house so she could see around her and look at some sheep nearby. Although so small, she was very interested in the animals. This was a good sign. We called her Linda and she learnt immediately to sit and come to us. She quickly grew and before long was able to accompany my husband when he inspected sheep in the paddocks further away.

He was quite surprised by her intelligence as she picked up the commands to sit and come back and so on. In no time Linda could round up a small number of sheep successfully. She always stood her ground if some stubborn animal stamped its feet—Linda always won. We had always had a good sheepdog but Linda was something special, and so obedient at all times. Before long we could trust her to go out of sight and bring a small mob of sheep without leaving any behind.

We had a small sheep stud and that meant the sheep were handled more than ordinary flocks. The rams were never far from the homestead and if we wanted to check them over at any time, my husband could tell Linda to bring them to the homestead gate by pointing to where they were. While she was away he would have a quick cup of tea before walking out to see how she was coping. She would always have the sheep at the gate and would be lying down facing the mob so she could watch any sheep likely to try to escape. If they did they were soon brought back to the fold again.

When autumn came, the showery days meant the stud rams and ewes had to be shedded. There was only a small mob of ewes so they went into a small shed a short distance from the shearing shed where the rams were put. The usual procedure was to put the ewes in first, then go down the hill and bring in the rams. We would call Linda and point to the ewes and off she would go to put them into their shed. By the time we had caught up to her she would have them on their way, bound for the shed, and we just had to help them run up the ramp into the shed. She would instantly set off for the rams and, although they always protested, Linda got the upper hand and sent them to the sheepyards, up a race and into their shed. The only time she queried our orders was if the rams were closer to the shed than the ewes were. She would still want to put the ewes in first, but would reluctantly obey when we insisted.

In the north-west corner of the property we had a yard made from old branches off the trees nearby. The gate was also made from a couple of branches of jam tree. Once the sheep were inside, we pulled the branches across the gate and the sheep were secure.

One day I walked up over the hill to this makeshift yard to give my husband a phone message about a sheep sale. I waited until the sheep work had been completed, then pulled the branches back so the sheep could go out quietly. We set out for home, stopping to look at the only old quandong tree still alive on the property. I put the kettle on for morning tea and my husband had a good wash.

Suddenly he looked through the flyscreen door and outside the house but he couldn't see Linda. He called her as this was unusual, but she wasn't there.

Then the penny dropped. He remembered that he hadn't told her we were finished and that she could come home with us. Although the brush gate was open, Linda had apparently remained there, guarding the sheep in the yards. When my husband arrived back at the yards, he felt so sorry for his lovely dog. He gave her a great pat and set back home.

Another example of Linda's devotion to duty was when my husband and son Geoffrey rounded up a fair-sized mob of sheep in the middle of a paddock near the house. They examined the animals and dressed the lightly blown ones, then decided to go back to the house to have a cup of tea. Again, because they were talking about farm doings, my husband overlooked telling Linda that the job had been completed. When they got back after remembering the error, there she was, busily keeping the animals all in a circle. Poor soul, she would have been very occupied as the sheep would have seen the men leave and would have tried repeatedly to break away.

By request from the local show society my husband taught Linda to yard three sheep in a pen in the middle of a paddock. She did this perfectly, so he gave a couple of exhibitions at our local show but refused to take her to Perth because he was worried about loud noises from the sideshows that might frighten her.

In time we purchased an early Landrover with a canvas hood which was often removed. One day on the highway to Carnarvon my husband passed a large transport in a cutting six or seven miles from home. It was crawling very slowly up the hill but he quickly left it behind as he went down across the sand plain, where he met another large transport going south in a great hurry. The road was narrow so he suddenly had to pull right over onto the edge of the highway.

A few miles after this incident my husband glanced back to find, with horror, that Linda was no longer in the back. He thought she must have overbalanced when he'd swerved to the side of the road. He turned back and stopped and whistled in the spot where he had veered sharply. There was no answer. He checked the short shrubs bordering the road to see if she was lying there unconscious.

The slow-moving transport which he had passed earlier came by and my husband tried to stop it, but the driver ignored him. He didn't know what to do, so he returned home and rang the police. The policeman informed him that Linda hadn't been picked up, but he added that another farmer's sheepdog had recently been stolen by a truck driver. He believed sometimes these dogs were sold to station hands for stock work. What a horrible thought!

We wondered if the transport that passed going north, which wouldn't stop, had picked up Linda. The police in Carnarvon said they would stop the truck south of the town around midnight, when the transports usually got there, and see if they had a dog that looked like Linda. Next day we did another search of the area where Linda must have fallen off, but no luck. The whole household was feeling so sad. The Carnarvon police hadn't had any luck either.

A couple of days passed and then early one morning when one of us opened the back door, there was poor Linda, looking drawn and covered in bright red mud which was caked on her long fur. She was lying down on the step. Her feet were raw from walking on stones. We had no idea how far she had travelled.

The police were pleased to hear our news and said that she must have come from near what we called the Half-Way roadhouse, now called The Overlander. It's between Northampton and Carnarvon and was the only area that had had a thunderstorm in the past couple of days. Otherwise she could not possibly have had a bath in a puddle, which clearly she had done. The roadhouse was nearly 100 miles away.

Linda could hardly hobble. I bathed her feet with warm water and put some ointment on them but, as with most dogs, it was soon licked off. We fed her a light diet for a few days, wrapped her up in a blanket and put a covered hot brick with her at night.

She was back on deck in about a fortnight, ready to help with the sheep, but we did not use her for a while longer. What a wonderful, faithful animal she was, and how lucky no-one else picked her up. Perhaps she kept herself hidden in the scrub at the side of the road until the way was clear. We would never know.

When my husband died suddenly she mourned her loss by lying sadly at the back door. She did not live many years after that and died in her sleep. Linda—a valuable, loving animal missed by all who knew her.

SALUTE TO A HERO

Barbara Arnold, Goolwa, South Australia

When we lived in far north Queensland, we kept three Rhodesian ridgeback/red heeler dogs for culling wild pig numbers for station owners. Pigs were a terrible menace up there. They would tear down fences, eat the cows' feed, kill calves and savage people if they got a chance.

My husband was a truck driver at a wolfram mine 50 miles from Mareeba and 100 miles north of Cairns. Most weekends we would head off along the river banks where the rubber vines grew so densely that they created hollows where pigs would hide.

My husband would drive and the children, Shayne and Deanne, and I would keep a lookout. The three dogs would lean out, sniffing the air for pigs. As soon as they picked up a scent they would jump off the vehicle and run it its direction. We would follow on foot until the dogs had located the pigs and bailed them up in a rubber tree hollow. They would then distract the pigs to prevent them charging at my husband as he came in close with his gun.

Some people taught their dogs to bite the ankles of pigs, but my husband taught ours to stand back and distract them, so he could aim and shoot without having the pigs turn on him. The biting type of dogs, because they came in close, often got gored and killed. Since our dogs were also our friends, we didn't like to make them take too many risks.

One weekend when we had just shot a mountain dingo, we spotted a huge boar disappearing into the scrub. My husband grabbed the .222 we keep in the Toyota all the time and went after him on foot, followed by Shayne, who was then twelve.

We lost the trail in the dense rubber vine. Just as my husband was bending down in the river bed, looking into the scrub at a level with the bank, the boar came charging at him. He didn't have time to fire before he was knocked over backwards, smashing the gun barrel on Shayne's head. A hole was gouged in my husband's elbow and he grazed his knee. Before he knew what had happened the pig was standing over him, ready to rip open his stomach. I was watching all this from a distance and was frozen with terror.

Suddenly, in a flash of red, Sam, the big male dog, appeared from nowhere, grabbed the pig's flank, turned him away from my husband and distracted the pig. My husband was then able to quickly find his gun. He fired all the bullets remaining in it and killed the pig.

We regrouped after that close call, checked all the injuries and bound up Shayne's head with my shirt. He later had to have stitches. Very shaken by the experience we made our way back to the Toyota, and when we got home we gave Sam an extra serve of dinner to reward him for his loyalty. Without doubt my husband would have been killed had the dog not charged in when he did. The feat was all the more remarkable since the dogs had been trained not to bite, yet Sam had recognised a time when he should.

AS POPULAR AS A NEW GOVERNESS

John Hawkes, Yaraka, Queensland

In 1985 at Mt Marlow station near Yaraka, Quensland, I was walking a mob of about 2,000 sheep down the Barcoo River when the overseer, Steven Gray, brought down a pup he had just got from Arno, the neighbouring property.

He dropped it on the ground to see if it would show any interest in the sheep. An hour later, four of us eventually caught it. In that time he had circumnavigated the mob a dozen times in an orderly fashion, never pursuing too hard or once cutting off a sheep.

Although some tempers were rising, I was very impressed and next week went over to Arno. After a carton of home brew, I eventually persuaded Billy Morton to part with the last of the litter, a black and tan kelpie dog. I named him Jess after Jessie Owens, the athlete.

As a contract musterer, I travel extensively with Jess. He is as popular as a new governess at every place we go. He is a natural backer, will unload trucks and swims rivers to get to sheep in a tight spot.

One day I was mustering at Diamond Downs for John Parkinson. I was in my Cessna 150 and my wife, Neen, was on the ground with Jess, John Parkinson, his daughter Kerry, and Tony Morley. They were all on motorbikes. We were mustering four paddocks as though they were one—20,000 acres in all—as the fences were shot. As it turned out, the main mob (about 1,500) ended up on one side of the fence, and little mobs of a dozen or more were scattered through the scrub all over the other paddocks.

One by one people were directed to other mobs until four stockmen were in one paddock putting together 500 stubborn sheep while Jess was in a paddock by himself with 1,500. He was, I could see from the air, also going through the broken-down fence at every sweep of the tail of the mob and working into the mob any that were getting through. With about two kilometres to go to the corner, everything looked pretty well under control, so I radioed the boss and told him I'd fly home.

He said, 'Well, I've only got a hundred or so here, and I can see Tony hasn't many. Who's with the main mob?'

'Jess has them in the next paddock,' I replied. 'He'll block them in the corner and wait for you there.'

And sure as eggs, that's what he did.

Someone later volunteered to give Jess his headset, so I could tell him what to do from the air.

'You hang onto your headset,' I said. 'Jess knows what to do.'

THIRD TIME UNLUCKY

Marjorie Atkins, Bayswater, Western Australia

Many years ago my father had a sheepdog named Bluey. He was a good dog and as well as working the sheep, he would also lead my father's horse back to the house after it had been saddled.

One day the dog went missing for rather a long time. When he came home, he had a fit. He had eaten a poisoned bait. The remedy which my father had recently learned from the Aborigines he worked with was to cut off the tips of his ears and tail. Unfortunately, it was the third fit the dog had suffered, so he died. Apparently this remedy would have worked if it had been the first fit the dog had had.

YOU TELL 'EM, MATE

Jule Nancarrow, Broken Hill, New South Wales

When former station owner Wreford Whitehair befriended Mate, she was on an outback station property out from Tibooburra in the far north of New South Wales.

She was suffering from malnutrition, had infected sores around her neck which had been rubbed bare of hair by a chain, sores on her body, and was timid and frightened when approached. She could not stand the sound of a whip and cowered at the sound of a shouted voice. Somehow she knew that Wreford was different. He healed her wounds, he fed her and gave her love. Today she is known as The Wonder Dog.

Wreford now works as a station consultant, and on his travels Mate sits up front in the passenger seat to observe the road ahead. Whenever she sees kangaroos, cows, sheep or emus, she barks to warn them to get off the road.

She is a remarkable sheepdog and will work in the shed, in the yards or in the paddocks. When the sheep have to be hurried along, Wreford says, 'You tell 'em,' and she starts to bark. If he wants her to cease barking, he says, 'Take five.'

When they are travelling together in the outback, Wreford contacts station properties on his UHF radio to advise them of his impending arrival. But once he's found the right channel, he leaves the communication to Mate.

'You tell 'em,' he tells her, and she does. She barks into the mike, and from the other end gets the same customary, cheery response from station properties all around the region: 'Hello, Mate! How are you?'

Both Wreford Whitehair and Mate are very well-known and respected identities in the Broken Hill area.

PART 7

FLEECE COUNTRY

The horizon shimmers in the hazy, dusty distance. It's hot. The trees are sparse. From the wooden verandah and its low, overhanging roof, you hear a windmill creak and gates clank.

In far-off runs measured in square miles rather than acres, hardy merinos graze saltbush and bluebush. Muster them, and they'll run like stags. They'll split, they'll sit down, they'll hide. Station dogs need to be cunning and tough and fast. Their feet get prickles and are cut by rocks. Troughs and dams are far apart. The shade is thin.

In the yards where the mobs are drafted at shearing time, urgent yaps of the yard dogs pierce through the indignant complaints of ewes and falsetto-voiced lambs. On the big stations, shearing will go for months—eight shearers working flat-out, rouseabouts sweeping the board, tossing fleeces and keeping pens full for each shearer.

Dogs get little rest in the shed and yards, and it helps if they use their initiative—although they sometimes go overboard. There are dangers and diseases. And some dogs, like Soda, end up looking 'like a hard-boiled egg'.

Dog and owner work as a unit and think as one. They know each other well . . . or, like Karla and Rover, they think they do. You also find unexpected gems like Midget and Kate—and humour as dry as a creekbed in drought to keep a sheepman hanging on.

And then there are the one-man dogs that don't recognise wives and jilleroos as part of the plan . . . dogs like Pudden, Fred and Jinny. The returns from wool are bad enough—but to have the dog on strike because its treasured boss is away can really strain the friendship.

CELEBRITY ON THE ROOF

Blanche Niemann, Mildura, Victoria

Growing up on a south-western Riverina wool property called Mindook station provided me with many, many wonderful memories—the country, the river, the lifestyle and especially the animals.

Looking back on my childhood, no memory is stronger or more vivid than that of our gallant sheepdog, Pudden—a legend, a friend and an outstanding working dog. He had been a soft, wriggly, licky puppy, coloured grey, black and many other earthy colours all mixed together, with one blue and one brown eye. He learnt fast, displaying the intelligence of the German coolie breed and the timid demeanour of his kelpie cross. He watched the other dogs and copied—but a raised voice was enough to send him scurrying away, tail tucked between his legs, not to be seen again until the heat had passed.

He was my father's shadow, never to be found far from him. As he grew older, his personality also began to develop. He took up the unusual habit of travelling on the roof of the farm ute. He would leap into the back of the ute, then bounce up onto the roof, legs braced against the rough country roads. He wasn't even discouraged by the highway travel—nose pointed straight ahead, flop ears flapping in the wind. He became quite a celebrity in the district. Truckies tooted as they passed and described his antics to their mates over their CBs.

His endless movement began to take its toll on the tin roof of the Suzuki ute. Cracks began to appear which let the cold July rain cascade into the cabin. Something had to be done. Fortunately the local garage owner had heard of Pudden's exploits, so he designed and built a cover for the cabin which solved the problem.

Pud always had the ability to worm his way into people's hearts and avoid their wrath. I can see him still, returning home after a rendezvous with the neighbour's friendly bitch, standing calmly and proudly on the roof of Mr Murphy's new Commodore. The scratches in the royal blue duco hardly showed at all, but the tension on Murphy's face, although carefully veiled, was evident.

As older dogs died, Pud stood alone as 'the only dog worth his salt on the place', according to Dad. Mustering for shearing on one of those late March days that make you think that summer won't ever dissolve into autumn, Mum and Dad paused to discuss the best way to get the 'woolly brutes' home. They had 1,000 wethers in full wool to drive home, five miles in flaming heat. Mum was in the ute with Pud. Dad was on the bike. He decided to do one final check that they had got all the sheep, but told Mum to start pushing the mob homeward. 'Send Pud,' he told her.

Dad headed off, calm in the knowledge that the mob would be halfway home by the time he rode around for a final look. Unfortunately, like all good working dogs, Pud wasn't about to let

140

the mob move until the boss returned. This is where he left them, and this is where they'd stay.

'Come behind, Pud,' came the casual instruction from the ute. Pud stayed put.

''Hind, Pud,' Mum yelled. No response. The door of the ute creaked open as Mum stepped out.

'Pud! Come behind,' was the command, this time the frustration evident in her voice. Mum had never been renowned for her patience, or her gentle temper—and the heat and flies, combined with a hard morning's bumping around the rough paddock after 'maggoty sheep' had done little to improve her mood.

'Come behind, you bloody useless mongrel.' Mum started to stride around the mob. Like the fine example of a working sheepdog that he was, Pud loped around the mob to cover the opposite side.

Mum changed her tack. 'Here, Pud, come here. Good boy, jump up, come on.'

For the ensuing hour, Mum shouted, screamed, ran, swore, cursed and wheedled her way after Pudden, with no result.

After the hour of eternity, Dad returned looking for the mob, finding his wife beside herself with rage, and Pud, cool as a cucumber, tail wagging and smiling at his master. The sheep had not moved an inch. Mum maintains to this day if she had had a rifle, Pud would have been an ex-working dog.

As the seasons passed, Pud's limbs grew stiff and his sight dull. He was still master of the younger dogs and still a fine, proud sheepdog with a calm intensity and dignity in his soft eyes. There was a void in all our lives when he was gone.

THE STORY OF KATE

Alex Haley, Berrigan, New South Wales

I was travelling from my sheep farm at Tocumwal to Melbourne on a business trip, when I stopped off at Wahring Cottage Service

Station for fuel. John, the owner, came out to serve at the bowser, followed by his faithful corgi dog. But this morning there was an addition, a black and tan kelpie female about ten months old. She sat down just a couple of feet from my door to wait for the petrol to be served.

I looked at her and she looked at me and I guess she knew she had found her destiny. 'Who owns the kelpie, John?' I asked.

He said a bloke had dropped her off three weeks ago and was supposed to come back and pick her up. He hadn't shown up.

'I'll buy her off you,' I said. 'What's the price?'

'I'll ask the wife,' he said. 'And if she agrees, you can have her providing you bring her back if the owner turns up. Call back on your way back from Melbourne and if you promise a good home, I think you can have her.'

Seldom has the day taken so long to pass in Melbourne. I am usually short of time rushing from one venue to another and cursing because the day is going too quickly. My mind was with the little black and tan at Wahring. I conjured up in my imagination how, in my absence, the owner had returned to take her back—or worse, a truck had come in too fast and run over her.

I left Melbourne at 6 pm in the dark, and drove non-stop at the maximum speed the law would allow to cover the 130 kilometres as quickly as possible back to Wahring and the dog. Twenty kilometres before my destination, I eased back because I knew she had been killed or taken by someone else. I even felt anger that John hadn't given me the dog for safekeeping when I went to Melbourne that morning. I drove into the service station and couldn't believe my eyes. There, sitting out waiting for me it seemed, was the dog.

'Yes, she's yours, but a good home now.' John was all smiles as he knew that I wanted her. I opened the door of the car and, believe me or not, that dog knew she was going with me and jumped straight into the car.

'I'll be blowed,' John said. 'She hasn't accepted an offer to get into a car before, and she has been sitting at the end of the driveway entrance all day, as if she was waiting for you.'

'She's no good with sheep, you know,' John went on. 'The other bloke has a stock crate and she wouldn't work for him. Although he did say she was only ten months old.'

John's words had about the same effect as a bucket of cold water thrown over you unexpectedly on a hot day. 'She'll be right,' I muttered, a little flattened, and I drove away without a thank-you to John.

Kate sat next to me. I told her her name was Kate and she rode like a lady in the car. When we reached home she walked inside.

At the sheep farm the next day, I did my immediate tasks quickly as I wanted to start Kate's training. About 60 weaners were ravaging the lucerne paddock, so there was a genuine job for Kate. Woody, my faithful friend, had no idea what to do with sheep but liked to come along and try. Woody accepted Kate into the household without fuss. The three of us went to the lucerne paddock and I pointed at the sheep and told Kate to 'go away back'.

Kate looked concerned but stood there. I said 'go away back' again, and then, with Kate and Woody watching, I ran around the sheep. The neighbour yelled over the fence, 'The other way around, mate. You stand there and the dogs run around the sheep.'

Very bloody funny . . . the world's full of comedians. But foremost in my mind were John's parting words—'She's no good with sheep'. No good with sheep—hell, it doesn't matter. I like the dog anyway and I've managed without a dog this long—so what?

The sheep going out of the lucerne paddock turned left instead of right and ran the wrong way down the lane. ' Way back,' I shouted, and ran after the sheep to head them off. The sheep were fast and I was slowing and puffing and thinking I'd have to get the ute. A black and tan flash went past me to the front of the sheep and turned them, and then she stood there looking back, sending the message, ' What the hell do I do now?'

'Bring 'em up,' I coaxed. She stood there. 'Push 'em up,' I pleaded. She stood there. 'Bark!' I yelled. 'Ruff, ruff.'

Woody rushed to the sheep as she knew about barking, and barked. Kate barked too, and the sheep ran. Kate began running from side to side, and I realised that I now had myself a sheepdog.

Times are tough. The economy of the farm is on a sharp downhill slide with no bottom in sight. Every day things go up, fuel costs rise, wool prices drop, and every other person who can only survive by increasing his charges is doing so. The only way I was going to save this farm was to go contracting, foot-paring sheep. I advertised for work, and everyone who had sheep too rough to handle or too difficult to treat rang up. The established foot-paring foot-rotters wouldn't handle these sheep and the owners couldn't, so I accepted these jobs as I didn't have much choice.

I employed a couple of strong young men, set up my sheep-handler, and with Kate and a new pup, Bedee, onboard, we left for our first job. Kate had shown much improvement and an immediate grasp of her duty only three weeks after that first-day lesson. Kate and I drafted 300 sheep without any assistance from any human. A neighbour and friend who sometimes lent me his good dog saw Kate in action and was quite put out that Kate was turning out so well so quickly.

Bedee was a mistreated and cringing black bitch that I had rescued. After Kate, Bedee was a disaster. She wouldn't come when you called her and she just ran straight at the sheep, scattering them in all directions. But after sleeping inside for a couple of weeks and eating regular meals, she began to come when called and do simple things like sit down, come behind, get off the chair, and things like that. I let her out with the sheep to see what would happen and she killed the first of three sheep by chasing a crazy weaner into a strainer post. She killed two more in similar fashion before she became Kate's well-behaved apprentice.

So, with two young, inexperienced men, two inexperienced dogs and being a bloke who is getting a bit old for this sort of caper, we arrived at our first foot-paring job. Shock one was, they weren't sheep but long-horn goats, big and tough, moving restlessly around this high-fenced sheep pen. We discussed the situation and decided we needed the work, so we set up our handling machine.

One of the workers provided shock number two. These were feral goats captured at Wilcannia, and they had never been handled. Our special race would have been useless, so we set up the machine against the permanent pen. The worker said his job was to keep them up into the handler for us all day. We were ready to go.

I took Kate and went to help the workers move the goats forward. 'Get over,' I said to Kate.

'Stop!' the worker yelled. 'They killed the boss's good dog this morning.'

I yelled to Kate but she was already around them. One goat charged her but somehow she got out of the way. I got in the pen and a goat charged me. I ducked. The worker wasn't so quick and the goat crashed into his shoulder and broke his collarbone. I dragged him to the side of the pen as goats charged and leapt high all around us.

'Get me out before we're killed,' he yelled as we dragged him over the fence and put him in the car. The boss arrived.

'Haven't you bastards handled goats before?' he said.

'Not wild ones like these,' we said.

He asked us who was going to pen them up because the injured worker was the only one who would do it. Then he looked into the pen and asked what was going on.

Kate hadn't got out of the pen as we thought but had gone around and around and had the goats circling in the big pen. I was surprised but pretended I knew she could do it. Trying to impress the boss to gain future work, I said I'd pen them up.

Kate worked all day and the boys cursed and swore, and the boss worked all day in my place on the machine, so pleased that at last he had found someone that could handle wild goats. When the goats got their wide horns stuck in the machine another worker ran in with a saw and cut the horns off, and as they tried to pull away Kate nipped them on the legs to keep them up. The day was hot and dust swirled continually. At afternoon smoko Kate couldn't jump the fence out of the pen to have a break because she was so tired. She lay in the shade for the 20-minute break and I lifted her back in for the last two-hour run.

Kate had handled the goats, wild as they were, so well at her first attempt that I eventually told the boss she hadn't seen goats before. He replied that I wasn't a bad worker but it was a pity I talked so much rubbish. Kate was lifted out of the pen and lay down in the most privileged position possible—in the twin cab ute—for the trip home. Despite the two boys' bruising and aches, they patted and wiped Kate down with a damp cloth for the duration of the 30-kilometre trip home.

Next day the word had got around the goat farm's neighbours that a bloke had a pretty good dog that could handle goats, so a few people wandered in during the day to see her work. From that job, people started to ring more frequently with offers of work.

The next job was a relief for everyone—1,500 head of Suffolk ewes needing a manicure. We set up the machine with our specially designed twin race so that sheep walked up to the machine side by side. They went into a single race at the end as they climbed up into the handling machine. The trick is to keep both sides of the race full all the time and if this is done efficiently, the sheep will run and enter the race a lot more easily, causing less stress on the sheep and the workers.

Bedee was about to get her first turn as she hadn't been allowed near the goats, or there would have been a substantial grave for dead goats if not some persons as well.

Kate, I must point out, had never seen the twin race system work

145

before, nor had Bedee. So two boys worked on the machine as I was going to work with the dogs to teach them what to do. We filled the race and work started. As each race emptied I would walk up the side, push the stragglers up the front and then fill the race with more sheep. Soon Kate and Bedee both started pushing the sheep up the race on one side and I would get the other. I decided to make Kate stay on one side and get Bedee to work the other.

By 11.00 am on the first morning, the dogs knew what they had to do. Bedee would come around Kate's side and Kate would snap at her, nipping her to send her back. If they were filling the pen and Bedee stood in the wrong spot, Kate would go up and snap at her, biting her sometimes, until she stood in the right position. After several jobs and two weeks, the dogs had become as professional as one could believe.

We started work at 7.30 am and stopped for 30 minutes at 9.30 am, and then worked through until noon, breaking up the afternoon in the same manner. We were working in 40 degree temperatures in the Riverina, and the only way to survive was to pace yourself correctly. The dogs learned the work schedule fast. If we called 'smoko', the dogs would stop work halfway through a bark to go and have a cold drink and lie in the shade, until time was up to start work again. We carried iced water for the dogs to drink and we always put it out for them. It turned out they wouldn't drink water, no matter how thirsty, unless we put it down for them.

Some time passed and the reputation of the dogs seemed always to proceed us.

For one job, we arrived at the property of a very big sheep dealer, a noted dog trainer, animal lover and, in general, a great bloke. Coincidentally, the person that gave me Bedee was shearing on the property with his four-man crew, so the place was a hive of activity. Since the shearers worked the same times as we did, the bloke that gave me Bedee didn't get a chance to see her work, but listened with increasing interest as the owner of the property related some of the skills of the two dogs.

On the first day we were there, the owner told me I would ruin the dogs as I used to pick them up and pat them and make a big fuss of them after any particular job they did. The boys also patted the dogs and made a fuss of them. The dog-trainer owner explained that dogs that work hard can't be handled like this as they become too spoilt and soft and won't work. However, after working on this property for two weeks we noticed he was putting his young dog

146

in the front of the ute instead of the back, and he was also picking it up and patting it.

The owner's father had a champion dog that people talked about. He came over quietly one day and said he had to move some very valuable stud ewes and lambs. He wondered if I could lend him Kate. I said I had to come too as Kate would not work for anyone else, not even for the boys with me on the machine. He was very happy with Kate's effort and said if I was taking orders for pups, could I put his name down and he would pay me immediately.

All the sheep had been shorn and only the wild rams remained unpenned. The owner's dog had been run over six months previously by a car, and his young dog was too inexperienced for the job, so the shearers and other helpers came out to pen up the rams. The father's dog and one of the shearers' dogs wouldn't go in the pen, so I told my dogs to hop over. Kate got in the pen and got behind a gate as a ram charged her. Bedee went after the ram and they started to turn the rams around and around like the goats until they eventually went up the race. The chap who gave me Bedee called out that he had only been joking when he said I could have the dog. The shearers stopped for fifteen minutes just to watch them work.

The job was finished after almost three weeks, and the owner came down with a cheque and paid me for the job. I thanked him and then he handed me a cheque for $2,000 to cash at the bank in the local town. I was a bit confused because he had paid full price plus a bit extra for the job. He said, 'Cash that cheque on your way through town and leave Kate with me. She will have a good home.' No way, but thanks anyway.

Another time, we went to a place near Oaklands to do a job, one of the worst ever. We had to remove the dags, dried and large and copious enough to fill a plastic bucket, from every sheep. We battled along for days, with one of the boys quitting the job. However, a highlight was the farmer who had a dog that no-one could better. Talk about smart, this one was super-smart. He was so good he only went to work when he believed no-one else could do the job. He was big, same colour as Kate, black and tan, but heavier and about three-quarters the size of an Alsatian.

One of the many clever things he did was to run up alongside an escaping sheep, grab it by the wool on its shoulder and hold it until a human walked up and took the sheep from him. Bedee watched this with interest and ran out from her duties to inspect the technique more closely.

At the very next job we were doing, a sheep jumped the race and ran away. Bedee went after the sheep, grabbed it by the wool on its shoulder and held it until one of us came to take the sheep. From then on I called 'catch' to Bedee if I wanted a sheep caught in the paddock. Kate looked on each time. One day I was moving ewes and lambs with Kate on her own. I called out 'catch', forgetting Bedee was not there. Kate ran up behind the sheep I'd singled out, grabbed it by the back leg, flipped it over and held it until I came up.

When fly time was prevalent we took the gear to the paddock, circled the sheep, and I would point out a suspect fly-strike, call out 'catch', and one or two dogs would catch the sheep. They caught on so fast that, after we'd done this a couple of times, they didn't need to be told—as soon as we put the fly-strike equipment in the ute to drive to the paddock, the dogs would round up the sheep into a circle, find any fly-struck sheep themselves, and catch and hold them until we were ready.

They had become so skilled at every aspect of sheep handling that I took them for granted, talked to them like humans, always let them ride in the front of the ute—and they even slept inside the house— without ever a blemish to their great record.

People came and stood and looked in awe as the dogs continued to perform their duties with ever increasing skills. Once I had to move 3,000 head back home—a trek of about five miles. We set the sheep on the way, left the dogs with them, and I went home to do some other jobs.

The neighbour who'd laughed at Kate the day she came home called in and told me to keep an eye on my sheep because a big mob was coming down the road and no-one was with them.

'Hell, what happened to my dogs?' I said in panic. But the dogs were there and the neighbour couldn't believe his eyes that the young dog, who only a year or so earlier didn't know the meaning of 'way back', could move 3,000 sheep down the road efficiently.

The battle to keep the farm was eventually lost, and I now drive a truck for a living. Kate and Bedee take turn about to ride with me in the truck. No more sheep to work, no more applause from the crowd, no more excitement and challenge to do the impossible, but somehow the dogs seem to be happy to be with me—although sometimes I think they look at me and feel sorry for me because I no longer have the sheep to work nor do the jobs we loved doing.

AN ORIGINAL BILL

Bob Batchelor, Claremont, Western Australia

A drover gave me a big black dog,
He had a lot of white round his chest,
A friendly bloke, with an undershot jaw,
Always underfoot like a pest.

Living on me own at the shearing shed,
The Todds were both away.
Had all me dogs including this one,
And was working both night and day.

I tried him out—he had no idea,
I stuck with him day after day.
But in the end I'd had enough,
A 'twenty-two' would put him away.

I looked for a bullet, not one to be found,
It wasn't the day to be parted.
He began to work and never looked back,
This character's life had started.

I called him Bill, an original name.
He'd look up and smile at your face,
Then sneak up and piss on Jock Watson's leg
At orders—then step back a pace.

Jock never caught him, he was much too smart,
But he caught himself a bit later.
Fell out of a buggy and under the wheel,
I was sure he had gone to his maker.

But no—he woke up and gave me a lick,
Got into the box on the back.
He'd made up his mind he wanted to live,
And surviving's a bit of a knack.

I had him tied as a 'peg dog' one day
At a bridge high above water.
He went over the side and hung by his neck,
Archie saw him an hour or two later.

He looked quite dead. Archie left him there.
I didn't return until seven.
Took him back home to dig a grave,
You guessed it—he lived again.

He came on a train all the way to the West,
Settled into a different life.
Spent most of his time just sitting about,
It was hard to get into strife.

But he managed—was hit by a bullet.
Went walking, was shot in the chest.
Staggered home all bloody and helpless
And survived after treatment and rest.

I'm not sure I should tell this story
About Bill having ESP,
But he had it for certain in my mind.
It happened so often, you see.

I'd be out back driving a tractor
And see a sheep that had need to be done.
I'd think about Bill coming up the track,
And half an hour later he'd come!

We'd catch the sheep, fix up its flies.
Bill would lie around for a while.
Tractors were boring so he'd go home.
Does his story make you smile?

A HARD-BOILED EGG SODA

Garth Fragar, Little Hartley, New South Wales

In north Queensland's Longreach–Winton area during 1951, I had a black and tan sheepdog named Soda. He was a kelpie–collie cross with a lovely thick coat of not very long hair.

Following the advice of a local man, I treated Soda with mutton fat and kerosene for small brown dog ticks. Although I followed the recipe carefully, the treatment was far too severe and removed all the hair from his body, leaving him totally devoid of any covering. Soda was a pathetic sight but nothing could keep the smile from his face. He was a very happy, hard-working dog with plenty of spirit. As I wanted to work him at shearing time I made him a little sugar-bag coat to keep the sun from burning his bald back.

One morning we brought sheep to the yards at the shearing shed and I removed his little coat and tied him under a shady tree at the shed. After lunch I rode out in the 110 degree heat to get a small mob of sheep that had been missed about two miles from the shed. I left Soda tied up in the shade and took another dog to work the sheep.

Soda slipped out of his collar and followed me. He reached me just after I got to the sheep. This meant I had a problem—how to get Soda to the shed without him getting burnt and blistered by the sun.

It was a good season and there was water in a nearby creek, so I coated his back with brown-black mud and covered the mud with dry grass and we made it back OK. By this time, though, the mud had dried and it cracked off his back leaving him looking like a hard-boiled egg fresh from the shell, with every vestige of dried skin removed.

One of the shearers said his hair would not grow properly again, but in about two weeks he had a lovely new coat of crisp hair.

151

UNBROKEN BONES

Alison Chandler, Semaphore Park, South Australia

My son was helping to unload sheep from a four-tier semitrailer and was being assisted by his young kelpie, Boney.

They were working on the top tier and Boney was told to 'Get up front'. However, the dog had had enough, jumped overboard and crashed to the ground. There was consternation all around the yards.

Boney, fittingly short for Bonehead, lay still for half an hour. After being checked for broken bones, he went straight back to work, which kept the men talking for days.

ROVER'S ROPE

C C Cooper, Jamestown, South Australia

Many years ago my father was killing a sheep for the home table with, as usual, his dog Rover watching his every move.

When Dad reached the stage where he was ready to pull the carcase up off the ground, the rope which he always used was just not there. For a moment he hesitated, then walked off to get a rope.

He had not walked many steps when he met Rover coming to him dragging a rope in his mouth. It wasn't the right one, but Rover had realised what was needed.

A MEMORABLE PARTNERSHIP

Don Dufty, Albany, Western Australia

Alf Dufty, my late uncle, was a happy but firm boss and always had exceptional dogs. His best dog, Jeff, he had through the 1930s till about 1943.

Alf looked after the sheep on Hope Glen, which was about seventeen miles north of Nhill. The property was the estate of J C Dufty and extended almost to the southern boundary of the Big Desert. Most of the times I was with him he drove a 1939/40 Chev ute that had a wide parcel shelf at the back of the seat. This is where Jeff used to lie, with his head near the open driver's side window.

Going round a mob, Alf would just say in a conversational way, 'Looks like a blown sheep there, fella.' Jeff would jump out the window and catch the sheep out of the mob, almost always without any further direction. It seemed as though there was telepathy between them. When, now and then, Jeff caught a very daggy one that was not blown, Alf would say, 'No, not that one', and Jeff would let it go and find the one Alf wanted. I never heard my uncle yell or scold Jeff harshly. On the rare occasion that Jeff did the wrong thing, Alf would say, 'Hey, come back, you mad sod. You can do better than that.' And he invariably did.

It was more than six miles from the back paddock to the homestead, but it was no problem for Jeff to move a mob this distance on his own. Alf would let the sheep onto the road, say, 'Bring them home, boy', and a few hours later they would be in the yards, with Jeff sitting in the gateway waiting for Alf to shut it. The pat and few words he got were a quite sufficient reward from his point of view.

One day Alf drove down the road and was halfway home when he saw a sheep that looked flyblown. Leaving the wide wire gate open, he drove into the paddock only to find about fifteen or so blown sheep. With his young dog he pushed them into the yards in a patch of mallee about half a mile from the road. He was still working on the sheep when he saw Jeff's mob nearing the open gate. Jeff was slowly trotting from one side to the other, keeping the stragglers up with the mob. Suddenly he stopped, went through the fence into the paddock and made a wide circle around to the

153

open gateway. He sat watching the gate about a chain back from the roadway until the last sheep had passed by.

Alf was amazed. How could he have known the gate had been left open? He went later to the spot where Jeff had left the mob and gone through the fence. It was impossible for him to see a wire gate lying on the ground—even less so from a dog's height. Alf swore that as he passed Jeff and the mob on the way home, Jeff gave him a look that said, 'Why did you leave that b . . . gate open?'

TOO CLEVER BY HALF

Bruce Mills, Tumby Bay, South Australia

In the first book of *Great Working Dog Stories* there is a story about Karla, a blue and tan kelpie and how I came to own her. She was a dog of exceptional intelligence, loyalty and natural ability.

One afternoon, however, her talent rather overextended itself. My wife had advised me when I got home that we were having relations for a barbecue lunch the next day and we had no meat left. Not having any killers handy, I called Karla and went in the ute to the bottom dam, thinking there would be wethers in for a drink. There were none at the dam, but a few hundred metres further on, there were about twenty just moving away.

I held Karla up above the bluebushes and pointed in the direction of the sheep and bid her to bring them back. Away she went and I waited. And waited. I then decided to climb the windmill to see what was going on. There, at least two kilometres away, was a pall of dust. The main mob of sheep no doubt had left the dam much earlier and was spread out over that distance. Karla had kept breaking out until she had reached the lead.

By the time the sheep were returned to the dam and I had caught a suitable killer, the sun had set. I called to Karla to let the rest go, and as she jumped into the front of the ute, as she always did when she thought she had done well, I cursed her for being such a stupid old bastard and that I would now have to kill and dress the sheep in the dark.

Karla wriggled her ears and thumped the seat of the ute with her tail. She knew by the tone of my voice that my blasphemous words were really praise and my heart was filled with pride at owning a dog that displayed the attributes of a true mustering, self-motivated, working kelpie.

MIDGET THE MIGHTY

Alan Masman, Lake Cathie, New South Wales

The working dogs most spoken of in the Australian bush are the kelpies, the cattle dogs, the border collies. However, the working dog in this story is a miniature black and white fox terrier, the runt of a litter with such small legs that her height when fully grown was only about seven inches. Her name was Midget.

She was born in Mudgee, New South Wales, and when she was old enough she was taken to Wamerawa, our 8,000-acre sheep property at Carinda in the north-west. She was to be a house pet for my wife and teenage children. This was the case for only a very short time, however, because she became very attached to me and my motorbike. She was soon riding with me, her front legs hanging onto the handlebars. She exuded an air of supreme confidence and an impression that she, not me, was overseer of the entire operation.

The sight of sheep sent her into a frenzy of continuous yapping, which became her hallmark. She became a brainy and very game paddock and yard worker, but because she was so small, she tired quickly. Ten minutes of frantic work at a time was about her limit, but she would put it to good use. She ran from one side of the sheep to the other, yapping constantly to give them a good hurry-up. When she needed a rest, she would come and nip my boot to tell me she needed to be picked up. In the sheep yards, she worked continuously and could even jump up onto the sheep's backs, yapping the whole time. She really got some action from the sheep.

On those occasions when I had to lift a sheep into another yard, I would often feel a small weight in addition to that of the sheep. Looking down I would find Midget fastened onto the wool. She would stay latched on until I was about to drop the sheep on the other side, and then she'd sit and look up at me for a pat. I think she believed she was actually helping me to lift the sheep!

Midget's skills impressed a drover passing by so much that he inquired if she was for sale. He liked her ability to yap and wanted her as a 'peg' dog to block off a laneway or gateway when the stock were camped at night. I refused the offer, of course.

Soon after this, though, Midget went missing. I had been running in the horses with Midget's help. As was the usual practice, when the bike reached the bridge near the house yard, Midget jumped off to return to the house. This time, however, the horses raced past the horse yard and took off to the far end of the paddock, so I wheeled round and took off after them. I didn't realise it at the time, but Midget must have followed and run among the trees where a wedge-tailed eagle was sitting on eggs.

Twelve months later I found her jawbone, with its double fangs in the bottom jaw, under a tree bearing the nest. There was no doubt that this was Midget's jaw as we recognised her teeth.

The household was never quite the same again and many a tear was shed for a quaint little dog who was not only a loyal and trusted buddy but an outstanding little worker as well.

SONNY AND THE ESCAPEE

Jennifer Coathupe, Kingston, South Australia

Our working dog Sonny is a big black and tan kelpie with a waggy tail that contorts his whole body when he's excited and happy. He wouldn't win any beauty contest, though, as he looks a little like a Doberman and he's a bit forbidding except when he knows you.

One time we were shearing our rams, and it had been a long day for my husband and the station hand. On the very last pen one of the rams decided he didn't want to be shorn. He shot out of the pen while the station hand was getting another ram out.

Bob, my husband, was busy shearing, so this renegade was able to canter out across the board. I saw it coming out and attempted to corner it with my broom, but he turned to face me, took one look at me and the broom, and decided I didn't present too much opposition—he charged right through, leaving me sitting upside down on the board wondering what had happened and where the ram had gone.

Sonny had been lying under the wool table having a kip, but he got up and sauntered out of the shed after the escapee.

We finished the rams in the shed and were cleaning up when our stock and station agent called in to have a talk about what was going on in the markets. Bob and the agent were leaning against the wool table talking. The station hand was tidying up around the wool bins, and I had almost finished sweeping the board.

Suddenly there was a clatter from behind us and, on turning around, we saw that Sonny had done his job well. He had gone after that ram, cornered it, overpowered it and brought it all the way back into the shed. While we watched him, he hunted it across the board to where the station hand grabbed it and proceeded to shear it.

Needless to say, we were all stunned. We knew he was a good dog but hadn't realised quite how good till that day.

ORDERS FROM ON HIGH

Natalie Broad, Cue, Western Australia

Fred was a little, red, rough-coated kelpie dog belonging to Eric, my brother-in-law. He was top dog of the seven we had at the time, but very definitely a one-man dog who worshipped the ground Eric walked on.

157

I have a funny little story to tell about Fred during mustering time five years ago. Eric was flying the plane, so Jenny, the jilleroo who was working with us at the time, decided to take Fred because she had seen how useful he was. She thought he would be able to help out. We have an 800,000-acre sheep station in the Murchison, so we travel a lot of miles, especially at mustering time.

Eric directed Jenny onto a large mob of toey sheep. They started to go in about ten different directions at once, so she screamed and signalled to Fred, 'get back there.' All he would do was run along next to the motorbike, waiting to jump on for a free ride. He wasn't going to work for her! According to Fred, he only had one master— and it definitely was not Jenny.

Eric flew over again and saw that Jenny was still in difficulty trying to control her mob. Over the mustering radio attached to the front of the bike, he asked her what the matter was. She tried to explain her plight. The other musterers were too far away to come and assist, plus they had mobs of their own to control. The only option was for Fred to lift his game.

Jenny called Fred back to the bike and Eric whistled into his radio and told Fred to 'get back round there'. Fred shot off the back of the bike like a bullet and did what he knows best. Jenny stared in amazement at this extraordinary little dog who, after taking his orders from his boss in the air, had the mob under control in no time at all.

WINNING OVER THE RIVAL

Betty Thompson, Bylong, New South Wales

When I married 43 years ago and came to live with my husband, I felt everything was perfect and the love we had for each other was sublime. Alas, I never dreamt I would have to fight for that love with a dog for two years and be treated with such dislike.

Jinny was my rival right from the very first day I took up my position as a loving wife. She was my husband's shadow and obedient servant, following at his heels wherever he went. There was some doubt about her breeding but she showed a mixture of cattle and sheepdog in her appearance and in her ability to work both cattle and sheep. She was really good to watch, biting as directed by my husband—either just a nip or a really good bite, first one heel and then the other—but she never bit the sheep and was quite handy in the yards as well.

Several months after I married she still eyed me off with suspicion and would have nothing to do with me. Even when it came to her feed-time she would not accept it from me and would wait until I was out of sight before she very gingerly ate it with distaste. If my husband put his arms around me she would slink off and refuse to follow us another step.

Having lived on the land all my life, I was accustomed to animals and the work associated with them. Naturally I helped with all the outside work when needed, which was often and especially with the stock. One day I went to help with the muster and, as my own horse was lame, my husband caught one of his horses for me to ride. Normally it was Jinny's habit to spin and bark with excitement, then rush off ahead of us as we mounted. This day, however, as I was about halfway onto the horse, Jinny unwound and, as quick as a flash, darted in and with all her pent-up hatred bit my horse on the front foot. Well, you can just imagine the result. My poor horse let out a wild snort, leapt in the air and at the same time spun sideways. How I managed to land in the saddle remains a mystery to this very day. When I finally quietened my horse and abused the dog, she smirked back at me as if to say, 'I got you that time.'

Her jealousy went on for almost two years and I had given up trying to win her over.

On one occasion we had a bad outbreak of bushfires, and my husband and all the available men had to be on the job both day and night while I was left at home to cope with the chores. We had just begun shearing and had just started into a mob of ewes and lambs and could not stop. As we only had a small two-stand shed, we did the rouseabouting ourselves and, in the absence of my husband and workmen at the fires, I had to turn my talents to being the shed hand.

Jinny was left at home with me and her spirits reached rock-bottom. She went into deep mourning for her master and true love, staying put in her kennel. About the third day, though, she actually followed me to the shed and watched me pick up the fleeces and throw them on the table and sweep the board. Now and again I gave her a pat and said, 'Cheer up, old girl, he will be home soon.'

Each time there was a small response from her—just a slight wag of the tail—but it was the first ever, and I began to wonder what would happen next.

On the fourth day, she began following me and when I picked up a fleece, she would pick up a piece of wool, bring it back to the table and drop it at my feet as if to say, 'There, I am helping too.' I would tell her she was a good dog, and get a big tail-wag.

By the end of the week she was keeping close tabs on my every move. She came to help me start the engine to run the generator for our lights at night. As I cranked the motor she would rush in and bark at the handle until it started. Then she would sit down and look at me with her head on one side as if to say, 'There, that helped you get it going, didn't it?'

The final capitulation came when she followed me to bed and slept outside the door all night. I knew at last I was accepted, but I did wonder if she would change when my husband returned.

It was a great surprise that when he finally arrived—exhausted and smelling of smoke and gum leaves—and took me in his arms, she barked her approval and jumped up and licked, first him, then me.

I had at last won the day and she was willing to share her master with me for ever.

TO OUR TRIXIE

Maureen Turner, Old Junee, New South Wales

She was only a little red kelpie bitch,
Only a dog, that's true.
The kind that was bred for working sheep,
She was loyal through and through.

160

She came as a hungry, gangly pup,
And didn't grow very large,
But the stubborn old ewes in the mob would move
When that little dog took charge.
Clever and cunning and competent,
Working all day in the sun,
Till the lengthening shadows and cooling breeze
Would tell her that work was done.
And only then would she come to my side
And tongue at her master's feet,
Knowing the jobs of the day were done,
Her tasks were all complete.

A HUGE VOCABULARY

Greg Walcott, Horsham, Victoria

I am one of the fortunate sheepdog owners to have been lucky enough to have owned the 'freak' dog whose intelligence was simply outstanding and quite unbelievable. I have owned several good or very good sheepdogs, but Whisky was extraordinary.

He was largely a self-taught dog. I trained him with the basics as a pup but rarely had to teach much else as he simply picked up things or worked things out for himself. His powers of reasoning and comprehension often amazed me.

His vocabulary was huge. I once read in a national daily newspaper that dogs could not learn more than twenty words, but simply reacted to tone of voice. As a result I wrote down in excess of 400 words in Whisky's vocabulary and quite often tested the tone of voice theory by including, in a conversation with someone, a simple order to Whisky in the same tone that I was using. He would invariably stir from his half sleep and do as suggested.

I was able to teach him many names—of people, pets, sheds, vehicles and so on. This was often very handy as I quite often used him to run messages to people. I would tie a note in a rag to his collar and send him off in search of a particular person—and he always found them.

One day I was having trouble drafting ewes. Whisky and I always drafted by ourselves with little or no trouble. This day, however, was very hot—the sheep were not running, the dog had his tongue out and I was getting hot under the collar. In desperation I decided to change the pens around to try to make things easier. In the meantime I told Whisky to 'Go and get a drink. Go to the dam and have a drink'—which he was only too pleased to do.

When I had sorted things out in the shed I called Whisky to start drafting again. There was no sign of him. I was really starting to get annoyed. I looked out of the shed to see Dad driving up from the house, which was about one kilometre away. He arrived looking very concerned and with Whisky on the front seat.

Whisky had knocked on the kitchen door demanding entry. When Mum opened it he marched straight past and up to the kitchen table. No sign of Dad so back past Mum, out through the lounge and up through the front room to where Dad was working at his desk. With a demanding couple of barks and an anxious look he about-turned and marched out with Mum and Dad watching in utter surprise and bewilderment. Thinking the worst, Dad followed him out to the car and promptly drove up to the shed to see what was wrong.

To this day I do not know if Whisky mistook 'dam' for 'Dad' or simply took it on himself to go and seek Dad's assistance with the drafting. Mum and Dad couldn't believe the assertive way he got his message across.

WHERE'S THE 'OFF' SWITCH?

B E Madden, Girilambone, New South Wales

Some years ago, for some mysterious reason quite beyond me, the station was experiencing a shortage of dogs. It's usually the other way around—an abundance of half-starved dogs that drove me crazy trying to fatten them.

The boss always maintained a good dog was infinitely better than two ordinary station hands—but they were in short supply also. Therefore my husband was instructed to keep his eyes and ears open for a good dog to *buy*! A few weeks later the sheepdog trials were on in town. What better place to find a dog suitable not only for sheep work but with good breeding potential? My bloke not only found the kind of dog needed, he paid real money for him—his first ever cash purchase for a dog—$100 no less.

On their arrival home, we all admired this sharp, alert-looking dog. He certainly looked the part and we could hardly wait to see him perform. On the weekend our daughter and family arrived, providing the perfect excuse to try the dog—they needed some killers.

Daughter, son-in-law and kids all climbed aboard the truck, hoping to see some fancy dog work, and after the dog had been tied up on the back, I jumped in the front determined not to miss the display. We got to the paddock and quickly spotted a likely looking mob of sheep. When the truck stopped we were all warned to stay still and quiet while my bloke let the dog go and sent him off to round up the sheep.

With ears pricked and a swift look around, the dog set off in a rush for the sheep. We were all very impressed with the way he rapidly had the sheep rounded up and brought back to the master. We were even more impressed with how he held them in a tight little bunch while the three killers were caught and tied up.

The master then whistled the dog to come behind and started off to bring the truck over and load up the sheep. Looking around as he got to the truck, he was a bit astonished to see the dog was bringing the sheep along too.

For the next half hour kids, daughter, son-in-law and my husband himself ran themselves ragged and yelled themselves hoarse trying to get the rotten dog to 'come behind' and let the sheep go. In utter frustration, my husband finally roared, ' The boss had better pay another $100 to stop this bloody dog!'

I have completely forgotten what the name of that dog was— but I do remember he didn't last here very long.

BACKING THE BLOCKAGE

Frank Bawden, Tumby Bay, South Australia

Friend, sharefarmer and shearer Andrew Mills comes from a family of noted kelpie breeders, owners and trainers. Accordingly, he has a particularly good dog called Boy.

During shearing we were filling the shed from outside when the sheep baulked in one of the catching pens. Andrew sent Boy up onto the backs of the wethers, up the ramp and into the shed to look for the blockage.

My brother Bernie, who is big and hairy, was the shed hand. Unbeknown to us, he was bending down, nailing the grating in the catching pen into place.

Boy, true to form, darted over the backs of the sheep and landed with a big 'woof' right on Bernie's broad back. It's still debatable today who got the bigger shock. Bernie leapt into the air with shouted obscenities, while Boy must have suffered a good deal from shock also.

We spectators had considerable difficulty controlling our mirth. Needless to say, Bernie was at a loss to see what was so funny.

PART 8

CATTLE COUNTRY

Swirling dust, beasts roaring like an angry football crowd, yards with fortress fences, the crack of stockwhips and the drumbeat of hooves—these are the essence of cattle country. Shiny-coated cattle, herded by helicopter, horse and dog, jostle and bellow and always await that moment to revolt. Dogs with jaws like rabbit traps eye them, alert to the slightest hint of insurrection.

Bred to cope with droughts and long distances between waterholes, Australian cattle are some of the world's toughest. To tackle a cow fiercely protecting her calf, or a wild scrub bull, takes guts. The dogs of cattle country, if they are going to survive, also have to be fit, intelligent and agile.

It's not all grime and sweat though. Out of the dust come the unexpected hilarious moments such as the time emus ruined the muster, as described by young Kathy Boyden of Charters Towers. And Errol Munt says he nearly fell off his horse laughing so much at his dog Gundy standing on top of an angry bull in a dam.

The ringers in Fred's team, though, might not have been laughing when the horse-biter gave them a bit of a nudge along.

For Rags, however, who was seriously injured while saving his owner, there is deep gratitude.

THE DAYS OF NO DOGS: SHIRLEY JOLIFFE'S STORY

Angela Goode

More Great Working Dog Stories included a story called 'I Had Got Myself a Beauty' by Shirley Joliffe who, after she had got her children off her hands, went mustering. She left a comfortable job in a town to return to the bush, swapping pens for mobs of cattle and a desk for a horse and dog.

In the course of putting together this book, I heard from Shirley's cousin Beryl Thomas (whose story 'Old Don of St Kilda' appears in Part 6 'Back of Beyond' in this book) that Shirley, 59, was one of very few female contract musterers in the land. So I gave Shirley a call at her home in Mitchell, in south-eastern Queensland, and caught her in the middle of cooking a meal for some of her six grandchildren.

She told me that when she got Ned, the cream and tan bitzer of her story, in 1975, she had in fact headed straight out to Forest Vale station with a contract to muster 60,000 acres of wild cattle. That's some change from working in a newsagency and raising three daughters in a town. She employed three or four men and took over the cooking and the running of the stock camp as well as spending her days in the saddle running down wild cattle and quietening them in small mobs of coachers.

Shirley was no stranger to the bush, however. She had been brought up on her parents' 30,000-acre beef cattle property not far from Mitchell. She broke in her own horses, rode in camp-draft events, won a few and took out a Queensland championship.

She moved to another cattle property when she married. After the stint in the town, she and Ned took off and worked together until Ned was put down in her old age. As well as continuing to regularly muster cattle for Forest Vale, where she keeps her plant of twelve stock horses, Shirley takes on casual jobs as a musterer all round the Mitchell area.

This gentle-sounding woman, who admits to a love of fashion and who has no plans for retirement, not only runs down wild and stirry cattle, but in her early days at Forest Vale, even used to throw them. 'It's fairly rugged work,' she says in an understated way. ' The boys do it very well. I never had quite enough power to pull them over quickly.' Nevertheless, she did throw about six on her own.

These days Shirley and her men have the Forest Vale cattle under control, so there's no longer much need for such heroics. They spend a lot of time riding around the mobs and domesticating them. From August each year she spends twelve weeks mustering the station so the calves can be weaned. In January, another 12-week cycle begins, doing the branding muster.

On her own 1,500-acre place at Roma—which, like everywhere else in the region, is devastated by drought—she is handfeeding the few cattle that remain on the place. Her 45 breeding cows have been sent away on agistment.

Shirley knows of no other woman in charge of a mustering team, although she is sure there must be some. Many women these days have been forced to take up mustering to help their husbands out because of the financial disaster caused by interest rates, drought and the wool crash. But few opt to take up mustering as a full-time occupation.

Shirley admits she does get some strange looks from time to time when she's out on a horse . . . not so much because she's a woman, though. It's more because she wears the biggest felt cowboy hat she can find—with the brim turned down right over her eyes. Then, like some wild west outlaw, she ties a bandana over her nose and mouth, so all that's visible is a pair of eyes. 'It's not for looks. I just like to be protected from the sun,' says Shirley, who also wears gloves and long sleeves out on the job for the same reason.

Sadly, the days of dogs out in the mustering camps seem to have passed. Although Shirley has a blue stumpy-tailed cattle dog that would love to work, she doesn't dare risk it: 'Most people put out 1080 these days for dingoes, and I just couldn't bear to see my dogs poisoned,' Shirley says. 'It's getting very hard to use dogs out in this country because there is so much bait around—not that I blame them. It's good that they're trying to control dingoes, but I'd certainly use heelers in my work if I could.'

It's a pity indeed. The sight of a heeler retrieving a cow and then, as Shirley wrote in Ned's story, 'floating through the air like a trapeze artist on the brush of a cow's tail' is no doubt missed by many.

DANCES WITH EMUS

Kathy Boyden, Charters Towers, Queensland

I live about two hours out of Charters Towers in north Queensland on Moonlight Creek station. I am eleven and do correspondence lessons through the Charters Towers Distance Education Centre.

On one of those typical Aussie working days in the bush, my sister Jody, twelve, and I were allowed to take time off school to join in a muster for mickey bulls. It took a while for Dad to get all the kids and workers saddled up. The men were really looking forward to getting stuck into chasing the bulls and everyone was impatient. Probably keenest of the lot, though, were our nine eager blue healers, led by Dad's dog Ned. Even though they were often called 'the useless mongrels', no mustering gang would be complete without them.

Finally everyone was settled and ready, so off we went on a hard day's work. It was a day we were always to look back on and have a really good laugh about—although at the time, Grandad and the other men didn't see the funny side of things. We had finally mustered a herd of scrub cattle together and all the troublemaking micks had settled down to a make-believe peacefulness when suddenly we had visitors.

The first we knew of this was when our working dogs, who had been taking a breather under the shady trees, sat up with a start and pricked up their ears. Of course Ned, the boss dog, couldn't resist the fun of a chase on a hot day. So off he dashed with bristles sticking up a mile high and that awful bark of his that always sets Dad in a bad mood. All the commotion was over just a few inquisitive emus who had seen the mob of cattle and the ringers, and had decided to join them. Of course Ned had other ideas that unfortunately didn't come true.

The poor emus, who had almost reached the cattle, were suddenly being mustered up by Ned and the mates in his clan. But you all know that emus can't be made to do what they don't consider dignified, so instead of running away so that Ned could have his bit of sport, the frightened emus turned in a semicircle and headed straight for the mob, with Ned and his team hot on their tails.

For the next ten minutes there was one mighty commotion, what with emus flat-out through the mob of cattle and 'the useless mongrels' right behind them. The dogs were letting out such a howl and whine that you can imagine what happened to that mob of cattle. I can tell you—those micks didn't hang around to see the fun!

By this time the emus had had enough and decided to give the dogs a bit of a fright, so they screeched to a halt, did a tight circle and darted straight for the dogs. Ned, despite being such a brainy dog, couldn't even guess what was in store for him. With a snarl and a brave bark he stood his ground but, honking as loud as thunder, the emus advanced with deadly intent. You should have seen those dogs with tails between their legs head straight for the horses. Ned, however, was the oldest and slowest of the lot and he wasn't quick enough to escape the kick of the leading emu's powerful legs or the cruel peck of his beak. The rest of the dogs found sanctuary under the horses' bellies.

Until this time, the men on their horses had enjoyed the spectacle of the dogs and emus and had been laughing their heads off. But all of a sudden they found themselves caught up in the turmoil too. What with dogs and emus running around the horses and the horses starting to have a good buck, there wasn't much peace and quiet. The men were yelling at the dogs to shoot through way out yonder, while the emus were stomping their feet to the beat of a drum. The dogs, meanwhile, were cringing on the ground like cowards. Just when the chaos was at its height, the emus turned and strutted away with necks held high, never to be seen again.

When the men had finally controlled their horses and discovered that their mob of cattle had disappeared completely, their tempers were up pretty high. Dad needed something to take his fury out on, so his keen eye roved around for the instigator of all the mischief. But Ned, the trusty, hardworking packleader was nowhere in sight and he stayed invisible for quite a few hours. No-one had ever said he was brainless.

PUTTING A BITE ON
THE RINGERS

Graydon Hutchinson, Alpha, Queensland

Chris was in his forties, single and semi-retired. He always had a few horses and cattle on his small block and did an odd day's outside work, but he spent most of his time sitting in a deck chair on his front verandah, or down town talking to someone.

He paid big money for a well-bred cattle dog to help him with his stock work but the mutt wouldn't look at cattle, let alone bite one. He would bite horses though—he was always chasing and biting them. He would even bite the saddle horse when Chris was riding him. Despite numerous beltings with sticks and whips, the dog persisted in his terrible habit. Chris had threatened to shoot him a few times but never got around to it.

One day Chris's best friend Fred arrived for a short visit. He was about ten years younger and led a much harder life. He ran wild cattle on a large property and for his efforts he received half the proceeds of the sale of the cattle. From these he had to pay wages to several men and maintain horses, dogs, saddlery and so on. Even with these expenses, he still made big money.

One of hig biggest problems was finding suitable men and dogs. The men had to be able to ride fast in rugged country when running cattle into the coachers and be able to tie up a cleanskin cow or bull. The dogs were needed to bite a beast that had broken from the coachers hard enough to frighten it back into the mob, or to hang onto the nose of a bull while someone got onto his tail to pull him down. Fred went through a lot of dogs—and men.

Fred spotted the horse-biter tied up near the empty 44-gallon drum with the end cut out. 'Hell, that's a good sort of a dog you've got there,' exclaimed Fred.

' Yeah, mate, he's good but I haven't got the work for him,' Chris said. 'Take him with you.'

It was about a month later that Fred dropped in again. Chris was hardly game to mention the dog but eventually got around to asking how it was performing.

'Bloody beauty, mate—best dog I've ever had,' came the unexpected reply.

'Fair dinkum?' muttered the unbelieving Chris. 'Will he bite cattle?'

'Hell, no,' laughed the cheerful Fred. 'He won't even look at a beast, but by hell he can bite horses. That couple of slow riding ringers that were always hanging back on the tail are up in the lead on every run now.'

HEELING INSTINCT
ON HOLD

Les Evans, Borden, Western Australia

Many give credit to dogs that is not strictly justified—dogs work after training and repetition. However, there are some who seem to have a brain.

When I was a boy we had a little red kelpie bitch. She was the only heeler, with horses and cattle, we ever owned. On this occasion my father was doing some fence repairs along a little-used road. He had two horses standing unattended on the road hitched to a wagon. Normally they would remain like this indefinitely, but on this day a limb broke off a tree and startled them. Away they went. When Dad saw Lassie take off after them he thought, 'Oh well, that's that. I won't see the horses for a while. The wagon could break up and I'll have to walk home.'

However, instead of heeling the horses as she had always done previously, Lassie went to one horse's head and bit and barked till she had them jammed against the fence. When Dad finally got to them, Lassie was jumping up and down and her tail was thrashing happily. She had caught them and she was very pleased with herself.

It really was quite an extraordinary act since it was such a significant departure from her normal method of working. She had overruled her natural instinct to heel the horses in order to stop them. That seems to me to be using brainpower.

SHY AND WHITE

Enid Clark, Singleton, New South Wales

Shy was so named because she would whimper and squirm when I picked her up. She is almost completely white and has two blue eyes. I hadn't wanted a white dog but she turned out to be better than I had ever hoped—a tough, intelligent worker, a gentle and loving friend. She worked for five years at Singleton saleyards in between mustering wild cattle in the mountains.

Not having wanted a white dog initially, I have found they have great advantages over red or black dogs. Cattle can see them better and can therefore be stopped more easily. In scrubby country a white dog is very easy to see in the distance and I have noticed that they don't feel the heat as much as a dark-coloured dog. Some of these factors may account for Shy's talent with cattle.

We have a small place and work casually for other graziers. On one property we mustered there were some very steep and dirty gullies and if the cattle broke we sometimes had to spend half a day getting them together again. As we approached some of these gullies, Shy would leave the mob and go ahead to wait for the breakaways. She would meet them face to face with force, rushing and jumping up and barking in their faces—which would alter 99 per cent of their minds.

Once, on another property, a breakaway heifer about eighteen months old all but knocked my husband's horse over and made for the scrub. The dogs were sent to block it, but when we noticed that it was useless, we called them back as they were needed to take the mob to the yards a couple of miles away. We usually work two dogs each in bad country and one each in average country. This was bad country but only three dogs came back and Shy wasn't one of them. We put the mob in the yard and had lunch, then went on drafting—and still Shy hadn't shown up.

After about three and a half hours we noticed a beast coming around the mountain about half a mile away, just a few feet at a time. Then, as it got closer, we could see Shy rushing in at its head. It would charge and stop. She brought it all the way into the yards. It was the wild heifer and it hadn't gotten any quieter.

174

It had taken her approximately four hours to bring it the two miles.

Shy is ten years old now and only does the little jobs around the house. It makes her feel important to still be needed. She gets the house cow and educates our weaner cattle in and out of the yards. She keeps our calves and our neighbours' calves sorted out if they get through the creek block when it rains. If we truck a new house cow from our other place, and she hasn't come along to help, she makes sure the neighbours end up with it the next day. She thinks it is a stray and that it must be sent back. If she helps us bring it home, then she'll leave it here.

A couple of months ago we bought three small black calves to rear. We put them in the calf yard under Shy's supervision. Next morning, one was gone. When we let Shy off her chain, we didn't notice where she went until we heard a cow roaring and saw her coming 300-400 yards away, bringing a little black calf with the mother in hot pursuit from our neighbour's paddock. She worked the calf through the fence and brought it right to our calf pen. We didn't like to disappoint her, so we put it onto the truck to take it back to the neighbour's place.

When we arrived we were surprised to discover they had our calf tied up at their yards and were wondering who owned it. Shy must have seen it get out of the yard and head off into the night, so was determined to retrieve it as soon as she was free.

SWAM HER IN

Jean Richards, Upper Lansdowne, New South Wales

The men were working in very hilly and heavily timbered country and they were mustering the top paddock. After getting all 150 head of cattle to the top of the hill, a heifer broke away. Nigger, the black kelpie, went after her.

The boss said not to worry about the heifer as they would first take the mob to the yard, then go and get her after lunch. Just as they finished lunch, they heard Nigger barking. The men followed the sound to the river and were astonished to see Nigger swimming along in the middle of the river with the heifer right in front of him. When the dog and heifer got to the shallow water at the crossing, the heifer left the river and Nigger drove her up the bank and put her in the small paddock near the yard.

Nigger must have swum her about two miles down the river, because there was nowhere else they could have entered the water because of high banks, fences, rocks and trees along that distance.

THE BULL-RIDER'S DEBUT

Errol Munt, Toowoomba, Queensland

This story happened some fifteen years ago and involved Gundy, a cattle dog I had been given as a pup by my uncle, Mr Norm Ehrlich.

I was on horseback and Gundy and I were trying to shift a Droughtmaster bull across the highway to the yards on the other side. We almost had him enclosed in the yard when he decided to break away and head back across the highway, which was about 250 metres away. The determined bull gathered speed and took no notice of either the horse or Gundy as we tried to block him.

When he reached the first road fence he leapt across the grid and over the highway and then smashed through a piping gate on the other side. By then I suppose he thought he was home and safe. This was not the case as Gundy and I were in hot pursuit. The language from me was 'blue' with rage, and Gundy was heeling him every step he took. By the time I opened the gate at the first fence and got across the highway, I could see the bull heading for the supposed safety of a dam. After a brisk gallop to catch Gundy and the bull, I arrived to see the bull make a leap into the dam. Gundy duly followed.

In the next twenty seconds I changed from being extremely angry to laughing so much that I couldn't sit straight on the horse. Imagine seeing your dog swim up alongside a bull, climb upon his shoulders, stand there on all fours, and bite the bull on the back of the neck. A bull-riding dog—I hadn't seen that before.

Deciding the water was no longer the best place to be, the bull swam to the edge of the dam, with the dog still aboard. Then he climbed up the bank and stopped some three metres away from the water. At this stage, Gundy jumped off. He had ridden his eight seconds and got top points from the judge!

If only dogs could talk—in between eyeing off the bull, he would occasionally look back across the dam at me with a pleased look upon his face that seemed to say, 'I got him for you.' After a minute or two's rest so we could all regain our composure, the bull was willing to be driven anywhere without resentment.

DREAM LOVER

Doug Allison, St George, Queensland

Lover was named after Rain Lover, who won the Melbourne Cup, but he was also a good lover by nature and produced many smart sons and daughters. He was a working freak capable of working big and small mobs, ewes and lambs, or lambs only, and with limited instructions. As a yard dog he had no superior. However, my story is of cattle mustering.

My horse-racing partner, Jack Dyball of St George, had a property called Peppercorn which was divided by Buckenbah channel. It had a 4,000-acre back paddock mostly consisting of thick mulga scrub in which eight head of grown, branded cattle plus four young calves had twice eluded two experienced stockmen. They had tried to muster them on horses but gave up, saying they couldn't be coaxed out of the mulga.

Following an overnight inch of rain I asked Jack to give me the four fresh sheepdogs and his utility so Lover and I could go out to retrieve his scrubber cattle. He replied that I was stone crazy.

'How are you going to get cattle out on foot that two good men can't get on horses?' he said.

The cattle were easily tracked, and with the burrs on the ground softened from the rain, Lover and the four sheepdogs were sooled onto the cattle as they took off. With Lover in the lead and the station sheepdogs barking and the calves bellowing, the mob soon bailed up.

Armed with a stockwhip, I followed, and after half a dozen times of bailing the mob up, I had manoeuvred them onto the road. With Lover controlling the lead and the station dogs helping when necessary, I walked behind the cattle for six miles through three gates and eventually put them across a single-lane bridge 50 yards long. Jack Dyball was amazed. He couldn't believe a man on foot with five dogs could have achieved what we did with such stirry cattle.

Lover was a genius or a dream dog. He always helped me in my job as sheep and wool officer for the Department of Primary Industry in St George. Several times I classed and drafted mobs of up to 1,400 sheep with only the dog to help. Once, with the owner helping, we classed 3,600 sheep in one day. The owner voluntarily paid for 4,000 sheep, suggesting I should shout Lover a rum that night with the extra pay.

YOU LITTLE TRIMMER

Geoff Hamilton, Legume, New South Wales

In 1950 I was fortunate enough to be given a part-kelpie black pup from Mr Whaley Funnell of Jackerbulbyn. I called the pup Trimmer. His father, a fantastic dog named Spud, together with his master would muster the property of some 20,000 acres of coastal forest country.

When Trimmer started work, he was so hyperactive it took sixteen days straight mustering in the mountains and then a droving trip to settle him down. Among some of the amazing things he did was

178

the time he took a mob of cattle along a road, not collecting any other cattle on the way providing I was in front—although I might have been ahead by as much as two miles. I would canter along and enjoy a cup of tea with the neighbours until the cattle caught up, and then I would let them through the gate and go on again.

Another time I had 68 Hereford weaners on the road to Tabulam, just the second day weaned from the mothers. By 8 am I had them settled down and descending the ridge towards Rocky River when the lead, about a mile away, went through a gate to visit some Jersey cows. I sent Trimmer after the calves and he proceeded to bring them out steadily, but it seemed he'd left one behind. I cursed him profusely and got the Hereford calf—same shape, size and colour as my own mob—out of the paddock. I then realised from the earmark it was not one of mine.

In 1951 my cousin Jim Apps and I mustered 96 Hereford three-year-old heifers on Bungawalbyn Creek. We had considerable trouble separating them from other cattle in the same paddock where they had been on agistment. It was 3 pm before we set off to drive the heifers ten miles along an unfenced forest road. Jim took the lead and I kept the tail moving. I had two dogs with me, Trimmer and his mother, Smuttie.

Once we had lost our daylight, it was a hard, slow trip, travelling through thick scrub in the dark, especially as there were two calves with blight who would wander from the mob. I had to rely on my ears to work out where the cattle were, listening for movement in the leaves. To tell which dog was which, I'd call and get them to jump up on my foot in the stirrup so that I could feel their collars. I would then send one dog to each side of the mob. It was a real battle, especially as half misty rain was falling and added to the confusion and frustration. We yarded the cattle at eleven o'clock that night.

It was a great relief next morning to find all the heifers were accounted for, and without doubt credit for that was almost entirely due to the skill of the dogs.

SPOILSPORT

Ron Cherry, Armidale, New South Wales

I had a blue cattle dog named Ned. His favourite job was to bring up the rear of the mob. If they slowed a little, he'd rush in with his mouth wide open and bite hard and fast—and always seemed to enjoy the result.

We were droving a mob of sheep one time and I decided to let him have a run. Every now and then he'd open that great big mouth of his and rush at the sheep.

'No, Ned!' I'd yell, and you would hear his mouth suddenly snap shut and he'd crash right into the back of the surprised sheep and fall in a heap.

He'd pick himself up looking very annoyed, then glare at me as if to say, 'Bloody spoilsport.' Before long he'd be off for another try.

RICH GIFTS FROM RAGS

Carolyn McConnel, Esk, Queensland

Rags was a black and white, speckled, mostly cattle dog, but with a dash of border collie. She was given to me when I was first married and had just moved in from sheep country to the Brisbane Valley in southern Queensland where we ran all cattle. She was just a tiny pup then and quickly became a great mate and a fair cattle dog.

The only other dog on the place was a golden labrador, but together these two could outwit any bull that ever bailed up. Sandy the labrador grabbed the tail and Rags would go for the nose and, with an almighty crash, the bull would be down on the ground and these two would sit back and wait until he got up. If he headed in the wrong direction, they'd throw him again.

Rags was also very useful when we were repairing flood fences. One of us would go to the other side of the creek and she'd swim the creek as many times as you wanted her to with a cord attached to her collar. Whenever we needed such things as wire or a hammer, we tied them onto the cord and hauled them over. It saved us hours of wading through flood water and mud, and she thought it was great fun. She would lie on the bank just waiting to be called across.

Rags earned my deep gratitude when she saved me from serious injury when she was an old dog. We were working with touchy heifers, and the dogs accordingly were all sent out of the yards since the presence of dogs can make them even touchier.

Without warning a heifer suddenly rushed out of the mob and knocked me over. I hurt my hip and was unable to get away, which meant I was very vulnerable to another charge. However, Rags ran straight into the yard from wherever she had been lying and attacked the heifer, which forced it away from me. I was then able to get to the fence and safety.

Unfortunately, one of the heifer's charges broke Rags's hip. Despite the pain and the fact that she was able to use only three legs, and had disobeyed orders about being in the yards, Rags was determined to protect me. However, even with all the best care our vet could give her, she changed from being a carefree, happy-go-lucky dog to a very snappy dog with everyone but me. It was obvious she would always be in pain, so with great sadness we had her put down.

PART 9

KERR'S TERRITORY

Up near the Gulf of Carpentaria, at hot and steamy Borroloola in the Northern Territory, I spent a few days yarning with Ron Kerr about dogs, his days of mustering wild cattle, of droving, of horses and the crocodiles he once hunted.

Drinking strong tea made by the gallon, we sat in a kitchen where a baby brolga squawked for food, a galah and a sulphur-crested cockatoo perched on chairs and a few dogs walked through. It was not hard to imagine we were sitting in Ron's camp out bush, yarning around the fire.

You might remember from *More Great Working Dog Stories* that Ron's evocative story of Sandsoap was judged winner from almost 2,000 stories received. I wanted to know more about this man who has lived out bush all his life . . .

THE LAST OF THE OLD-STYLE STOCKMEN: A PROFILE OF RON KERR

Angela Goode

Born under a wilga tree alongside the Namoi River near Gunnedah, Ron Kerr spent all his childhood on the track, listening to stories around campfires and following mobs of sheep or cattle with his drover parents and six brothers and sisters. He was a useful stockman by the age of four, left school at twelve, had his own horse plant at fifteen and went off droving on his own at sixteen. He married Mavis, the daughter of another droving family, when she was fifteen.

He's walked cattle from Collarenebri to Coonamble, and he trapped rabbits in the 1950s for 30 pounds a week. In 1952 he took cattle from Dirranbandi to Bourke, broke in horses when there wasn't much droving work around, then picked up mobs of sheep which he shifted around between Bourke and Cunnamulla, Hungerford and anywhere a dollar could be made. He took sheep from Broken Hill to Tibooburra, and took cattle from White Cliffs to Fowlers Gap. He started on wild cattle in 1959 as a contract musterer, being paid a half-share of what he caught. He's seen the land from a saddle, and stock routes from Swan Hill to Quilpie and Borroloola.

It's been a spartan and independent life of rolling a swag out under the stars and cooking on an open fire, and following the mobs. He makes his own pack saddles and repairs his saddles. Dogs and horses have been his life.

'If you don't have horses, you don't have money. But if I don't have money for something, then I don't need it,' says this man with the tanned, wiry body, bushy beard and thick explosion of hair on his head. 'I don't need a wage,' he says, adding that he has never been beholden to governments or banks. 'I can always eat from the bush, things like berries, turtles, kangaroos, goanna, fish. One time, when we were really hungry, we even had a brumby.'

Droving, despite the romance of it all, is an unforgiving game where only the best stockmen will survive. Ron, Mavis and his team had a near disaster in 1960 in desert country when he was droving down the Cooper and he missed a bore during three days of dust storms. Instead of travelling 30 miles between bores, they went sixty. The stock were two and a half days without water and 'I nearly killed my horses,' he says. He made the decision then to never again be anywhere near drought, and in 1962 he headed for the Territory. When he crossed the border, he and his team had a pound between them.

He soon got work at Balbirini station to muster wild cattle and from then on he was in demand. Those were the days when the station country was being cut up and the sale of feral cattle was the only source of income the new settlers had in their early years. In the late 1970s, during the government-sponsored eradication of feral cattle to control brucellosis, blue tongue and tuberculosis, Ron and his team of mainly Aboriginal stockmen, horses and bull terriers were in demand: 'I've mustered just about every property from here to Roper River,' he says in a drawl honed after 57 years on the track.

These days Ron is the last of the old-style musterers. No-one else still works with dogs and horses on wild cattle. They use

186

helicopters and four-wheel-drives for speed and efficiency. Ron is critical of these fast and noisy methods, but in a quiet bushman's way: 'The helicopters are making cattle wild again and they run all the fat off them. You have to keep them twelve months longer to put the fat on again before you get your money.'

On top of that he reckons mustering with horses and dogs is at least 50 per cent cheaper and sees a continuing role for him and his two sons who work with him. He also thinks that the days of the drovers could come back because of the high costs of transport. He says he could take cattle 100 miles for $2 a head, get them fat on the way and handle them gently. The 'ball-bearing drovers,' as he calls the truckies, can't compete with those prices but they are, of course, quick. 'It's a hell of a lot cheaper with a horse that runs on grass,' he says. 'Everyone's got to come back a peg or two.'

Ron still throws the occasional wild bull out on Lorella Springs station, 300 kilometres west of Borroloola, where he has a mustering contract. About 2,000 wild cattle still roam there among rocky creeks and thick scrub where, in places, only dogs can go and vehicles certainly cannot.

For about six monts of the year, Ron, with a team of men and a plant of about 90 horses, ties up bulls and quietens them down in coaching mobs before yarding and trucking them away for sale. In this, the toughest job in the cattle game, injuries and accidents are frequent.

'There are plenty of falls from horses, and horses that fall on people. I'd average one a week of those,' he says with a laugh. He's been stabbed by sharp horns, trampled by bulls, skidded on his face 'and come up with no skin on it. Jumping off your horse has got to be timed right—you mustn't leave too early,' he says about the knack of grabbing a beast's tail and throwing the animal before tying its hind legs with straps.

The risks for the bull terriers, whose instinct it is to grab onto nostrils and hamstrings, are even greater. At the end of each bull-catching season, Ron has to start breeding and training more dogs. Not all the hazards, though, come from cattle. One of his newest dogs died before he even got out to Lorella Springs. A cane toad, part of the recent invasion from Queensland, got into his bowl and poisoned the drinking water.

Ron has recorded much of his life from his earliest memories right through to the present in a series of old exercise books that travel with him out to his stock camps. Following are just a few stories lifted from those memoirs. They give not only an insight into the role of dogs in the Territory, but also into an increasingly rare breed of stockmen.

MORNING MUSTER AT BALBIRINI

Ron Kerr, Borroloola, Northern Territory

I had the men bring the seventeen head of quiet cattle and put them in the yards overnight so we could get an early start. We would be back late for our midday dinner after a short muster.

Because we were short of horses, I told Dimond, the oldest fellow in the team, that he looked like he knew how to fix a yard so cattle couldn't get out. It would be no good knocking our horses about getting cattle if they were going to get out of the yard again. He readily agreed to stay behind and make the yard strong, saying how 'those younger blokes don't know much about making good yards'.

The evening before I had talked to Pludo, the head Aboriginal stockman, about doing a short muster. I quizzed him about the rough cattle we'd seen along the river, where they would leave the river and where they would run into the cane grass. It helped to have a plan in your mind.

Next morning we set off. I went to within two miles of some flat ground with the coaching mob, then sent them on with four men to set themselves up between two hills on that flat site. Three others of us and three dogs waited until the coachers were in place, then we went into the river. Ten minutes later we found between eight and ten head in the water. They went up the bank and into the cane grass. I sent one of the boys up the creek and cut around through the cane grass.

He came back saying he couldn't see or hear anything, but thought they were planted where they went into the grass. So I sent in the dogs. Within minutes there was a bellow and the cane grass came alive. There could have been 40 head in the grass, which was six feet high. Heads bobbed and because the cattle were panicking they didn't bother looking for their walking pads through the grass.

For 300 yards they ploughed through the grass, chased by the one dog that wasn't already hanging onto a beast. Our little brumby horses were flat-strap to keep in hearing distance. They ran about a mile before we caught sight of them, but by then they had dropped back to a trot. Pludo came up alongside to tell me that the open country was just ahead and that the cattle would pull up and try to turn back. We eased up to a trot too, and waited for the dogs to catch up.

They caught up in about two minutes. The three weeks that they had been on near-starvation diets had obviously done them good. They still had their tongues in their jaws and looked like they could run another mile if they had to, but we were only 100 yards away from the cattle. When I sent the dogs, they took off like they knew there would be reinforcements to help them out at the end of the run. They hit a big spotted bull on the tail and I swear the bull 'dozed' a half-dozen cows and weaners ahead of him.

The cattle didn't have time to turn back—besides, they were bunched so tightly they couldn't turn. They came out about 300 yards from the coachers. It was hopeless to try and bend them into the coachers. It's not easy trying to manoeuvre 40 head of cattle in a tight bunch, especially when they're all in overdrive to get away from the snapping ivory behind them. To head them at the coachers meant that they would pick up the coachers and take them with the mob. If the boys didn't have horses any faster than the ones we were riding, then the cattle would take the coachers with them too, especially as the mob of scrubbers was much larger than the coachers.

The boys with the coachers could see that we were making no attempt to wheel the mob their way. They moved between the coachers and the galloping scrubbers, which by now the little run-out brumbies were up on the tail of. Their legs were working like pistons. One of the boys started dropping back even though he was throwing everything at the horse to get a bit more out of him. I yelled out to him to hold the coachers, as we were getting close and the fellows holding them had fresh horses under them. The idea was for us to blow the wind out of the scrubbers as much as possible. I could see that the four fellas holding the coachers had cottoned on to what we were about.

There was nothing to stop us throwing at least one beast each as everyone was carrying two straps around their waists. The fellows stayed behind the coachers, leaning low over their saddles out of sight of the galloping mob while waiting for them to go past. Then they, too, could join the fray of the throwing spree. The blokes with the failing horses had turned toward home, knowing their horses wouldn't be much good for throwing.

With six of us now in behind the scrubbers, it was every man for himself. Already Punch, one of the boys on fresh horses, was right up on the tail of a young bull, one hand flat on the pommel of the saddle on the offside, foot clear of the iron. It was only a matter of yards now and he would leave the horse. With any sort of luck he would get two head of this mob so long as his horse stood still when he jumped off.

My horse was still holding on, not getting any faster but not losing any ground. The scrubbers were dropping back fast. Punch was off his horse and in three or four strides he had the bull's tail. The brush of the tail was wrapped around his hand, and the heels of his riding boots were going in for brakes as he sat back. The bull stopped his forward movement as Punch stepped out to one side. The bull had woken up to why he couldn't keep going and his head came around to get rid of the load on his tail. When his nearside front foot suddenly left the ground to spin around for the man on his tail, Punch pulled the tail towards the head. The now completely off-balance bull only had one place to go—flat on his side. When the hind leg came up stiff from the fall, Punch had the leg in his hand. With his knees over the short ribs, Punch used one hand to tuck the tail between the hind legs and over the flank, to hold the bull flat on his side, while the other hand took the strap from around the waist.

The strap—or the bull strap, as they are called—is a double-buckled strap one and a half inches wide and around three feet long. Once you've got it properly in place around the two hind legs, you can stand up and walk away from a tied bull, and he'll still be there when you bring the coachers around to pick him up. After you have left a bull tied up for ten minutes, he'll get

190

his wind back and sit up. In a short time, he works out how to stand up with two hind legs strapped together. He may hop a little way, but he won't be far gone when you come back several hours later, unless the strap has been left too loose.

Looking around to see what was available for me, I found, right in front of my horse's nose, a big old bottle-tit cow with big curled horns, like a speedwheel racing bike. She was going to be mine. As I grabbed the tail, I had a name for her—Bikehandle Bertha. By the look of the horns, I would say Bertha had been doing the disappearing act for ten years or more and had served her time as a school mama to the younger cattle in how to dodge the stock camp.

I ran back to my horse in the hope of getting another one out of the mob. A quick look around indicated there were cattle in straps all about. Some of the boys were on their horses again. Pludo and Punch were well up in the lead, both on foot, going for a tail 100 yards away. Most of the cattle were now climbing the rocks up the hill in front. It was little use throwing anything up in the rocks as they would only knock themselves about too much in the straps. I waved to the boys to pull out and it was then that I realised that everything had gone like clockwork. No more than half a dozen words had been spoken. Eight head had been tied up by one hour after sunrise.

The boys were all talk about the dogs getting the cattle out of the long grass, each one giving his version of what the dogs had done. It was only then that I missed the dogs, and the boys said that they weren't still chasing the cattle. As we drew nearer to the coachers we could see the dogs sitting behind Norman's horse.

As we got closer I noticed that a fresh cow had joined the coachers. Norman said that she had come out of the long grass behind us and had trotted into the coachers. When she saw him she had taken off again. When the dogs that were following us saw her, the big white dog had grabbed her by the nose, then another dog had got her by the ear, and a third had caught her on the back leg. That cow just stood there singing out, so Norman had brought up the coachers and the dogs let go of the cow. She ran into the mob and only came out once. A bite on her nose made her quickly retreat.

We sat around there for another half an hour and the boys reran the whole episode in their own lingo. Each one had his own story. As we now had nine head and eight to pick up, I told the boys that we had better get started, and that the big scrubber cow would only keep her horns if she stayed with the coachers. The ones on the ground had no choice—to get one of our horses horned now would mean a man on foot. Three of us were carrying horn saws under our saddle flaps. There would be eight more homemade polled cattle on Balbirini that night. The scrubber cow made one more desperate attempt for freedom, but within ten steps she had one dog hanging off her jaw and in five more steps another hanging off her flank. She made it back into the coachers before the third dog arrived.

We eventually stood up all the bulls we had caught, after giving them a bit of a horn trim, and joined them in with the coachers. We walked them around the little sandy flat to get the fresh ones used to what was going on.

The station yard was no more than three and a half miles and it wasn't yet midday. I thought I should have another look in the cane grass not far from my own camp. Beyond the cane grass there was a creek and a sheer wall of sandstone rising some 600 feet and quite inaccessible to cattle. At the base of this wall was a cattle pad going down towards the McArthur River. I felt sure there were more cattle along the river, plus I was curious to find out more about this part of the station.

With seven of us spread out around with two riders in the lead, plus three dogs, we headed back. The young bulls tried to make a half-hearted break for the long grass but didn't want to have too much to do with a man on horseback, and even less to do with the dogs. After two miles there was little difference between the coachers and the nine fresh cattle, so I left four men with the coachers and took Pludo and Punch and two dogs. The third dog was older and never liked leaving the cattle that were being driven.

We crossed the river and rode along the back of the wall as quietly as we could in order to see cattle before they heard or saw us. At the bottom of the rock wall it was like a tropical rainforest—big paperbark trees, four to five feet through their butts, and water trickling out of the rock walls. The temperature was about ten degrees cooler and there wasn't much humidity as the high sandstone wall seemed to funnel a light breeze along the river.

We had struck fresh tracks indicating a few bulls were around and we found where they had been eating the bark off the trees. The bark tastes salty and most times that you find paperbark, you find bulls. The bark has a lot of uses for Aboriginal people and they can light fires with it very quickly.

About a mile down the river we found four bulls chewing hunks of paperbark. The boys assured me that when the bulls spotted us they would charge across the river, which was only six inches deep, and then go into the cane grass on the other side, and most likely hide in it. A few minutes later, they did exactly as predicted.

We didn't go charging after them as a bull in hiding likes to draw first blood. If you come on to them quickly, they charge first and retreat second. Then they go for the belly of the horse. We could hear them in the cane grass. How many there were, no-one knew, so I sent the two dogs in. Seconds later, the cane grass erupted. None of the dogs was a barker and the cattle didn't know they were coming until they latched on to the hamstring. All we could do was follow the sound of the cane grass being trampled and hope that all the bulls were ahead of the dogs, and that we didn't meet any stragglers head-on. The bulls were heading across the cane grass, which was about 100 yards wide, making for open country to get away from the dogs.

On the other side of the cane grass there were bulls going everywhere. We saw four going in the long grass and there must have been fifteen others which came out in fifteen different directions. The dogs had three going close together, so we went after them. After a bit we had them running in one direction. There were some clumps of cane grass to go through before we could get them out into the open ground.

On the last patch of cane grass before the open ground, the two dogs had the bulls really wound up. We were cutting to the left to meet them on the other side when we struck a washaway with steep sides and had to go further down to a pad going across. On the other side, there were only two bulls in front of the dogs. We never did work out how the third one gave us the slip.

Meanwhile the two bulls were out on open country and I thought they wouldn't be too far from where the coachers were. Riding up to the bulls we put them into top gear for 50 yards until they were showing signs of tiring. One bull stumbled and ploughed along on his nose with his front legs buckled under him. By the time he regained his feet the dogs were gaining on him. The bull saw this and decided to stand and fight. His first lunge at the dogs was his first mistake. The old white dog, Bull by name, had him by the nose and Boofhead, the other dog, had him by the hamstring. I could see by the faces of Pludo and Punch that they were a little confused about what to do, so I waved them both on after the lead bull before he got his second wind.

I took my horse away from where the two dogs and the bull were dancing around. I left my horse behind some bushes to give the dogs plenty of time to educate the bull, who was by now just standing still and bellowing. Taking my leg strap, I walked up behind the bull. I intended to tie the bull's hind legs while he was standing up. I had done this many times before with these two dogs and I knew they wouldn't let go until I did.

Boof had a neat way of holding a bull by the hamstring. He grabbed it on one side then worked his body around to the other side. Then he leaned against the other leg, keeping his front feet pointed outwards to stop his toes from getting stomped on. When he got into position, both hind legs of the bull came together and it was simple to wrap the strap around them and pull tight. Then I took the tail of the bull and pulled so the hindquarters came over and the bull overbalanced and flopped on his side. Then I called the dogs off.

Bull terriers have interlocking fangs, with two large teeth on the top jaw and a single one on the bottom that close up together. When they get them locked up they cannot let go while the beast is pulling against them. Sometimes they don't want to let go, and teaching young dogs to hold on and then let go again has its problems.

Anyway, after tying up the bull the two dogs had caught, I went to see if Pludo and Punch had caught the other one. I found their horses not far up in the open country, but there was no sign of the boys or the bull. A bit further on I found a hat and, a little further, a shirt. I could see their tracks and also the bull's tracks. There was a little stony knob not far away and from there I could hear them singing out to one another.

I knew that if they were foot-walking the bull, he must have bailed up on them. They would have had one bloke on horseback and the other on foot in an effort to make the bull chase him. The one on the horse would then have had time to get off, run in and grab the bull's tail. The shirt and hat with the smell of 'man' would have been thrown under the bull's nose to make the bull charge. If one bloke has a chance to go for the tail, it can be very dangerous at times when a bull is in a fighting mood.

Just over the ridge, Pludo was on the tail. I pulled up and kept the dogs back while Pludo and the bull were having it out. Pludo was crouched fairly low to the ground and the bull must have got some of his wind back, for now both were spinning fast. If he could hold the weight of the bull long enough, sooner or later he would get the bull off balance. If he couldn't he would have to pick his time to let go so he could get a head start to the nearest leaning tree. Anyone coming to help right at that moment could do more damage than good. Pludo and Punch's horses were 100 yards away and there was no hope of taking the bull away.

I waited to see if the bull would come down or Pludo would let go. It seemed like minutes, but it was probably only a few seconds before I saw the bull's horn go into the ground and over he went. Pludo twisted his tail between the hind legs and Punch came racing in with a strap. The look on their faces showed how happy they were with the win. It was as good a catch as you would see anywhere.

Half a mile out we found the other boys waiting with the coachers, which we then drove back to the two bulls tied up. We tipped their horns and let them up into the coachers. We were within three-quarters of a mile of my camp and a mile from the station, and it was still only just after lunchtime.

Dimond had done a good job on the yards, so when we had all had food, we worked the mob around, settling down all the freshly caught beasts. Just before sundown I told the boys we would start yarding, in case we had trouble. Pludo rode across and asked if I was going to bring the dogs which I had tied up at dinnertime. I told him to start the cattle off and that I would let three fresh dogs go. I had three specially for yarding. One was a stumpy-tailed dog, called Stumpy, and the others were young dogs with a bit of pace.

All went well until we got to the gateway, then back they came. We turned the lead back to the gate the first time. The next time around, the cock-horn cow and two bulls went between the horses. The cock-horn cow made the mistake of trying to jump over the little dog, Stumpy. As she went in the air, he went for her bottom jaw. He was between her front legs and when they touched the ground, her nose and horns hit the ground together and her hindquarters kept on going. She landed with four feet in the air and she was about 30 feet in front of the gate. Stumpy held her bottom jaw. Both horns were buried in the dirt and he wasn't about to let her go. One of the boys had a strap on her before she knew what was happening.

Punch and I were on the shoulder-blade of a bull each and had a dog as a rear gunner, picking up one leg then the other, and their bellows were fairly flying out of them. I think they were glad to have a horse alongside to guide them. We pointed them at the gate and took them right into the coachers at a hand gallop. The whole mob went straight through the gate. Only the cock-horn cow lay outside in a strap.

Don Rory wanted to know if we would be able to drag the cow through the gate, but I said that we should get the horns off her and that Butch, the big red and white dog, would lead her in. I tied Stumpy to the fence as Butch wouldn't go on the nose while another dog was free. When they had dehorned the cow, we turned her around so she would be facing the gate. Taking her tail, I asked one of the boys to take off the strap. As she came to her feet, I held her facing the gate and called in Butch. He went straight for her nose and when I knew he had a good grip, I let go. The little white dog was wailing her tune as the cow tried to bunt Butch. He jumped back, still hanging on.

The white dog, Jill, was a heeler and when she bit, they really knew they had been bitten. Forward motion was started. Butch was on his hind legs letting the cow carry him along and Jill was making her keep in step through the gate and into the coachers, where they dropped off.

I think that if you had asked the boys to share their supper with the dogs that night, they would have let the dogs have first pick. They reckoned they hadn't seen dogs work cattle like that before.

Likewise, Laurie Morgan hadn't seen dogs working like that. A few weeks later we had an almost identical problem with another cow. Laurie was standing outside the yard when we put Butch on the cow and he came dancing through the gate, leading her. Laurie then started screaming about getting the dog off the cow. When no-one took any notice of him, he jumped into the yard and ran up, trying to kick the dog off the nose. The dog let go and the only thing in front of the cow was Laurie.

Just as well she had no horns, as she would have driven them clean through him. You could hear the wind come out of him when the cow butted him right in the solar plexus. Laurie held his stomach and crawled through the yard, heading for the homestead, without saying a word.

UNDERSTANDING THE WORKING BULL TERRIER

Ron Kerr, Borroloola, Northern Territory

Bull terriers have powerful tools of destruction in their big boof heads. They should only be used for the job they were bred for, which is biting.

They can be very docile, but they can also change to be the opposite. If they're tormented or someone has upset them, a bull terrier can lock on. While the person is trying to get away, the bull terrier can't leg go. His teeth are locked in there and they can really do a lot of damage on a human leg. As well as that, nine out of ten bull terriers close their eyes once they grab hold. They just shut their eyes and hang there.

A good working bull terrier is a valuable dog and it takes a long time to get a dog working properly. Because they are doing such dangerous work, many of them get injured and killed, so I try to have new dogs coming on continuously. The older a dog gets, the slower his reflexes, and he's more inclined to hang on a bit longer than necessary. If a bull can get him out in front while he's hanging on the nose, the bull's got a chance of ramming him into the dirt or swinging him against a tree. If you get a good dog, you really miss him if he gets killed.

Pure-bred bull terriers are only used on one side to start off a working breed. The other side can be pure blue heeler. I also like a second cross blue heeler as a foundation bitch to breed a bit of colour into the dogs. White pups often get sunburnt. With five-eighths on both sides, you get a good type of working dog— a lighter build for speed and travelling long distances, while retaining the jaw strength of the bull terrier.

If you have quiet cattle, you won't need to use bull terriers. Blue heelers will do. Wild cattle need heavy biters as they have to go through a crash course of education. Bull terriers also help take a lot of work off the horses.

The breeding pair should be the non-barking type. Pups should be taught to follow a horse at about ten or twelve weeks of age. I take them far enough away from home to ensure they follow me and don't try to return home.

If the breeder owns the bitch, she can play a major part in training the pups to follow a horse. She can also help get the pups used to cattle, which initially should always be without calves. Otherwise the cows charge at the dogs and can destroy a pup's confidence. Children should not be allowed to play with any of the pups undergoing training.

During training a few things must always be in the trainer's mind. Firstly, a pup should never be allowed to run in front of a horse and, secondly, it must always be under control. The first is simple to teach. I just ride through timber country and if a pup runs in front of the horse, without saying anything I just break off a small stick and throw it at him. If he does it again, I use a heavier stick or improve my aim. You may find it easier to teach him if you take him out on his own. You'll know you are making progress when the pup gets back behind the horse as soon as he hears the stick being broken off the tree.

The importance of training pups to stay behind a horse cannot be overemphasised. Usually riders have to get off the mark fast, but if a dog is running in front, it could bring down a horse and rider, or the dog could be injured. Dogs have to know their place. The right sized stick and aim will give you control without saying a word. A fellow bellowing at his dog is worse than a barking dog.

Never force a young dog to go in on cattle. He will go onto them when he is ready. You may make the mistake of encouraging a pup to get in the way of a dog that is working, leaving the older dog no leg room and no way of escape from the horns. Alternatively, you could make the pup start barking before he gets a chance to latch on.

You should never hit a dog to get it off a beast. If you do, you could end up defeating the purpose you bred the dog for, by making it scared of latching on. I like to put the beast on the ground and have someone hold it down. I then take a strap and put it around the dog's neck. With the other hand, I push the buckle down tight and cut off the dog's wind. When the dog gulps for air, I pull the dog's jaws clear of the beast and hold him away. When the dog realises the beast is going nowhere, he is prepared to stand there and watch. It is important to keep him out of reach of the beast and call the dog behind. By now, with the beast quiet and restrained, he is able to hear you if he wants to. Breeders and trainers should be aware that bull terriers have a hearing problem—or they are just headless. Avoiding the pure breed solves some of the problems.

I also teach dogs from a young age to be aware of the stockwhip. I crack this over their heads to break up any fights among them around the camp. A whip is the safest way, as it is hopeless trying to pull them apart. When there is a mob of dogs, you could finish up with a dog hanging off the seat of your trousers.

We are also careful to tie up the dogs before feeding ourselves. Dogs are a problem in any camp when you are cooking over a fire. With open pots and pans around, it's easy to end up with a mob of pan-licking dogs.

Mavis devised a quick method of training dogs not to do this. It might sound tough, but you can't have dogs eating your tucker when you've got no spare supplies, and the men have to be fed. She used to have a billy of hot water on the fire all the time and, right from when they were pups, she would flick a spoonful of hot water on them if they got too close. It worked all right. If the dogs were loose, you would see them lined up twenty paces from the fire or food table, and they wouldn't come any closer. There were also very few fights over any scraps of food thrown to them.

When they're not working, you should tie your dogs to a tree to ensure they get a good rest after working all day and don't spend their time fighting. And leave them tied up until you've settled your horse next day. I've seen fellows let their dogs off the chain before catching their horses in the morning. When they've climbed on their horse, which might be stiff or bad-tempered and not going well for the rider, the last thing they want is a bull terrier hanging off the horse's flank.

Working bull terrier cross dogs have been taught to grab hold of anything madder than themselves. No-one has yet taught them that a bucking horse with a rider on top should be excluded.

199

STUMPY

Ron Kerr, Borroloola, Northern Territory

We always preferred storms to come in late afternoon as it would give us time to be dry again by the time the sun went down. Night storms coming in on strong winds meant you would have to get up and roll up your swags and wait out the storm, which could last two hours. After a hard day's riding and throwing bulls, we needed our sleep. Plus during daytime storms, every man was already mounted and able to hold the cattle in the open—far safer than trying to rely on a yard holding them, which would be the case at night.

Late in 1966 we were mustering wild cattle on Balbirini station not far from the McArthur River. I had started the season with a pack of thirteen bull terriers that I used to pull down bulls so I could catch them, tip their horns and force them to join up with our special quiet mob of cattle, the coachers. I only worked two bull terriers at a time and spelled the rest back at the camp. It was tough work for the dogs and very dangerous. By December, at the end of the bull-catching season, I often didn't have any catching dogs left because they were all injured or had been killed.

The first storm for the season hit us at about 2.30 one afternoon and lasted for an hour. It couldn't have been a better time as we had just thrown about six head and they were still tied up in the leg straps. The weather had been hot and sticky and we still had to manhandle the cattle in straps. As the storm broke we were able to get the cattle up and into the coachers in the rain without the danger of overheating them. If this was going to be the pattern of the storms, it would suit us.

It was one of those six bulls we were letting up that rushed Stumpy, the stumpy-tailed dog who was looking for shelter from the rain. He didn't hear or see the bull coming before it tossed him higher than a man on horseback. He landed on his side and I could see blood, but before I could get to him he was up and going back at the bull. This just happened to be the only bull we had ever let up with his horns on as we had broken the horn saw on the previous bull and the spare was back in the packs at the camp.

200

The dog had the bull by the nose and I sang out to the boy that the dog was hurt and to get the bull tied up again so we could get the dog away. He now had part of his stomach sticking out and as soon as the boy pulled down the bull I grabbed the dog, turned him upside down and carried him away from the cattle. Holding him down I could see the running gut, the small intestine, wasn't busted. The horn had pierced the skin, which had rolled with the thrust of the horn, then had gone into the stomach. I poked the gut back in and the skin rolled over the hole in the stomach wall. The two holes were not in line with each other, which meant the wound would stay relatively clean and secure. As it was still pouring rain, it was also fairly well washed.

The dog was now cold, so he was feeling the stiffness that comes with injury. He went into the long grass and lay down to lick his stomach. I left him there after making sure the bleeding had stopped. I intended to come back later, when I was sure the boys weren't going to have any more trouble with the cattle, and carry him on the horse. After moving on about two miles, and judging the cattle were under control, I rode back to Stumpy— but he was gone.

After singing out to him and riding through the grass, I couldn't find him. I thought he must have headed off towards the camp at the yards, about two miles the other way. I went back to the cattle thinking he would be better making it back to camp at his own pace. Sometimes when the dogs were hot, I would leave them and they would come into camp after dark. The only thing that worried me was that the smell of the tracks was washed out by then, but it wasn't far to where we were now camped compared with where we had come from that day with the horses. He would know where he was once he came onto the pad going to the waterhole. It was 30 miles back to the main camp.

That night the dog didn't turn up, nor the next morning. So I rode back to where he'd got horned and searched again. There was still no sign of him. We camped another day and the dog never came, so we moved camp toward the station as we had had another storm about the same time of the day and there would be cattle walking towards where the storms had come from, straight into the wind.

We came onto the edge of some country we had previously burnt, and already there was green feed about two inches high and plenty of cattle tracks. Just short of where we had built a yard we found probably the biggest mob we had struck at one time. There were 60 to 70 head of cattle—about the same sized mob as the coachers. They were just coming off water when we topped a ridge that had a sandy depression on top where we blocked the coachers. We left three boys with the coachers and went back down over the ridge we had just come up and rode downwind of the cattle.

Using the cover of the timber along the creek we were able to come up behind the cattle, which we started towards the coachers. Being full of water they were completely out of wind getting the half-mile up to the coachers. In the mob there were six big bullocks we thought we would have trouble with. All were about ten years old and still fat. Holding them in the coachers we could see the BAT brand standing out and knew that they were Tarwallah bullocks that Fred Ellis had owned a few years back. We had picked up odd bullocks of his before. If these six handled as quietly as the others had, they would give us no trouble.

True to form, as we moved them off to see how they would go, the six bullocks moved as one, coming out into the lead and walking right up behind my horse, following every move the horse made around logs or trees. As they were only three feet behind my horse, I let them walk a bit faster, then stopped to make sure that they knew I was there. All six would stop, only moving again when I moved. When I rode around a fallen tree they never lost a step turning after the horse. When a beast from behind looked like passing them, they threw their heads sideways and gave the beast a bump with those long sharp horns. Even the young bulls gave the bullocks room. The size of those bullocks attracted respect from the other cattle as if they were some sort of armoured tank.

Reaching the yard I rode through the gate and the bullocks never slackened their pace. They came straight through and right across the yard. I think all the fresh cattle were in the yard before they even knew a yard was there. We cut the mob back to 40 head of coachers, including the bullocks, and started back up the McArthur River to Bessie Springs. It was three days of mustering before we got to our camp and again the bullocks proved their worth—we got back to Bessie Springs with 60 head, an increase of twenty, plus two more brumbies joined the horse plant.

When we reached the new camp about twelve miles north of

where he had got hooked, Stumpy met us. He was as lively as a cricket, with only a small lump to show where the bull had got him. He had returned to the camp a few days after he had been injured, and Mavis and the kids had looked after him. I was pretty pleased to see him as he was a particularly good 'noser'. I had never seen him get flipped off a nose. He could even drop a bull to the ground by pulling the bull's head down between its front legs to throw him off balance. That dog could hold them down long enough for me to put a strap on their back legs. I thought so much of the dog that he was my main breeder.

The following year I went up to Nathan River station on the Limmon Bight River, very rough creek country. To get there we had to swim stock horses, pack horses and dogs over nine creeks and rivers. Among the dogs were two of my best, Stumpy and one we called Blue Bitch.

Within about six miles of our destination two brumbies came out of the scrub. They were good types and we decided to run these in as they'd be a couple more breakers and could join the horse plant. I was on a good horse and was able to head them off all right. Stumpy and Blue Bitch came too, but they couldn't keep up. I lost sight of them when they dropped back. That night we put all the horses, including the two brumbies, in a holding paddock, and settled down to wait for the dogs to show up—but they never did. Next day I went back as far as Rosie Creek, thinking that they could have gone back to where we had our last camp. Since it had been raining each night, there were no tracks for them to follow and I didn't find them back there.

Six weeks later the local copper sent a message that my two dogs had turned up at the police station—160 miles back at Borroloola. They had gone back through all those creeks and over that tough, stony country. The message came through on a two-way radio at Nathan River station, so I told them to hang on to the dogs and look after them until I returned.

It was quite a few weeks before we got back. It was then that I found out that both dogs had eaten a poisoned goat carcass. It had been put out for the dingoes which had been killing goats kept to provide milk for the Aboriginal people around the town. The stumpy-tailed dog died, but Blue Bitch survived.

The death of Stumpy meant the last of that good strain I had been breeding from. But I got hold of more good dogs, trained them up and started over again for the next season. It's a story that just repeats itself.

LADY AND RED

Ron Kerr, Borroloola, Northern Territory

In 1949, when I was thirteen, my father, my brother Colin and I were returning to Scone after taking a mob of cows and calves from Aberdeen in the Hunter Valley to Quirindi, up over the Dividing Range. I was chief cook and bottle washer. Colin was horse-tailer, responsible for getting the horses unhobbled and brought to the camp by daylight.

When the cows and calves came off camp just after daylight, and after the wagon horse was caught and tied up, Colin would have breakfast. The rest of the horses would be put into the mob with the cattle and driven along with them, and Colin and Dad would leave camp. I would be left to wash up, pack the wagonette, top up the water keg and harness up the wagonette horse to follow the cattle to the dinner camp.

Dad had a red kelpie sheepdog that never missed a droving trip, whether he was needed or not. His name matched his colour— Red—and he worked either sheep or cattle. Red had taken a holiday on this trip because Dad wouldn't let him near the cattle. There were a lot of old cows who hated dogs. They really gave him a rally around the flats, protecting their calves. So instead, Red trotted along under the wagonette, taking in the sights.

Dad reckoned that every time Red came near the cattle he lost about an hour of travelling time. The old cows would chase Red then go back into the mob in a panic searching for their calves, which would be halfway into the middle of the mob. The cows would then have to sniff every calf to get the right smell.

Along with us in the horse plant we had Mum's pride and joy, a brown mare called Lady which she drove in the sulky. She

204

was also Red's best mate. They both used to take us to the pictures on any Saturday night when we were at home—a place a bit of a way out of Scone. On those nights out, we would unhitch Lady from the sulky and tie her to a tree with a nosebag of chaff and oats slipped over her ears. Red always sat down alongside Lady and we knew they would be there for the trip home.

So after this droving job, we came back over the range past Murrundi. We camped just short of the Burning Mountain, about one good day's travel from Scone.

Next morning Colin brought the horses into camp with the news that Lady was missing. Dad had already eaten so he saddled a horse, telling us she couldn't be far and for us to pack the wagonette while he searched. Horses often feed off on their own, so we weren't too worried, just annoyed that we had to waste time looking for her.

As the foothill of the range was fairly stony, even a full plant of horses didn't leave many tracks. One horse would therefore be really hard to pick up, so Dad arrived back at camp about dinnertime without Lady. We then informed him that Red was also missing and that it seemed highly likely to us that Lady and Red were together and had headed towards Scone.

We arrived home just before dark and the first question we asked Mum was whether Lady and Red had turned up, but she hadn't seen them. We searched for them for two weeks and couldn't understand what could have happened to them.

Three weeks after they had gone missing from the camp, a car pulled up at home and a bloke asked Dad if he had lost a brown mare and a red dog. They had been up at his place for the past two weeks, where the mare had found some pretty good feed. The dog wouldn't leave the mare's side, so this man had taken food out to him.

Next day Colin and I rode 40 or 50 miles to the foot of the range to collect them. They were both in good shape. The dog was pleased to see us, but he still wouldn't leave the mare's side. It is unusual for a dog to attach itself so closely to a horse, but we've had it happen more than once.

Another dog, Emmie, was so fond of the wagonette horses that she always used to trot in the small space between them, right under the centre pole. We couldn't understand why she never got trodden on. She seemed to be tuned into their minds and to know when they were turning.

PART 10

OUT ON THE TRACK

The big sheep and cattle droves are a thing of the past, but that doesn't mean that the dogs of the bush don't keep travelling. They hit the track to search for their masters. They cross rivers to meet their heart's desire. They keep a weary truckie, the modern drover, company in the front seat as the miles roll by. And they also ride pillion on a motorbike like the best of the Hell's Angels, even in defiance of the law, and sometimes without permission—like Jet and the postie.

Those epic droving trips, however, from which the legends grow, are when a dog comes into his own. Lionel Hewitt tells of taking sheep on the road in the drought of 1958, and how Rusty averted tragedy only to suffer agonies of his own.

Then there was Peter Richardson's trip in the 1940s with sheep destined for a ship at Onslow. When the droving cart broke down his dog—also called Rusty—was left behind, too footsore to continue and not expected to find his way home. Life can be terribly unforgiving for dogs and people out on the track.

DROVING UP TO ONSLOW

Peter Richardson, Toodyay, Western Australia

I was in the pastoral game in the Gascoyne for a good number of years and owned and saw many dogs. This story is about a red cloud dog of mine called Rusty.

In the late 1940s, when I was 23, four of us were contracted by Elders to take a mob of sheep from Carnarvon to Onslow. It was a distance of more than 400 miles on back tracks to collect wethers from properties along the way, to be shipped to the Middle East. We collected the first mob from a property called Wandagee. From there we went up the track to Midialia, Williambury and Lyndon to end up with about 2,000 head. We followed the Lyndon River most of the way, and as it was winter we had plenty of water for the trip, which took in total about five weeks. For most of the way, the going was terribly rough.

209

Each man had a dog and of the four, Rusty was the best. As well as our stock horses, we had two pack horses and a cart pulled by two other horses and a mule. On the cart we carried all the swags, cooking gear and food, as well as big rolls of hessian with which we made temporary night yards for the sheep using steel droppers to keep it in place.

About twenty miles out of Lyndon, the track was so rocky and rough that our cart broke an axle and fell apart. We had no choice but to load all the gear from the cart onto the two cart horses and the mule. Since we had no spare pack saddles, we had to use the most extraordinary improvisations imaginable. We folded the hessian over each animal and bundled droppers each side and tied the rest of the gear on top. In this fashion, we continued on with the sheep to Onslow.

Once we'd delivered the sheep and rested up, we set out on our long trip back to Carnarvon to return the plant. Normally the dogs would have travelled home on the cart after their weeks of work, but because we had no cart, they had to walk. About halfway between Onslow and Lyndon, the dogs were so tired and footsore, they could not travel any further. We couldn't carry them on the horses because of all the extra gear we had to carry, so we had no choice but to leave them there on the track—much to my sorrow. Some weeks later we reached Carnarvon and I returned to Wooramel, where I was the overseer.

About two or three weeks later, I got a phone call from Tim D'Arcy, the manager at Lyndon, to say my dog Rusty had turned up there. I felt this was remarkable as he had obviously pushed on after me as best he could. He must have come the best part of 100 miles.

Tim D'Arcy put him on the mail truck and I picked him up in Carnarvon. We enjoyed many a good year together after I thought I had lost him. None of the other dogs made it back.

A CHORD OF
UNDERSTANDING

H H Cay, Coonabarabran, New South Wales

First appearances were not promising, but I was desperate. Next day
I was starting work as boss musterer at Portland Downs on the Barcoo.
It was a place of 250,000 acres and I had no dog. What was worse,
I had sandy blight and couldn't see more than 150 yards.

The dog, called Binky, was slate grey in colour, dejected in
appearance and his ears were blocked and swollen by a massive
infestation of blood-sucking ticks. Nevertheless, he greeted me gamely,
wagging his tail if not with enthusiasm then at least with courtesy.

'Yeah,' I said. 'I'll take him.' I thought we might just make a team:
he could hardly hear and I could hardly see.

That was the inauspicious start to a friendship that lasted for eight
years. It stretched from the gibber plains of central Queensland to
the high hills of the Hunter Valley and beyond. And what a team
we made! I never had a better mate, four-legged or two, while Binky
had a boss who knew and loved him for what he was—the best,
gamest kelpie ever bred on the western plains.

Once well-cared for, his coat was shiny. And go . . . that dog could
outwork the rest of the dogs in camp and leave them belly-deep
in the bore drains. By the time Binky was two years old, I was the
envy of the stock camp. Some dogs can be taught, some have to
be bullied, but Binky, well, he was a natural. He knew when to
stop, what to do, and could out-think the crankiest ewe. Binky was
always a bit deaf but that didn't worry either of us. We were linked
by an umbilical cord of understanding that surpassed words, whistles
or signals.

Years passed. I left central Queensland and crossed the border into
the south-west of New South Wales. Binky and I hitched a ride
in a cattle truck down to the Hunter Valley. Barsham, a steep property
on the mountain slopes of the Hunter, was a massive contrast with
the plains of Queensland. What a challenge for the poor dog. But
I needn't have worried. Once he had mastered the art of lifting his
leg on a slippery slope, he had no problems. Instinctively he worked

wider, always blocking the cunning, paddock-wide wethers, never panicking the ewes and lambs.

Again the years passed and we were still inseparable. Only the scenery was different. Now the cliffs and rugged ranges of Arizona on Upper Mauls creek in the Manilla district replaced the green Hunter hills. In dog terms, Binky was getting on in years. He was worn by the hot Queensland sun and frozen by the cold nights of the mountains. But what a mate. He was always waiting as I tightened the girth straps, though now he trotted an inch behind the heels of my horse and left the younger dogs to cast ahead.

One morning Binky didn't answer my whistle. I found him stiff as a board under the saddle rack. Thirty years have passed, and I still dream about the dog that shared my mustering years.

THANKS A LOT, MICK

Neil Macpherson, Tamworth, New South Wales

There is no doubt in my mind that a dog is surely man's best friend, but not just any dog—a kelpie, a working sheepdog. In my life on the land I have had control of numerous sheepdogs—some good, some not so good—but I am going to try to relate a story about one of my highlights of the sheepdog world.

I had got myself a new truck in 1965 and went stock carrying, something I had always wanted to do. A chap from Bendemeer gave me a small red kelpie pup. I liked the small breed of kelpie because, as truck dogs, they could manoeuvre around the pens and run in under the sheep easily. This pup's brother and sister had been sold for high prices and finished up in New Zealand. So I had high hopes for Sandy, as I called him. As time went on, I was proved correct.

Sandy was put in that new truck when he was six weeks old. He sat or lay on the floor and later, when he got a bit older, he sat on the pasenger's side which I had covered with a blanket. In those days heating wasn't considered necessary in a truck, but one dog was as good as a heater. Sandy travelled in that truck for five and half years and was never sick or smelly. Mind you, every time I got out, so did my dog.

I needed to spend every Monday at the Tamworth saleyards where about 10,000 sheep and lambs went through each time. Among other jobs, I would cart about six or seven loads of sheep to the abattoirs. Sandy and I could load these with the minimum of work and trouble. He was an outstanding truck dog. I would leave the side window down when I arrived at the saleyards and Sandy would stay in the truck until I gave him his special whistle. Although there would be 100 trucks and about 200 dogs and all the noise of the sheep, gates banging and men shouting, he would somehow find me.

One day Sandy didn't answer my call, so I asked around: 'Have you seen my little red dog?' Everyone knew him but nobody had seen him that day.

After some time, maybe two hours, I was convinced he had jumped into some other red truck and that I wouldn't see him again. The next thing, along came Sandy, full of apologies and very wet and tonguing. He had just had a cool-off in the trough. Mick Pullman, one of Jack Smyth's right-hand men, came hobbling after the dog and said to me, 'Thanks for the loan of your dog, Mac. He is a real little beauty. He and I have just drafted 2,000 sheep on our own.' That was high praise indeed, because Jack Smyth was second only to Sir Sid Kidman as a cattle dealer and dealt in hundreds of thousands of sheep, so Mick would have seen a lot of dogs in his time.

But thanks a lot, indeed, Mick. Despite the flattery, my dog had done a day's work for someone else and I still had six or seven loads of sheep to put on my own truck. Nevertheless, I was proud of my dog, but he was pretty tired that night.

Sandy was never tied up in later life. He always slept near that truck and everywhere the truck went, so did Sandy—even carting wheat from local farms into the silos in Tamworth.

When eventually I sold the truck and business, the buyer turned to me after he had given me the cheque. 'Righto, Mac,' he said, 'how much do you want for the little red dog?'

I was moving to town and town life is no life for a dog, let alone a working sheepdog, so I informed the new truck owner that he didn't have enough money in the bank to buy Sandy. But if he promised to give him a good life and let him ride in his truck, then he could have him for nothing.

I saw that dog ten years later when he was very old. He answered me when I called him and we had a bit of a cuddle-up. He was happy.

SITTING PILLION WITH THE POSTIE

Helen Firth, Nambour, Queensland

Jet was a highly strung black kelpie of ours that spent many an hour running beside a horse or riding pillion on a bike. She was an excellent working dog and devoted to her master.

Many years ago my husband and I went on a working holiday. We took Jet and her daughter Scubie, whose father had been a bull terrier. We decided to work in Brisbane for a couple of months, so we moved into a caravan park in Hawthorne, on the banks of the Brisbane River. The caravan park wouldn't allow the dogs to stay there even though we promised faithfully that they would not be a problem and would stay tied up whenever we weren't there.

Next door to the caravan park was a shipbuilding yard, so we approached the people there and asked if it would be OK to tie the dogs there. They would be in easy reach of us for feeding and regular exercise. They agreed to the arrangement, so we took the dogs over and tied them up where they wouldn't be in the way. We stressed to them that the dogs should not be let off under any circumstances.

The next afternoon, when we went to take them for a run, we heard the following story. City people, being what they are, couldn't resist feeling sorry for the dogs, so while the men were sitting about at smoko break, they decided to let them have a run and some scraps. Scubie didn't leave their side because of the attraction of the food, but Jet, being the highly strung type, decided to have a sniff about the yards.

She then heard the sound of a motorbike—actually it was the postie, delivering mail. Something must have twigged in her mind and made her think that it was her master. So off she went, running after him. A few of the employees started after her on foot.

It must have looked like classic comedy with the motorbike tootling along, followed by a black dog with several men running behind her in frantic pursuit. She led them a merry chase through the streets of Hawthorne before she managed to spring up on the bike with the postie—who hadn't been aware he was being chased. Imagine his amazement to be going along, quietly delivering mail, and suddenly to find a strange dog sitting pillion on his bike.

She finally disembarked and managed to find her way back to the shipyards with the men hot on her heels. Meanwhile, Scubie was still having smoko with the rest of the employees. They didn't let the dogs off again, but thoroughly enjoyed telling us all about Jet's ride.

IN CONTEMPT OF COURT

George Stewart, Toowoomba, Queensland

I was acting as Presbyterian minister in Mt Isa in July and August of 1991. While I was there I met Bill Hartley, who had formerly been self-employed as a bore-drain cleaner in the Goondiwindi district during the late 1960s and 1970s. As I had been a minister in Goondiwindi from 1956 to 1960, I knew the district well. Accordingly, Bill Hartley and I found we had a great deal in common regarding the district and its people. Bill, now retired, told me of an incident that took place while he was bore-drain cleaning on the New South Wales side of the Macintyre River west of Goondiwindi.

Bore drains run out at long distances from artesian bore heads which are, in most cases, never turned off. The water coming up from the artesian basin is extremely hot as it emerges above ground. Bore drains serve two purposes—to take the water considerable distances to stock for drinking, and to allow time and distance for the water to cool sufficiently so stock are able to drink it.

Naturally, over a period of time the drains tend to clog up with vegetation and silt and require attention to keep the water flowing. Bill Hartley's job was to maintain the drains. To save time and money commuting from where he was working to where he was living, he purchased a small motorcycle. Because of his age, he was given a restricted licence which prevented him from carrying a passenger. However, Bill was devoted to his kelpie dog Booker, who Bill found invaluable for clearing stock, especially sheep, away from the drains when he was cleaning them. Accordingly, Booker soon became Bill's pillion passenger.

At the time there was a somewhat officious police officer aptly nicknamed Radar by the locals. One day on the Mungindi road, Radar stopped Bill riding his motorcyle with his dog sitting behind as a pillion passenger. He checked Bill's licence and pointed out the nature of the restriction and informed him that he was not qualified to carry any passenger and that included his dog. Then and there the dog was removed from the pillion seat and Bill continued on his way at a speed slow enough for the dog to run along beside the bike.

When Bill had gone a mile or so further and was out of sight of officialdom, he stopped and Booker once more resumed his customary seat. However, the zealous officer of the law, suspecting such an event would occur, had followed Bill. Coming up quickly behind the bike, he pulled Bill over and promptly issued a ticket for a traffic offence.

Bill decided to contest the indictment and on the day set down for the hearing at the Boggabilla Court House, he came armed with Booker. As Bill ascended the steps of the court house, an attendant stopped him and told him the dog was not allowed into the court. When Bill informed him that the dog was the chief figure in the case, he was somewhat grudgingly allowed to proceed. Booker immediately showed his contempt for the court by lifting his leg against the doorpost as he entered the building.

Bill's appeal was disallowed and he duly paid the fine. However, the law was seen by the locals for the ass which it so often is and Radar's reputation was further dented.

STOPPED IN HIS TRACKS

Dorothy Harrison, Geraldton, Western Australia

My son owned a very good black shorthaired collie–kelpie dog called Pedro. He was never far from his heels in crowded places like sheep sales, bars or on beaches. He could handle a single sheep or a thousand, and would run along the backs of sheep to force the lead when drafting, filling the shearing pens or loading trucks. He would grab the front leg and toss a sheep that needed treatment when the animal was pointed out to him.

Throughout the district he was well known and when he mysteriously disappeared one day, my son spent weeks phoning and visiting farms for miles around, hoping for a lead. Advertisements placed in papers brought no answers.

Eighteen months later fencers on a large property 50 kilometres away were having lunch in an out-camp when a strange dog, hungry and thirsty and with a piece of rope around his neck, walked in. They took him home, fed him and, after testing him out, the manager took him on as his new working dog.

I sighted the dog with others on this manager's utility one day when he was in town. I was sure it was Pedro for he had ruptured a salivary gland under his jaw when he was younger, and the dog I saw had the same affliction.

On hearing this my son travelled to the manager's property early next morning and waited in his car for him to arrive and give out instructions for the day to his men. The manager whistled and half a dozen dogs raced for his vehicle. My son gave his particular whistle, which caused Pedro to stop in his tracks. On hearing the same whistle a second time, he raced back and jumped through the open window of the car onto my son's lap for a joyous reunion.

All who witnessed this were satisfied that it was the dog stolen eighteen months earlier. It was deduced that he was trying to find his way home when he met the fencers in their remote camp.

ABSENCE MAKES THE DOG WORK BETTER

Margaret Bell, Taralga, New South Wales

In the early days of the last war, my husband Joe left our property to join the Light Horse and start military training.

Joe had a particularly good and faithful sheepdog called Tong. He was a cheeky little fellow, a dedicated worker and one who knew every gate and paddock of the family properties. One place was ten miles from Goulburn and another, newly acquired place was about 50 miles to the north.

Tong always thought he knew more about mustering, droving and working sheep than any man, and often he was right about that. But when he was wrong it took an awful lot of whistling and shouting before he would bow to his master's commands. He also would always rather work sheep than have a meal any day!

When Joe joined up, Tong could not comprehend the absence of his working mate. Any opportunity he got, he would head off to the other property to find him. He would wait by the front gate of one or the other property until someone found him and tied him up again. The two old retainers on the newly acquired property were amazed when Tong first turned up obviously looking for Joe. In those days there were no telephones and mail only once a week, so there was very little contact between properties.

When Joe returned, Tong seemed to be transformed into an absolutely new dog in his sheep work. Instead of always thinking he knew best, he became a devout follower of Joe, only too ready to do as he was asked.

QUEENS OF THE ROAD

Fred Eldering, Crookwell, New South Wales

I was returning home after a sheep show around midnight, towing the canvas-covered trailer behind my ute. Beside me, stretched out on the seat with her head resting on my leg, was my old border collie bitch, Stardy—still travelling after eighteen years, mother of many champions and veteran of many sheepdog exhibitions and trials.

Since 1947, a Stardy had always been on the front seat of the truck or ute with me, keeping me company during the long, lonely hours on the road trucking cattle and sheep. They all carried the stud names of Greyleigh Stardust, but the Stardy on my seat that night was the last of the original strain that had formed the basis of my stud, the oldest registered working border collie stud in Australia, founded in 1947.

The lights of the ute shone down the highway and I fondled the old girl's ear and smiled. Coming up behind me, I could see in the side mirror the fairyland lights of a big rig. I pulled down the mike of the CB: ' You're clear, mate,' I told him. The rig passed and pulled over to the left and back came the words of thanks from the driver.

The CB crackled again. 'That you, old Freddie?' the driver said. It was an old mate, Mac. So as the kilometres rolled by, the two of us, whose paths had not crossed for a few years, chatted on.

'I don't suppose old Stardy is still on the seat beside you, Freddy?' he said. 'She would have passed on by now. I would sure like a quid for every mile she's shared in the cab with you.'

Back went my reply that she was indeed sleeping in her usual place. We both swung off the highway and drew up in the parking area of a truck stop. The rig driver came over and we greeted each other warmly, then he gently lifted the old dog from the seat and hugged her before placing her on the ground for her wee break.

Inside the truck stop, the woman on duty insisted on taking 'the offsider', old Stardy, her usual two sausages—before she even got our black coffees. We settled down for a bit of a chat and, seeing the fuss that everyone had made over my old dog, I told Mac the story about how I had got a replacement for old Stardy, for the time when she would no longer be with me in the cabin.

About eight months earlier, Stardy had picked up a virus and was

219

very sick. The vet had advised putting her down, but I took her home, treated her and nursed her through her illness. One day when she looked like she was never going to get back on her feet, I whispered to her to hang on. 'I don't want to lose you yet, old girl,' I told her. 'Who will be my truck dog? I've got no-one to take your place.'

Extraordinarily, some weeks later my top breeding bitch, who was then twelve years old and had not been in season for over three years, came on heat and mated with a young dog I had. She never looked pregnant at any time, yet presented me with two beautiful pups and reared them well. In all my years of breeding dogs, I had never seen an old bitch come on heat after such a break.

When the pups were ten days old, I was looking at them when the old girl walked in. 'Mac, you know how the old girl is with pups that are not hers once they are three weeks old?' I said. 'She savages them.

'Well, I picked up the bitch pup, showed it to her and told her to look after her as she was my next truck dog. She nuzzled the pup, put her head under my arm and looked up as if to say, "I understand boss".

'From the time the pup was a month old, she shared the old girl's mattress, sleeping between her legs and sharing her feed. Old Stardy never once snapped or snarled at the pup, the way she does with all the other youngsters. When the pup was old enough, Stardy allowed her the privilege of sharing her rug on the front seat of the ute—a thing that was taboo to all other dogs. She had never let another dog into the front of the ute or truck before.

'The pup is now four months old. The old girl has taught her how to behave in the cab—a quick snarl usually pulls her into line. The only reason the pup is not with Stardy and me tonight is that I have been away for a few days and my grand-daughter insisted the pup stayed with her.

'So, Mac, although I thought I knew animals, I cannot explain how it is that both bitches seemed to work together to produce a new truck dog for me. It was as if they knew of the big hole there would be in my life with the loss, eventually, of the old girl.'

We parted after we had finished our meal, but not before Mac had opened the door of the ute and fondled the old dog's head. 'See you, old girl. If not, thanks for the memories.'

Stardy lived on for another year and was nineteen when she died. The new truck dog carries the name of Little Stardy, but we also know her as The Miracle, because that's what we reckon she is.

I am nearly 70 now, but I still do sheepdog exhibitions in Sydney at the Castle Hill Show, and Little Stardy is one of my stars. I also give overseas visitors at conferences a look at how our dogs work. One of my recent escapades was to drive some sheep into the Regent Hotel in Sydney, put them into the lift, then shepherd them among the tables in the dining room where the delegates were enjoying dinner. That went down really well!

In 1979 and 1981 I won the Australian Championships at Mudgee with Greyleigh Mist and Greyleigh Snoopy—but I still reckon the way my old dogs produced a truck dog for me was one of the really special things that has happened in my life.

WHY GET WET?

Jack Rossiter, Bellbrook, New South Wales

We live on the wrong side of the river in flood time, and on one occasion we had a power failure. It was necessary for a couple of county council men to be transported by boat to attend to repairs.

On arriving at the river bank, the two men and a dog waited for us to pick them up. The dog was the first in the boat. When we reached our side, the dog was first out.

That afternoon when we arrived at the river to transport the men back, there was the dog, sitting on the bank waiting to get across. He was first into the boat again.

As the men left the boat we mentioned their dog. They assured us it was not theirs and that they had never seen it before. When talking about the incident some days later, we found that the dog had come from about three miles away and had been visiting a lady friend on our side of the river.

Now a dog would be just too silly if he swam a flooded river twice when there was a boat service running to a suitable timetable, wouldn't he? So there he was, home and dry, after a pleasant day's dalliance—and he went back to doing his cattle work the next day.

The strange part about it was that the dog, from all accounts, had never been in a boat before.

SERVED ON A PLATE

Marjorie Noll, Ballina, New South Wales

As soon as the working dog's pups were ready for solid food, my
father trained them never to take a bait.

The food and bones were always placed on a dish. After three
or four days of getting the pups to eat from the dish, my father
would then wrap some tobacco in the meat and throw it to the
pups on the ground. This would make them very sick. Sometimes
he would have to do this two or three times, but eventually the
pups would learn never to take food unless it was on a plate. This
meant he could take the dogs away droving for many days at a
time without their ever taking a bait.

When I lived in Caringbah with my husband, I trained our house
dog the same way. Even though there might have been bones and
food on the ground and he was hungry, he would never touch them
unless they were on a plate.

THE 'BLUE BLOOD' OF
THE BORE DRAIN

Lionel Hewitt, Kapunda, South Australia

I was travelling by car to St George in Queensland from Southampton
station, where I was a jackeroo in 1952. By the 17-mile bore drain
out of St George was the poorest long-legged brindle pup one would
ever expect to see in a lifetime. The drain was dry so I gave him
a drink from my waterbag and left him there.

On my way home that night, I found him sitting in the middle of the road. He was so weak that as his tail wagged, his whole body wagged too. So I picked him up and took him home with me. The boss, George Watson, came out on my arrival and immediately told me, 'Take that Alsatian and shoot the thing before it starts killing.'

It took a lot of explaining that I thought he was a kelpie-German collie cross, but I convinced the boss and so began an association that lasted for fifteen years. After a month of good feed, Rusty, the name I gave him to suit his colour, was fit enough to start work. I took him and another dog to muster the big back paddock. As happy as Larry he was to follow the horse.

I found the first mob of sheep at about 7 am, and they promptly headed for the mulga. My other dog went to the lead to head them off and Rusty went in behind them, barking wildly. He scattered them for miles. I ran him down on the horse, whistling and yelling, but to no avail. So I left him and mustered with just the one dog— and got home in the dark as usual. It wasn't a good beginning.

At about 9 pm the station dogs all started barking, so I went out and quietened them. It was, of course, Rusty returning home. I took him by the ear, shook him and carried him to the chain.

Next morning I had to go and get the sheep we had lost because of his actions. I took Rusty again, plus my .22 rifle. I found a mob and sent the good dog to the lead. This time, Rusty went with him, straight to the lead, stopped when I whistled—and brought the mob back. He never ever gave any more trouble or bit a sheep for the rest of his life.

Rusty worked with me on stations until 1958, when we had to take mobs of sheep on the road because of drought. We were heading towards St George on one trip and I made a habit of going on ahead to cut scrub for the mob. Rusty would take care of the lead. Not far from the bore drain where I had found him back in 1952, the dog started barking furiously, as though he had found a wild pig. When I investigated, I found the corpse of a man which had been in the sun for a week. After reporting our find, we went on to St George, Nindigully and Talwood, then to Boomi and Garah in New South Wales, travelling six miles a day or less.

The Macintyre River had flooded a lot of country and we saw the first grass in the six months we had been on the road. We agisted the sheep on the stock route and camped in one spot for three months. Rusty would go to the lead every evening and bring the sheep back to camp.

One evening a violent storm with thunder, lightning and sheets

223

of rain hit us. At about 4 pm I took a horse and went to help Rusty turn the sheep back. When I got to the lead, I couldn't find him. I thought he must have returned to camp as the storm was getting worse. I turned the sheep back into the wind on my own and left them. Back at camp, still no Rusty. Nor next morning. I went around the sheep on horseback in deep mud. I did the same for the next four days and still there was no sign of him. I cursed every living being in New South Wales for taking my dog.

Droving friends George and Jean Kelly came by with a mob of bullocks from Midkin station, near Moree, which they had brought out of the flooded country. George's wagon was full of dogs, but Rusty wasn't among them. I told him the story. Then, with a silly grin that only George could produce, he said, 'I'll give you 300 quid for him!'

'Where is he?' I piped. He told me that six miles down the road at a dam on the left, there were 70 or so sheep, mostly with long tails, being looked after by a big brindle dog.

So that was it. The pet sheep we had in the mob had walked fearlessly past the peg dogs we tied up on the roadside. We hadn't seen their tracks because of the rain and it had been too wet to count the sheep in the mob and realise some were missing—and possibly work out that Rusty would be with them.

When we got to the dam, the lambs were on the dam bank. The water was a mile wide around it, so Rusty hadn't been able to get the pet sheep to return. I left the sheep there and Rusty reluctantly came back to camp with me feeling, I suppose, that he had let me down.

We went south to Moree and found that the Gwydir River was in flood. We camped on a sandhill in the bend of the river. Just on daybreak one morning, I got up to make a cuppa. It was still raining and water was everywhere over the black plains around us. The sheep were in a temporary yard made out of pig netting. I picked up the billy and, without thinking, threw out the cold tea and leaves. SPLASH!—onto the soggy ground they went, disturbing the deep quiet of the morning.

Every sheep hit its feet at once. They flattened the yard and rushed. Some went straight into the river, never to be seen again. Others went down the lane. The further they went, the faster they ran, taking fright at the ones following behind them. In all my lifetime around sheep I have never seen or even heard of sheep rushing like that.

But Rusty came to the rescue again. He went to the lead and held them until I could get a horse and catch up to them. Sheep were bogged for two miles along the track. We eventually got them back to the sandhill, but only after Rusty had brought them a few at a time to the road where I could collect and hold them. It was a long day's work mopping up after inadvertently frightening them that morning.

Droving dogs work hard and need their sleep, but even night-time can bring unexpected dangers. Rusty never got tied up so he always slept near the campfire. At the same Moree camp one night, I was cooking a four-gallon drum of meat for the dogs. A log that was supporting the drum had slowly burnt away and the next thing we knew, there was an almighty yelp. The drum had tipped over and boiling water sloshed under Rusty while he slept.

He levitated and rushed straight for the flooded river and out of sight. The night was very dark, the bank was steep and slippery and there was little I could do to help him get out of the river. I could hear him paddling, yelping every now and again when he hit some debris or something. Two days later a poor scalded Rusty came back to camp. One complete side of him had no hair. I sprinkled talcum powder and borax on him and kept him warm and dry for a week with plenty of warm food. He healed up wonderfully.

We went northwards from there to North Star and then southeast to Wallangra. The sheep were shorn there, at a farm we had just purchased called Hidden Valley. From there we went south to Warialda where we were going to truck them to Inverell so they could be sold to raise money for the farm. On the way there, the grass was four foot high and we had no hope of driving sheep through it. All we could do was rush them down the bitumen at daybreak for five or six miles, then make camp. We would always meet a truck coming one way or the other, so Rusty would run over the sheep's backs, drop down in front and come back through the mob to part them and let the truck through.

One evening when we were camped behind the Warialda golf course, I whistled to the dogs to fetch the sheep into the yard. There was no response, so I went around the mob thinking a bitch must have been in season or something like that. Instead I found all my dogs lying dead—except for Rusty, who was in a pretty bad way. He was having fits but I saved him with some of the salt that I always carried in my saddlebag for that very purpose. He took months to recover from the poisoning, so we bought another dog to help

225

load the sheep and truck them down the Gwydir Highway into Inverell.

When Rusty got better he worked at Hidden Valley and we found he also loved working cattle and rounding up wild pigs for me to catch or shoot. He continued helping with the mustering and yard work until he was fifteen. Then, on 9 March 1967, we dipped 3,000 sheep on Ena station, which was about twelve miles from Hidden Valley and which I managed.

Next morning Rusty was asleep on his bag at the back steps where I put on my boots every morning. He sat up and put his head on my lap. I patted him and went off to milk the two cows. When I came back he was dead. I buried him beside the patch of cacti out from the cottage on Ena station, near Wallangra, on the day of my 33rd birthday.

PUTTING THEM TO THE TEST

Yard Dog Trial Results

The dog trialling world falls into two camps—the three sheep triallers who continue the traditions of a century or more, and the yard dog triallers whose sport got under way in Tasmania in 1980.

Three sheep trials require a dog to manoevre sheep around and through obstacles on an oval in a studied and refined manner. Yard dogs have to push ten or more sheep through a series of yards, a drafting race and load some on a truck. Some three sheep triallers regard the yard dogs as lacking in finesse and subtlety. Many yard dog people dismiss the three sheep trials as irrelevant in determining the most useful farm dogs.

Certainly there's a lot more room for exuberance in a yard dog trial. Dogs can display their ability to jump over gates into pens, run over the backs of sheep and, unlike in the three sheep trials, are encouraged to bark if the situation warrants it.

Not wishing to raise the hackles of either camp, I will leave it to Lance Clifford of Pyengana, Tasmania, to explain why he staged the nation's inaugural yard dog trial on 2 August, 1980 at St Helens.

'For a number of years I had organised sheep dog trials on the Martha Vale property at St Helens. Despite having trained, quiet sheep, much time was wasted gathering up the sheep lost and chased away by over-keen and forceful dogs. The farmers would later give the excuse, often heard at three sheep trials, that their farm dogs at home would clean up those sneaking trial dogs if they had to move a mob, or work in the yards where a bit of force was needed.

'So the following year, I decided I would give these farmers the opportunity to show how good their dogs were in the yards. It was partly run as a novelty event, but by the time we came to hold it, it had become the Tasmanian Yard Dog Championship and the concept took off straight away.

'The initial competition attracted extraordinary interest and the following year, in July 1981, ABC *Countrywide* televised the competition. Soon after, I travelled to Victoria, South Australia, Western Australia and Flinders Island to assist in setting up similar competitions.

227

'The dogs are tested doing the sort of everyday things done in sheep yards such as drenching and drafting sheep. Judges look for the dogs' ability to back sheep, bark as required, force and block sheep as well as obedience. Points are deducted for pulling wool, biting, assistance from the handler and the dog leaving its work or lacking interest.

'Probably one of the greatest boosts for yard dog competitions was that the first event was won by Miss Peta Bushby, 20, and her dog Nicko. It was the first sheep dog competition either had entered and their win gave intending participants confidence that all they needed was a good farm dog to be competitive. Peta was the only female competitor, but she showed her win was no fluke by later winning an event at Launceston show.'

Because results of the Working Sheepdog Association's National Trials in Canberra were listed in the first book, Great Working Dog Stories, it was thought yard dog champions should also be listed. So, from the records of yard dog association secretaries far and wide, here is the first almost-comprehensive list of their champions. If you can help fill any of the gaps, write to me c/- ABC Enterprises, GPO Box 9994, Sydney 2001.

YARD DOG CHAMPIONSHIP RESULTS

Tasmania

1980 - St Helens
1st - Peta Bushby   *Nicko*
2nd - Bernard Boot   *Tramp*
        Lance Clifford   *Pace*
3rd - Max Semmens   *Tige*
1981 - St Helens
1st - Max Semmens   *Tige*
1982 - Campbelltown
1st - Wes Singline   *Yank*
1983 - Bridgport
1st - Stan Smith   *Ben*
1984 - Campbelltown
1st - Irene Glover   *Red*
2nd - Stephen Crosswell
3rd - Daryl Pritchard
1985 - Ag Fest, Simmonds Plains
1st - Michael Green   *Bernie*
2nd - Stan Smith   *Ben*
3rd - Len Rigby   *Bronc*
1986 - Bushy Park

1st - Irene Glover   *Barney*
2nd - Stan Smith   *Ben*
3rd - Michael Green   *Bernie*
1987 - Bushy Park
1st - Irene Glover   *Glen*
2nd - Irene Glover   *Curley*
3rd - Michael Green   *Bernie*
1988 - Ag Fest, Carrick
1st - Michael Williams   *Maverick*
2nd - Stan Smith   *Ben*
3rd - Michael Green   *Bernie*
1989 - Campbelltown
1st - Irene Glover   *Glen*
2nd - Irene Glover   *Don*
3rd - Irene Glover   *Curley*
1990 - Bushy Park
1st - Irene Glover   *Tod*
2nd - Irene Glover   *Don*
3rd - Irene Glover   *Curley*
1991 - Evandale

1st – Gordon Brooker   *Ben*
2nd – Michael Williams   *Teena*
3rd – Geoff Elmer   *Shep*
1992 – Campbelltown
1st – Robert Brown   *Shep*
2nd – Michael Williams   *Teena*
3rd – Irene Glover   *Curley*
1993 – Evandale
1st – Matthew Johnson   *Kell*
2nd – Michael Williams   *Jock*
3rd – Michael Green   *Bernie*

South Australia

1982 – Lucindale
1st – Neil McDonald   *Max*
1983 – Lucindale
1st – John Gedye   *Scoriochre Gunga*
1984 – Lucindale
1st – Rick Sims   *Feng*
1985 – Lucindale
1st – Mick Rudd   *Norm*
2nd – Rick Sims   *Jock*
3rd – Neil McDonald   *Spark*
1986 – Lucindale
1st – Mick Rudd   *Norm*
2nd – Neil McDonald   *Spark*
3rd – Sally Stanley   *Kurleigh Kip*
1987 – Lucindale
1st – Rick Sims
1988 – Lucindale
1st – Rob Macklin   *Tasman*
2nd – Steve Weyman   *Alice*
3rd – Jens Pedersen   *Bamse*
1989 – Lucindale
1st – Lyndon Cooper   *Nacooma Gus*
2nd – Sally Stanley   *Kurleigh Kip*
3rd – Drew Barr   *Major*
1990 – Lucindale
1st – Peter Moore   *Tiger*
2nd – Lyndon Cooper   *Nacooma Gus*
3rd – Rick Sims   *Wyreema Jock*
1991 – Lucindale
1st – Rick Sims   *Wyreema Jock*
2nd – Lyndon Cooper   *Nacooma Gus*
3rd – Lyndon Cooper   *Pomanda Kelt*
1992 – Lucindale
1st – Lyndon Cooper   *Capree Sledge*

2nd – Wayne Gelven   *Glen Avon Spero*
3rd – Rob Macklin   *Sherwood Ace*
1993 – Lucindale
1st – Lyndon Cooper   *Nacooma Gus*
2nd – Sally Stanley   *Kurleigh Kip*
3rd – Lyndon Cooper   *Pomanda Kelt*

New South Wales

1985
1st – Steve Weyman   *Barambogie Mack*
1986
1st – Chris Stapleton   *Glenlogie Lucky*
1987
1st – Steve Weyman   *Barambogie Mack*
1988
1st – Chris Stapleton   *Glenlogie Lucky*
1989
1st – Jim Luce   *Phils Creek Sam*
1990
1st – Chris Stapleton   *Joe's Pride*
1991
1st – Michael Johnston   *Noonbarra Butch*
1992
1st – Jim Luce   *Capree Minute*
1993
1st – Chris Stapleton   *Capree Target*

Victoria

1991 – Swan Hill
1st – Brian Harrington   *Dan*
2nd – Sally Stanley   *Kurleigh Kip*
3rd – Sally Stanley   *Tuppence*
1992 – Euroa
1st – Neil McDonald   *Beau*
2nd – Jim Luce   *Pat*
3rd – Brian Harrington   *Mac*
1993
Yard
1st – G. Halsall   *Roy*
2nd – Sally Stanley   *Kurleigh Kip*
3rd – Rob Macklin   *Ace*
Utility
1st – Rod Cavill   *Kye*
2nd – G. Halsall   *Roy*
3rd – G. Halsall   *Snow*

Western Australia

1984
Utility
1st – Steve Gray   *Willy*
2nd – David Sims   *Sonny*
3rd – Charlie Staniforth-Smith   *Craig Jenny*
Yard
1st – Steve Gray   *Willy*
2nd – David Sims   *Sonny*
3rd – Charlie Staniforth-Smith   *Craig Jenny*
1985
Utility
1st – Nick Webb   *Carter's Nellie*
2nd – Ray Sutherland   *Swagman's Pep*
3rd – Doug Connop   *Strathblane Sasha*
Yard
1st – Steve Gray   *Willy*
2nd – Doug Connop   *Strathblane Sasha*
3rd – Ray Sutherland   *Swagman's Pep*
1986
Utility
1st – Doug Connop   *Peejay Sadie*
2nd – Doug Connop   *Glenview Boof*
3rd – David Slade   *Tippy's Work*
Yard
1st – Doug Connop   *Peejay Sadie*
=2nd – Steve Gray   *Willy*
            David Slade   *Tippy's Mork*
1987
Utility
1st – Don Robertson   *Booroola Joey*
2nd – Doug Connop   *Sorrego Cannon*
3rd – Ken Atherton   *Glenview Cobba*
Yard
1st – Ken Atherton   *Glenview Cobba*
2nd – Don Robertson   *Booroola Joey*
3rd – David Slade   *Tippy's Mork*
Brace
1st – Doug Connop   *Strathblane Sasha &
    Glenview Boof*
2nd – Doug Connop   *Peejay Sadie &
    Glenomian Dinny*
3rd – Doug Connop   *Wundurra Steve &
    Sorrego Cannon*
1988
Utility
1st – John Charlick   *Lochsloy Glen*
2nd – Tony Boyle   *Boylee Pup*

3nd – Doug Connop   *Strathblane Sasha*
Yard
1st – Doug Connop   *Strathblane Sasha*
2nd – Tony Boyle   *Boylee Pup*
3rd – Doug Connop   *Peejay Sadie*
Brace
1st – Tony Boyle   *Boylee Pup & Boylee Boof*
2nd – Doug Connop   *Strathblane Sasha &
    Glenromian Dinny*
3rd – Doug Connop   *Merna Whisk & Peejay
    Sadie*
1989
Utility
1st – Doug Connop   *Glenromian Dinny*
2nd – Doug Connop   *Merna Whisko*
3rd – Pip Hudson   *Nib*
Yard
1st – Don Robertson   *Scoriochre Lady*
2nd – Pip Hudson   *Nib*
3rd – Ken Atherton   *Glenview Cobba*
Brace
1st – Doug Connop   *Strathblane Sasha &
    Merna Whisko*
2nd – Pip Hudson   *Morillo Nicky Webb &
    Windeyer Pippy*
3rd – John Charlick   *Cyprian Kiwi &
    Koonwarra Kanya*
1990
Utility
1st – Steve Gray   *Craig Pete*
=2nd – Doug Connop   *Merna Whisko*
            Tony Boyle   *Boylee Pup*
Yard
1st – Ken Atherton   *Glenview Toby*
=2nd – Steve Gray   *Craig Pete*
            Don Robertson   *Scoriochre Lady*
Brace
1st – Doug Connop   *Merna Whisko &
    Glenview Dinny*
2nd – Chris Stapleton   *Capree Watch &
    Joe's Pride*
3rd – Doug Connop   *Peejay Sadie &
    Glenview Sheik*
1991
Utility
1st – Ken Atherton   *Glenview Toby*
2nd – Ben Voskuilen   *Gleetfeet Roy*
3rd – Lew Noble   *Sorrego Joe*
Yard

1st – Ken Atherton   *Glenview Toby*
2nd – Ben Voskuilen   *Fleetfeet Roy*
3rd – Lew Noble   *Sorrego Joe*
Brace
1st – John Greenwood   *Alphadale Johnny &*

Alphadale Peg
2nd – Pip Hudson   *Morillo Nicky Webb &*
   Windeyer Pippy
3rd – Ben Voskuilen   *Scoriochre Genie &*
   Fleetfeet Roy

INAUGURAL NATIONAL AUSTRALIAN YARD DOG CHAMPIONSHIPS

1981 – Launceston Show
1st – Peta Bushby   *Nicko*
2nd – Lance Clifford   *Pace*
3rd – Michael Chugg   *Spike*

Renamed—Australian Yard Dog Association Championship

1982 – Launceston Show
1st – John Rosten   *Beau*
2nd – Rick Smith   *Kirribilli Shirley*
3rd – Michael Chugg   *Spike*
1983 – Cressy, Tasmania
1st – Len Rigby   *Bronc*
2nd – John Weir
3rd – Stan Smith   *Ben*
1984 – Scotsdale, Tasmania
1st – Steve Weyman   *Barambogie Mack*
2nd – Stan Smith   *Ben*
3rd – Michael Green   *Bernie*
1985 – Kilmore, Victoria
1986 – Millicent, South Australia
1st – Chris Stapleton   *Glenlogie Lucky*

2nd – Mick Rudd   *Liscannor Norm*
3rd – Brendan O'Connor   *Landmere Rex*
1987 – Western Australia
1st – Chris Stapleton   *Glenlogie Lucky*
2nd – Steve Weyman   *Barambogie Mack*
1988 – Launceston
1st – John Greenwood   *Alphadale Johnny*
2nd – Neil McDonald   *Spark*
   Irene Glover   *Curley*
3rd – Lance Clifford   *Le Cliff Pete*
1989 – Tasmania
1st – John Greenwood   *Alphadale Johnny*
2nd – Neil McDonald   *Wabba Kelp*
1990 – Euroa, Victoria
1st – Steve Weyman   *Boree Troy*
2nd – Chris Stapleton   *Joe's Pride*
1991 – Pinnaroo, South Australia
1st – Chris Stapleton   *Capree Watch*
2nd – Peter Moore   *Tiger*
3rd – Lyndon Cooper   *Nacooma Gus*
1992 – Bathurst, New South Wales
1st – Michael Johnston   *Noonbarra Butch*
2nd – Chris Stapleton   *Capree Watch*

A BIBLIOGRAPHY OF AUSTRALIAN WORKING DOGS

Helen Hewson-Fruend, Gunning, New South Wales
and Stephen Bilson, Orange, New South Wales

Many of the books below are available through Noonbarra Dog Products, PO Box 1374, Orange, New South Wales 2800.

DOG STORIES

Baker, I, *Monday Sheepdog*, Angus & Robertson, Sydney, 1987. The story of the sheepdog, Charcoal, with his master in a range of farming adventures set in the imaginary district of Coonara.

Davison, F D, *Dusty: The Story of a Sheepdog*, Eye & Spottiswoode, London, 1947. The story set in Queensland of a kelpie–dingo cross.

Finger, C J, *A Dog at His Heel: The Story of Jock, an Australian Sheepdog*, John C Winston Co, Chicago, 1936. The story of an outstanding sheepdog, a crossbred Airedale terrier, Jock, set in the late 1880s in Western Australia and South America.

Goode, A and Hayes, M, *Great Working Dog Stories*, ABC Enterprises, Sydney, 1990. A collection of previously unpublished stories about predominantly South Australian working dogs.

Goode, A, *More Great Working Dog Stories*, ABC Enterprises, Sydney, 1992. A collection of 145 stories from all round Australia.

Jones, G and Collins, B, *Way of Life*, Farming Press, Suffolk, UK, 1988.

Lamond, H G, *Towser the Sheep Dog*, Faber & Faber, London, 1955. The story of a sheepdog, probably kelpie, set in western Queensland.

McCaig, Donald, *Eminent Dogs, Dangerous Men*, HarperCollins, New York, 1991.

McCaig, Donald, *Nop's Trials*, Lyons & Burford, New York, 1984.

McGuire, F M, *Three and Ma Kelpie*, Longmans, Green & Co, Croydon, 1964. A story based on fact set on a sheep station near Broken

Hill. Ma Kelpie had three pups, but their owner and one of the pups were lost in the bush.

Patchett, M E, *Ajax the Warrior*, Penguin, Harmondsworth, 1953. Ajax was a wild dog rescued from a flood and raised on a cattle station on the Queensland–New South Wales border. Ajax was the canine protagonist in other Patchett stories: *Ajax: Golden Dog of the Australian Bush; The Call of the Bush; The Golden Wolf; Ajax and the Haunted Mountain;* and *Ajax and the Drovers*. All have been translated into several languages.

Pollard, J (ed.), *Wild Dogs, Working Dogs, Pedigrees and Pets*, Lansdowne Press, Melbourne, 1968. Reprinted in 1977 as *Great Dog Stories of Australia and New Zealand*, Rigby, Adelaide. A collection of previously published stories and poems about dogs from the previous 100 years. It includes several Henry Lawson dog stories and poems.

Webb, Z V, *The Shared Dog*, Georgian House, Melbourne, 1945. Originally published in the *Bulletin*. The story of Spot, a mongrel belonging to two swagmen probably during the 1930s Depression.

Willey, K, *Joe Brown's Dog Bluey*, Rigby, Adelaide, 1978. A story of a blue heeler cattle dog set in desert country in central Australia.

Wrightson, P, *Moondark*, Hutchinson, Melbourne, 1987. The story of an Australian cattle dog, set probably in Queensland.

TECHNICAL BOOKS

General

Brown, J G (compiler), *Dogs of Australia*, KCC of Victoria, 1973, 1984.

Hamilton-Wilkes, M, *Kelpie and Cattle Dog*, Angus & Robertson, Sydney, 1967, 1980, 1982.

Holmes, John, *The Farmer's Dog*, Popular Dogs, London, UK, 1989.

Kaleski, R, *Australian Barkers and Biters*, New South Wales Bookstall Co, Sydney, 1914, 1933. Facsimile edition, Endeavour Press, Sydney, 1987.

Sanderson, A, *The Complete Book of Australian Dogs*, Currawong, Milson's Point, 1981, 1987, 1988.

Cattle Dogs

Redhead, C, *The Good Looking Australian*, Readhead, Adelaide, 1979.

Robinson, N, *Australian Cattle Dogs*, TFH, Neptune City, 1990.

Shaffer, Mari, *Heeler Power*, Countryside Publications, Wisconsin, USA, 1984.

Sheepdogs
Border Collie
Bray, J, *The Border Checkpoint*, Bray, Mittagong, 1989.
Carpenter, E B, *The Blue Riband of the Heather*, Ipswich, UK, 1989.
Collier, Margaret, *Border Collies*, FH, USA, 1991.
Combe, Iris, *Border Collies*, Faber & Faber, London, 1978.
Larson, Janet, *The Versatile Border Collie*, Alpine Publications, Colorado, USA, 1987.
Moore, J, *The Canine King*, Standard Newspapers, Cheltenham, 1929.
Quarton, M, *All About the Working Border Collie*, Pelham, UK.
Swann, Barbara, *The Versatile Border Collie*, Nimrod Press, Hants, UK, 1988.
Vidler, P, *The Border Collie in Australasia*, Gotrah, Kellyville, 1983.

Kelpie
Austin, T and Zaadstra, P, *Our Australian Kelpie*, High Thunder, Mt Gambier, 1991.
Brody, J, *The Australian Kelpie*, Brody, Holbrook, 1980.
Donelan, M, *The Australian Kelpie*, Donelan, Wagga Wagga, 1982.
MacLeod, N, *The Australian Kelpie Handbook*, MacLeod, Altona, 1984.
Parsons, A, *The Working Kelpie*, Nelson, Melbourne, 1986.
Sloane, S, *Australian Kelpies*, TFH, Neptune City, 1990.

Other
Breckwoldt, Roland, *The Dingo: A Very Elegant Animal*, Angus & Robertson, Sydney, 1988.
Sims, David and Dawydiak, O, *Livestock Protection Dogs*, OTR Publications, Alaska, USA, 1990.

TRAINING, BREEDING AND CARE

Austin, T, *Breeding and Training Sheepdogs*, Austin, Coleraine, 1978.
Cavanagh, R, *Australian Sheepdogs*, Cavanagh, Whittlesea, 1990.
Dookie Agricultural College, *Dog Handling Workshop*, Victorian Department of Agriculture, Melbourne, 1981.
Glenormiston Agricultural College, *Working Sheep with Dogs*, Victorian Department of Agriculture, Melbourne, 1981.
Greenwood, G (ed.), *Farm Dogs*, Australian Government Publishing Service, Canberra, 1979.
Kelley, R B, *Animal Breeding and the Maintenance and Training of Sheepdogs*, Angus & Robertson, Sydney, 1942. Reprinted as *Sheepdogs,*

235

Their Breeding, Maintenance and Training, 1949, 1958, 1970.

Lithgow, S, *Training and Working Dogs*, University of Queensland Press, Brisbane, 1987, 1988, 1989, 1991.

Means, Ben, *The Perfect Stock Dog*, self-published, Missouri, USA, 1970.

Parsons, A, *Training the Working Kelpie*, Viking O'Neil, Melbourne, 1990.

Russell, D W, *Managing the Sheep Dog*, South Australian Department of Agriculture, Adelaide, 1975.

Taggart, M, *Sheepdog Training: An All Breed Approach*, Alpine Publications, USA, 1986.

Victorian Department of Agriculture, *The Working Dog*, Victorian Department of Agriculture, Melbourne, 1977.

GLOSSARY

backer   a dog that runs over the backs of sheep to help force or bunch sheep up in a race or yard

backing   the act of running over sheeps' backs

bark out   to flush out stock from inaccessible areas such as thick scrub or mountainous terrain with a dog that barks continously or on command

biddability   able to be trained to a high level of obedience

black sallee tree   Eucalyptus stellulata—spreading, many-branched tree growing in frosty, snowy areas

cane grass   tall, bamboo-like reeds growing in swampy areas in Northern Territory

cast   the wide arc a dog will make in a paddock to move in around a mob of sheep or cattle

chain   a distance of 22 yards or 66 feet, a common distance between fence posts

cleanskin   an animal without an earmark or a brand

coachers   a mob of quiet cattle used to lure wild cattle

coasty sheep   sheep with cobalt deficiency resulting in ill thrift

cock-horn cow   with one horn pointing up and the other down

cover   sheep dog trial term for 'control'

dags   locks of wool on the breech of a sheep heavily coated with dung

draw   the bringing of the sheep by the dog toward the handler in a three sheep trial

eye, to have   to be able to control livestock by the force of an almost mesmerising gaze

gilgie   a small freshwater crayfish, like a yabby, found in Western Australia

Gold Coaster   term for a dog allowed to roam free and lead a relaxing lifestyle around the farm

hand gallop   faster than a canter, but not a gallop at full stretch

headlands   sections of paddocks that initially miss being ploughed when machinery negotiates corners. These are ploughed diagonally when the rest of the paddock has been completed

hoggett   a sheep aged between one and two years

horse-tailer   the person responsible for ensuring the team of horses used in a droving or stock camp is looked after and rounded up for each day's work

jam tree small wattle-like tree with hard, sweet-smelling wood, found in various parts of Western Australia wheat belt

Keep-eggs eggs rubbed with a greasy proprietary compound which preserves them without refrigeration

killers sheep kept for household meat supplies

knocking them up wearing livestock out by moving them too fast

merino rig a male sheep that has been improperly castrated, thereby having the characteristics of a ram

mickey bull wild, cleanskin bull, often poorly bred

mules to cut strips of skin from breach area of lambs to prevent fly-strike. Named after J H W Mules who pioneered the procedure

night horse horse used to patrol livestock in a droving camp overnight, usually steady and unflappable

party line telephone line shared by two or more subscribers

peg dog dog tied up to block a gateway, road, gap in a fence etc.

red cloud a strain of working dog originating from the Western Australia dog Red Cloud, bred by King and McLeod, or from King and McLeod bred parentage. Red Cloud was a big, all red dog of outstanding ability. His name was used to describe his descendants.

ringer a stationhand. Also, fastest shearer in the team

run-out brumbies inbred wild horses

sandy blight inflammation producing sandlike grains in the eye

stag a male sheep that has been castrated after reaching maturity

stool out to throw out shoots from the roots

windrow hay etc. raked into lines to allow it to be dried by the wind